Scotland's International Football Referees

1872 - 2025

Drew Herbertson

Copyright © 2025 Drew Herbertson

ISBN:978-1-918264-73-9

All rights reserved, including the right to reproduce this book, or portions thereof in any form. No part of this text may be reproduced, transmitted, downloaded, decompiled, reverse engineered, or stored, in any form or introduced into any information storage and retrieval system, in any form or by any means, whether electronic or mechanical without the express written permission of the author.

By the same author

Football Refereeing in Scotland: A history of its Organisation and Development 1873-2023

Contents

Acknowledgements	v
Preface	vi
Introduction	1
Notes on Referees' Biographies	4
The Early Pioneers	6
Referees – 1890 to 2025	21
Linesmen/Assistant Referees	223
FIFA Linesmen/Assistant Referees – 1992 to 2025	225
Lists of FIFA Referees and Assistant Referees	247
FIFA	254
UEFA	258
SFA Nomination Process	260
The World Cup	264
The European Championships	283
A Internationals	286
British International Championship	290
Ireland	292
South America	294
The Old Firm	299
Around the World	302
Newspapers	304
Family Connections	305
Referees' Associations' Awards	306
Roll of Honour	306
Bibliography	320

Acknowledgements

A number of people are due my sincere thanks for the assistance they gave in helping me write this book: Richard McBrearty (Curator) and Callum Livingston (Visitor Services Officer) of the Scottish Football Museum, who enabled me to access a whole host of material in the archives, including SFA minute books, FIFA documents, Scottish League minutes and handbooks; Steven Harris (SFA) for providing information on refereeing appointments following my retiral from the SFA; Alex Jackson (National Football Museum) and Peter Watson (University of Leeds) for sharing information on the involvement of British referees in South American football, a project they are currently working on (having been put in touch with them by Richard McBrearty); the staff of Glasgow's Mitchell Library in respect of my researching newspaper archives; Michael Schmalholz (FIFA Football Museum) and Chris Wild (UEFA Referee Department) for the provision of information on appointments; Andy Mitchell and Gordon Mellis for allowing me to draw information from their respective books "The Men Who Made Scotland: The definitive Who's Who of Scottish Football Internationalists 1872-1939" and "The Remarkable Story of Peter Craigmyle – The Fearless Aberdonian"; Brian Robinson, the grandson of the referee Peter Fitzpatrick for giving me access to the latter's match appointment records and the Glasgow Referees' Association's Training Class Records from 1946-1962; Willie Laidlaw for providing information on his refereeing career in Canada; John Dearie, the grand old man of Lanarkshire referees, for providing some useful nuggets of information.

My final thanks go to my son Craig, for once again putting his great artistic skills to such good use in designing the cover of the book.

Cover Images: Alamy

Preface

The motivation to write this book was born out of my career in referee administration with the SFA and it runs parallel with that of the other book I have written – "Football Refereeing in Scotland - a history of its organisation and development 1872-2023."

In my job, I had responsibility for the administration of the international appointments received by Scotland's FIFA referees, which was a hugely interesting part of my role. It gave me a real sense of connection to the referees and I took great satisfaction in dealing with them on the appointments they had received and seeing their careers progress on the international stage. I came to realise that referees are special people in football given that an important responsibility is invested in them to take charge of matches, regularly involving famous teams and players and played before huge crowds in foreign countries. As was the case with my other book, I long felt that there was a story to be told about these referees. Referees are generally much criticised within football and are often taken for granted in that they are just expected to turn up, referee the match and go home. They can easily be overlooked. I felt that it would be appropriate if the spotlight could be deservedly turned on the international referees. A little bit of attention on referees would not go amiss given the focus given to players, managers and clubs in the football world.

The scope of the book developed along very similar lines to my first book. Initially, my intention was to focus on Scotland's FIFA referees from the late 1940's onwards. Fairly quickly, however, I realised that I should extend the project to cover all of Scotland's international referees from the start of international football in 1872. It was absolutely correct to do so. Each referee deserves inclusion and for his contribution to be recognised. The remembrance of referees will generally diminish as the years pass by and perhaps only a few of the really famous referees will be recalled by some. The book presents the chance to record all these referees and pay tribute to them.

It was a lengthy research process to establish all the referees and the appointments they fulfilled, particularly in the period from 1872 up to the Second World War. SFA records provided an excellent foundation and this was added to by documents held by the Scottish Football Museum. Multiple websites were used to trace and cross check appointments. The British Newspaper Archive was a wonderful source of information, not just on appointments but on the referees themselves. Hopefully, the book fulfils its aim and does justice to the referees.

Introduction

Beyond the primary aim of establishing all the referees concerned, I had to decide on the level of match appointments fulfilled by them. This, though, was largely decided for me as the situation clarified itself the deeper my research went. Straightforwardly, international matches from 1872 were the starting point. It quickly became evident that the development and growth of football would guide me. In the early days of football, for example, Inter-Association matches between Scottish and English local associations, such as Glasgow v Sheffield, were hugely important in football. These matches are taken into account as are League and Amateur Internationals, with these having started in the early 1890's and early 1900's respectively. Prior to the Second World War, international football in Britain essentially comprised the British International Championship, League and Amateur Internationals, and Inter-Association matches. When the SFA rejoined FIFA in 1946, the door was opened for Scottish referees to be included in the FIFA List of International Referees, records of which commence from season 1947-48. This simplified things in terms of capturing the appointments in competitions and international fixtures in which the referees officiated.

Scottish club football plays an important part too, given that the international referees handled so many of the top matches. Appointments to the various national Cup Finals and matches between the "Old Firm" of Celtic and Rangers provide an excellent barometer of the standing of a referee. With the presence of Celtic and Rangers in the Glasgow Cup and the Glasgow Charity Cup, these competitions, which had great importance for many years, are also included in the referees' records of appointments.

It came to light during my research that many of the top referees prior to the Second World War officiated also in Junior football, with the Scottish Junior FA appointing these referees to Junior internationals and to the Junior Cup Final. These appointments are included in the referees' records and, for continuity, such appointments received by the post-war referees are also taken into account.

It will be evident from the biographies of the FIFA referees that there are great variances in their careers at international level. Some did not receive any appointments at all during their time on the FIFA List and many received very few with these often just in amateur or youth internationals played in Britain. The advent of the UEFA Club Competitions slowly increased the scope for appointments but generally these were the preserve of the officials who were regarded as the top referees. That was the way things largely operated through to the early 1990's. In the last 30 years or so the opportunities open to referees have been hugely boosted as UEFA and FIFA increased and expanded their competitions, particularly in youth and women's football. Now, the modern day FIFA referee receives many more appointments than their predecessors ever did, even those who were in the top rank of European referees of their time.

Until the role of the referee was formalised in the Laws of the Game in 1891, the referees in international matches and Cup Finals were officials of the organising bodies. As club matches in football's early years were controlled by a neutral referee with each club providing an umpire, it was therefore natural to apply the same principle to international matches. Whilst these officials are not referees in the true sense, they are fully worthy of inclusion for their vital contributions to football.

These initial "referees" are the covered in the section "The Early Pioneers". The section on "Referees - 1890 – 2025" captures all the true referees. Five Scots who progressed to the FIFA List through other National Associations are also included. They fully merit recognition for gaining FIFA status. FIFA Linesmen/Assistant Referees, a role introduced in 1992, are not forgotten as they deserve to be recognised for the vital role they play in officiating. A section is devoted to them, providing details of their careers.

Other sections cover a variety of subjects such as FIFA and UEFA, to provide some context of the environment in which the FIFA referees operate. The SFA's approach to its selection of FIFA officials is addressed. A section features the World Cup, in which Scottish referees have an excellent record, and other parts provide an insight into the involvement of Scottish referees in Irish and South American football, both of which topics emerged through my research. The part played by the Old Firm in refereeing is touched upon. The closing section summarises the remarkable accomplishments of Scottish referees in international competitions at country and club levels. In his contribution to Glasgow Referees Association's 50th Anniversary programme Jack Mowat, in response to being regularly asked why he chose to become a referee, put forward that it was a "calling" rather than a choice. That will be understood by any referee. There is something about being a referee that engenders a special feeling about fulfilling the role, what it means to them and how they carry out all that they do. Dedication to the role comes naturally. An individual singular approach is a necessity right from the start of any referee's career. All eyes land on the referee at every match and all sorts of criticism and invective are directed at them. Referees at the very top accustom themselves to all that comes their way. Strength of character is a paramount requirement. By their management skills, referees lead games as much as they control them through the application of the Laws of the Game.

Refereeing a match though is but part of the equation. Commitment to refereeing is all-encompassing. Referees in the modern era have to undertake strict and demanding training regimes to maintain fitness levels. They have always have had to work around family life and their jobs to undertake their refereeing commitments. For international referees, having an understanding and good employer has always been vital. Each international appointment requires three days off work – travelling to the venue the day before, the match day, and the return journey home. At the lower end of international appointments, a UEFA Under age mini-tournament now lasts for 10 days. If a referee receives, say, four international appointments as a referee during a season and maybe two or three appointments as a Fourth Official or now as a VAR, that amounts to about 18 days. Factor in any UEFA meetings which have to be attended on top of domestic refereeing commitments and an understanding will be gained as to how much commitment referees at the top level give to refereeing and, of course, to football. All this will be little known about generally. Scotland has produced a great number of excellent referees down the years, with the really top ones easily staking a valid claim to be considered amongst the world's best. The book presents the opportunity to recognise all of Scotland's international referees. Some names will be well-known, some less so and, I suspect, many not at all. There is great pride within Scottish referees as to what is done in the context of their commitment to refereeing and to football. At international level, Scottish referees have much to be proud of. The book commemorates their careers and is a record of their achievements.

Notes on Referees' Biographies

Births-Deaths
For the majority of the referees, either their date of birth or the year in which they were born is provided. The same applies to the date of their death or the year in which they died. For a number of referees, these dates/years have not been established.

The List of Referees
The information on the referees' length of service on the SFA List of Referees prior to the Second World War comes from several sources – a small number of SFA List booklets from the 1920's and 1930's, Scottish League Fixtures & Rules booklets (1901-02, 1908-09 to 1932-33 and 1937-38 to 1938-39), SFA Minutes and references to referee appointments and articles on referees contained in newspapers sourced through the British Newspaper Archive.

This enabled the period of service on the List to be developed for the referees prior to the Second World War. It is accepted that in some instances the actual period of service may vary from what is recorded. The SFA List booklet for 1938-39 is the first where the term "Class 1" is used. Up to that point, the SFA List was compiled in alphabetical order within geographical areas. The Scottish League operated its own List, drawn from the SFA List. From 1931-32, the League categorised the referees as either First Division or Second Division referees. In some instances of referees of the 1930's, there is a slight variance in the recording of a referee's service, either recording the number of seasons on the List or setting out the first season on the List and the service at Class 1.

Information on the List after the Second World War comes from the SFA's records and is recorded up to the end of season 2024-25.

Amateur Internationals
The SFA was responsible for Amateur Internationals until the early 1970's at which point the Scottish Amateur FA took the reins. Amateur international appointments are taken into account up to the changeover.

UEFA Club Competitions
Abbreviations are used for the Club Competitions in the summary of appointments fulfilled by the referees and linesmen/assistant referees. These are:

ECCC	European Champion Club's Cup
ECWC	European Cup Winners' Cup
ICFC	Inter-Cities Fairs cup
UC	UEFA Cup
UCL	UEFA Champions League
UEL	UEFA Europa League
UECL	UEFA Europa Conference League
UIC	UEFA Intertoto Cup
PO	Play-off
G	Group match
LP	League Phase
R32	Round of 32
R16	Round of 16

Appointments
This information is recorded up to the end of season 2024-25.

The Early Pioneers

Sydney Broadfoot
Born: 24th January 1857
Died: 26th September 1931 aged 74
1 British International Championship match
1 Scottish Cup Final

Sydney Broadfoot was deeply involved in football as a player and as a legislator, with simultaneous roles for many years. He was instrumental in the formation of Lenzie in 1874 and played for them throughout his playing career, becoming its President in 1885. He was a versatile player, playing as a full-back, a half-back and more regularly as goalkeeper. As a full back, he was good enough to be selected for an international trial match in January 1880.

He served on the SFA Committee and was elected Vice-President for season 1883-84, continuing to play for Lenzie. During that season, he was chosen to be Scotland's umpire for the first international against Ireland in January 1884. He repeated the role in the home International against Wales in March. Two days prior to that game, he refereed the Wales v England International. His run of appointments continued with being chosen to referee the 1884 Cup Final between Queen's Park and Vale of Leven. However, the match was not actually played. Following a bereavement, illness and injury, Vale of Leven requested that the match be postponed but this was refused by the SFA as it did not wish to set a precedent. In protest, Vale of Leven did not appear for the final. A subsequent meeting of an SFA Committee decided to award the Cup to Queen's Park.

Broadfoot was an umpire in the 1879 Glasgow v Sheffield Inter-Association match and for the 1890 Scottish Cup Final. He operated as a referee in club football for a number of seasons, refereeing Queen's Park against Battlefield in the Scottish Cup in season 1884-85 when Queen's Park suffered a very rare defeat.

John Campbell
Born: 3rd April 1865
Died: 10th January 1906 aged 40
5 British International Championship matches

John Campbell was with the Thornliebank club and was elected as the SFA's Honorary Treasurer in 1888-89. He served in that role for five seasons and it was during this period that he officiated in his international matches, each of which involved Wales. His first was England v Wales in February 1889. He oversaw two England-Wales matches and three Wales-Ireland matches (one in Ireland).

Thomas Devlin
Born: 11th July 1855
Died: 2nd June 1935 aged 77
1 British International Championship match

Thomas Devlin, of Arbroath, represented the Northern Counties on the SFA Committee from 1881-82 and was elected Honorary Treasurer in 1883-84. He held that position for five seasons.
His one international was England v Wales at the Oval, London in February 1887. He was selected as an umpire for the Scottish Cup Final on three occasions – 1884, 1886 and 1987. The 1884 Final was not played, however, as Vale of Leven protested against an SFA decision not to allow a postponement by not appearing for the game.

William Dick
Born: 17th July 1850
Died: 10th April 1880 aged 29
2 A International matches

William Dick, of the Alexandra Athletic club, became the SFA Secretary at the young age of 24 in October 1875. He was the referee for Scotland's away international against Wales in March 1877 and for the home match against England the following season. He also officiated as Scotland's umpire in the international against England in London in March 1877. Dick acted as Glasgow's umpire in the away Inter-Association matches against Sheffield in 1876 and 1878.

Dick sadly died aged 29 after a long illness, having been confined to bed for 10 weeks. Tributes were paid to him on his untimely death. He had been associated with the rise and progress of football in his role as Secretary. He produced the first SFA Annual, a comprehensive publication. It was suggested that he knew the rules of the game better than anyone else in the United Kingdom. Charles Alcock, the then Football Association Secretary, sent a letter to Glasgow newspapers to express sympathy on Dick's death and lauded him highly for his contribution to the game, referring to his untiring energy and enthusiasm together with many acts of kindness received by the Football Association and of advice given.

A Memorial Fund was established by the SFA to commemorate his services to football, and a monument was erected in his memory over his grave in the Glasgow Necropolis. To assist in the fundraising for the monument, the SFA organised a match between Queen's Park, the Scottish Cup holders, and Clapham Rovers, the holders of the FA Cup.

Football had not been Dick's sole interest as he was associated also with athletics, acting as a judge at meetings.

Robert Gardner
Born: 31st May 1847
Died: 28th February 1887 aged 39
2 A International matches
1 Scottish Cup Final; 1 Glasgow Charity Cup Final

Gardner had a significant role in the early days of Scottish football. He was one of the founders of Queen's Park in 1867, serving as its secretary in 1868-69, and captained Scotland in the first ever international against England. He was a versatile player – in that game against England he played the first half in goal, swapped with another player to play as forward for a period in the second half before returning to being the goalkeeper. He was capped five times, all against England. Representing Queen's Park, he served on the first SFA Committee when it was formed in 1873. During that season he and some other players had a disagreement with Queen's Park and he joined Clydesdale. Clydesdale reached the Scottish Cup Final that season and the opponents were Queen's Park. Clydesdale lost, with Gardner playing in goal. He played for Clydesdale through to 1880 and represented the club on the SFA. He was considered to be an excellent legislator of some originality, putting forward potential changes to the Laws of the Game.

Gardner's first international as a referee was the home match against Wales in March 1876. Earlier that month he acted as an umpire in the home match against England. 1877-78 was quite the season for Gardner. The SFA President that season, he earned his final cap against England, and then refereed the Scotland v Wales international and the Scottish Cup Final between Queen's Park and Third Lanark. All these matches were in March, so it was a momentous month for him. To round things off, he refereed the Glasgow Charity Cup Final in May – Queen's Park v Vale of Leven.

Gardner died of tuberculosis when he was working as a clerk on the Forth Railway Bridge project.

Alex Hamilton
Born: 17th December 1864
Died: 11th June 1946 aged 81
1 British International Championship match

Alex Hamilton played for Rangers (1881-84) and Queen's Park (1884-89), winning the Scottish Cup with Queen's Park in 1886. A right winger, he was capped five times for Scotland – four times against England, and once against Wales. He was also selected five times for Glasgow FA Inter-Association matches. Forced to retire aged 24 due to a serious ankle injury, he joined the Queen's Park committee and served as President for 1893-94. He took up officiating, acting as linesman for Queen's Park in matches and refereeing also. His sole international appointment was refereeing England's 13-2 thrashing of Ireland in the 1899 match at Roker Park, Sunderland.

Donald Hamilton
Born: 17th December 1864
Died: 11th June 1946 aged 81
4 A International matches
1 Glasgow Charity Cup Final

Donald Hamilton, of Ayr's Parkhouse club, was the SFA's President in seasons 1879-80 and 1880-81. In that role, he was the referee of Scotland's home internationals against Wales and England in March 1880. A year later, he was Scotland's umpire in the away internationals against England and Wales. He returned to the role of referee for the Welsh match at Hampden in 1882. His final match came the following year when he refereed England against Wales at the Oval. From 1879, he was an umpire three years in succession in the Glasgow v Sheffield Inter-Association matches. In his first season as the SFA President he refereed Queen's Park and Rangers in the 1880 Glasgow Charity Cup Final (which went to a replay).

Robert Harrison
Born: 1856
Died: 22nd July 1937 aged 81
2 British International Championship matches
1 Scottish Cup Final; 3 Inter-Association matches; 1 Glasgow Charity Cup Final

Robert Harrison typified the commitment that so many of his era gave to football, turning his hand to playing, administrating and refereeing. He played for the Portland club of Kilmarnock from the 1870's and maintained a long connection with the club. He was a right winger and was good enough to be selected by Ayrshire FA and by the Scottish Counties to be a reserve in its team to play Birmingham in 1880. Harrison was associated with Ayrshire FA for many years, serving initially as its Treasurer and then as President for over ten years from 1883. He also served on the SFA Committee from 1882-83 and was President in his last season of 1895-86.

Harrison officiated at matches regularly from the 1880's, his Glasgow Charity Cup Final appointment being in 1886. He

refereed Edinburgh's Inter-Association matches against London and Sheffield in consecutive weeks in January 1884 and Glasgow's match against Sheffield in 1887. He acted as an umpire in matches played by Ayrshire.
He developed a good reputation as a referee and this led to his selection for his major appointments in the early 1890's. His two international appointments were both in Ireland, officiating at the games against Wales and England in 1891 and 1892. The following year, he was chosen to referee the Scottish Cup Final between Celtic and Queen's Park. To round things off, he was Scotland's umpire for three home matches between 1895 and 1897.

William Keay
Born: 20th June 1839
Died: 26th September 1901 aged 62
1 AInternational match; 1 Inter-Association match

William Keay may only have refereed one international match, but what a match it was: the very first international – Scotland v England at the West of Scotland Cricket Ground, Partick in Glasgow. Queen's Park provided the entire team for Scotland and Keay, a Queen's Park player himself, was a reserve player for the match as well as being the referee. He was the Treasurer of Queen's Park at the time of the game and served as the club's President for two seasons from 1874-75.
Keay enjoyed another taste of international football when he was Scotland's umpire in the home match against England in 1874. Keay also refereed the Glasgow v Sheffield match of 1875.

Thomas Lawrie
Born: 21st October 1854
Died: 19th November 1904 age 50
2 British International Championship matches
1 Scottish Cup Final

Thomas Lawrie can certainly be described as an "early pioneer" in Scottish football's formative years, given the roles he fulfilled and the significant contribution he made to the game. He played for Queen's Park and was a brilliant forward in the club's early years. Lawrie was selected to play for Scotland in the first international against England but had to withdraw due to injury. He was elected to the Queen's Park committee in 1874, became its first match Secretary in 1875, its Secretary two years later and President for two seasons from 1880-81. He was the SFA's President in seasons 1882-83 and 1883-84 and the Glasgow FA President for five seasons during the 1880's.

His appointments to the Ireland v England and Wales v England matches in 1884 and 1886, respectively, reflect his status in the game. Additionally, he was an umpire for Scotland in four international matches between 1880 and 1884, the last one being the home British International Championship match against England.

In his first season as SFA President, he refereed the 1883 Scottish Cup Final, Dumbarton v Vale of Leven (which needed a replay).

He acted as an umpire for Glasgow in six Inter-Association matches between 1883 and 1887 and also in a Scottish Counties v Birmingham match in 1883.

Given his football activities, it was remarkable that Lawrie found the time to be involved also in athletics, as he was the President of the Scottish Amateur Athletic Association in 1886-87.

William McAndrew
Born: 1869
Died: 3rd March 1956 aged 87
1 League International

McAndrew is an outlier amongst the "early pioneers" given that his international appointment came 11 years after the formalisation of the role of referee within the Laws of the Game. He has the distinction of being the last Scot to take charge of an international match whilst never having been an actual referee. McAndrew was the Secretary of the Scottish League and was appointed to referee the Football League's match against the Irish League in London in November 1901.

At that time, he had been the League's Secretary for two years, so must have garnered sufficient respect in his short time in the role to be entrusted with the appointment to the match. In his younger days, he had been a player and secretary with Rangers. He went on to serve a very considerable 48 years as the League Secretary, retiring at the end of season 1947-48, aged 78.

A retirement dinner was held in his honour, attended by all Scottish League clubs and representatives of the Football League, the Irish League and the League of Ireland. William Cuff, The Football League's President, paid tribute to McAndrew by saying that he was "one of the greatest football legislators of our time". In the latter part of his career, he had played a pivotal role in the introduction of the League Cup. In a magnificent gesture on his part, McAndrew donated cups to the Scottish League for the winners of the then A and B Divisions – inscribed with the champions' names from the start of the competitions.

John McDowall

Born: 2nd February 1861
Died: 6th September 1928 aged 67
2 A International matches; 1 British International Championship matches; 1 Inter-Association match

Born in Wigtownshire, John McDowall was Secretary of the SFA for a remarkable 47 years. He was a towering figure in British football, highly respected for his administrative abilities and having a supreme knowledge of the intricacies of football legislation. His meticulous approach to his job set the template for his successors, embodying all the necessary traits, such as diplomacy, tact and persuasiveness to mention but three, to execute his job to the highest standards. He was described as approachable, genial and having great integrity.

McDowall joined Queen's Park in 1879 and captained the club's Hampden and Strollers XIs. He was only 21 when he was appointed as the SFA Secretary in 1882. He helped transform the financial fortunes of the association, as it was almost bankrupt when he took up the post. By the 1920's, the SFA was a reflection of his efforts and acumen as he had kept pace with the developments of the game and, equally, kept ahead of them. He played an influential part in the development of the Laws of the Game. McDowall was also the Glasgow FA Secretary for many years and was instrumental in the creation of the Glasgow Charity Cup. He was also the driving force in the establishment of the Scottish 2nd XI FA in 1882.

McDowall was chosen to referee the second international between England and Ireland in February 1883. The match was played at Liverpool and was intended to introduce football to the city. In later years he recalled, with a smile, of nearly being out of breath signalling the goals for England in a 7-0 win. The following month he refereed Ireland again, officiating at its home international against Wales. His last international was in the British International Championship in 1885 when he again refereed Ireland against Wales. He took charge of the Ayrshire v Lancashire Inter-Association match in 1883.

McDowall, who served as a Justice of the Peace in Glasgow, died after a short illness. Representatives of the other British associations attended his funeral. A minute's silence was observed at matches played on the Saturday following his death, with all players wearing black armbands and flags flown at half-mast.

James McKillop
Born: 1845
Died: 10th March 1920 aged 75
6 British International Championship matches
2 Scottish Cup Finals

James McKillop, of the Renfrewshire club Cartvale, was the SFA's President for two seasons from 1884-85. He played his part to the full during his presidency by refereeing England against Ireland in the British International Championship in February 1885 and, that same month, the Scottish Cup Final between Vale of Leven and Renton, which went to a replay.

Over the next five seasons, he refereed a further five internationals – four in Ireland and one in Wales. Three matches were Ireland v England.

Whilst President, he was Scotland's umpire in three British International Championship matches – twice against England and once against Ireland. He was the referee for the 1886 Scottish Cup Final, Queen's Park v Renton, and acted as an umpire in the 1890 Glasgow Charity Cup Final.
During his time in office with the SFA, he was a leading voice in the fight against the advance of professionalism.

William Mitchell
Born: 23rd April 1847
Died: 22nd December 1919 aged 72
1 A International; 1 Inter-Association match

William Mitchell was another of the early pioneers who performed a variety of roles in football's formative years. A goalkeeper with Queen's Park (described in the SFA Annual of 1875 as "playing with great judgement and is completely void of funk"), he was also the club's secretary for season 1875-6 and its President in 1876-77. In that latter season, he was also the SFA's President.
He refereed the home international against England in 1876 and a few weeks later he was an umpire in the home match against Wales. Mitchell refereed Glasgow's Inter-Association match with Sheffield in 1877.
He regularly acted as the umpire for Queen's Park in the club's matches.

Tom Park
Born: 4th September 1861
Died: 22nd May 1939 aged 77
6 British International Championship matches; 2 Inter-Association matches
2 Scottish Cup Finals; 2 Glasgow Charity Cup Finals; 1 Old Firm match

Tom Park was a stalwart of football and contributed greatly to the game as a legislator and as a referee. With the Cambuslang club, he represented Lanarkshire FA on the SFA Committee from 1887-88 through to 1890-91 when he served as the SFA

President. After that season he moved to Linthouse and represented Glasgow FA on the committee until season 1895-96.

During his time on the SFA Committee, he refereed regularly in club football. His international appointments all fell between 1889 and 1895. He refereed England in five of his six internationals – three times against Wales and twice against Ireland. He refereed Ireland v Wales once. He acted as Scotland's umpire in three matches – once at home to Wales with the other two being away matches against Wales and England.

Park refereed the 1890 and 1891 Scottish Cup Finals, and the Glasgow Charity Cup Finals of 1891 and 1892, the latter accounting for his Old Firm match. That appointment reflected his capabilities as a referee and the regard in which he was held. Even just four seasons into the rivalry between the two clubs, the choice of referee would have had to be carefully considered. He took charge of two Glasgow v Sheffield matches, the last in 1895 bringing his major appointments to a close.

Bob Parlane
Born: 5th January 1847
Died: 13th January 1918 aged 71
1 British International Championship match
1 Irish Cup Final

Parlane was one of the founders of Vale of Leven in 1872, with which club he won the Scottish Cup twice. For his time, he was a giant of a man standing six feet three inches tall. He played as a goalkeeper and gained a great reputation in that role. Capped three times by Scotland in 1878 and 1879, Parlane played twice against Wales and once against England. An engineering job took him to Northern Ireland in 1881 but he continued to play, joining Cliftonville, gaining a runners-up medal in the Irish Cup in 1882.

After taking up refereeing, he refereed the Irish Cup Final in 1888 and, given his connection with the two countries, was an ideal choice to referee the Ireland v Scotland International the following week. He was also an umpire in the 1889 Irish Cup Final. He lived the rest of his life in Northern Ireland.

Archibald Rae
Born: 10th October 1845
Died: 16th August 1911 aged 65
1 British International Championship match

Archibald Rae had an influential and pivotal role in the initial development of Scottish football. A player with Queen's Park, he joined the club in 1870 and soon became a committee member and then the club's secretary. In February 1873 he called a meeting of the eight existing Scottish clubs to consider forming an association similar to that of the Football Association to manage the game and also to establish a Scottish Cup competition. Successful outcomes on both points were achieved at the subsequent meeting in March and Rae was appointed as the first secretary of the SFA, and also to the SFA Committee. He served only one year in the role, but was deemed to have been an energetic and capable secretary, bringing to bear the experience and knowledge he had gained with Queen's Park for the benefit of the SFA's organisation. In February 1874, Rae was chosen as a member of the Football Association's committee, representing Queen's Park.
Probably due to his connection with the two associations, he was chosen to referee the Scotland v England international in March 1874. The previous year, he had been Scotland's umpire in the away match against England.

James Robertson
3 British International Championship matches; 1 League International
1 Scottish Cup Final; 1 Glasgow Charity Cup Final

Robertson played for the 5th Kirkcudbrightshire Rifle Volunteers (the 5th KRV), based in Dumfries, before joining its rival club, Queen of the South Wanderers, for a few seasons. Through that club, he represented the Southern Counties FA on the SFA Committee for three seasons from 1888-89 before reverting back to the 5th KRV. He continued on the SFA Committee through until 1896-97. During this period he served on the Referee Committee for two seasons from 1895-96 and was a member of the Selection Committee in season 1896-97.

Resident in Glasgow, he was a prominent referee throughout the 1890's. He refereed games in England, Ireland and Wales for his British International Championship matches and was in charge of the Football League's match against the Irish League in 1899.

Robertson was the 1895 Scottish Cup Final referee. He has a very notable distinction as a referee – he awarded what is in all likelihood was the first ever penalty kick, just a few days after the International FA Board had approved the introduction of the penalty kick into the Laws of the Game. The match was the Airdrie Charity Cup Final, Airdrieonians v Royal Albert, on 6th June 1891.

John Smith
Born: 12th August 1855
Died: 16th November 1934 aged 79
1 British International Championship match

An Ayrshire man, Smith won the Ayrshire Cup with Mauchline in 1878. He studied medicine at Edinburgh University and help found the university's football club. Smith also played rugby whilst at university and was selected as a reserve for the national team in 1876. Football won out between the two codes and he won the first of ten caps in 1877 against England. He played six times against England, scoring a hat-trick in the 3-2 win in 1883 and the only goal in the victory the following year (his last international), and four times against Wales. Smith joined Queen's Park in 1880 and enjoyed five seasons there, winning the Scottish Cup twice. A job took him to London in 1886 and he played for a number of clubs there, most notably Swifts with whom he reached the FA Cup Semi-Final in 1886, repeating what he had achieved with Queen's Park the previous season.

In December 1886, he found himself suspended by the SFA for having played for Corinthians against Bolton Wanderers, a professional team, but the ban only applied in Scotland. Smith returned to Scotland to become a general practitioner in Kirkcaldy. Given his fine playing career, he was still much respected and the matter of his suspension was forgotten about when he was appointed to referee Scotland's home international against England in 1892.

Alexander Stuart
Born: 24th February 1865
Died: 23rd November 1891 aged 35
1 British International Championship match; 1 Inter-Association match

Stuart was the one of the first prominent officials to emerge from the east of Scotland. His club was Selkirk and he was President of Edinburgh FA in the early 1880's, representing that body on the SFA Committee. He was the SFA Vice-President for two seasons from 1884-85 and played his part in officiating at matches. He was the referee of the England v Wales international in Blackburn in 1885 and the following season he was Scotland's umpire in the home match against Wales. Stuart acted as an umpire in the 1884 and 1886 Scottish Cup Finals.
He refereed the Edinburgh v Cleveland Inter-Association match of 1882 and was an umpire for Edinburgh in its two matches against Sheffield in 1882 and 1884.
Stuart resigned as SFA Vice-President in April 1886 on moving to England to work.

James Walker
1 British International Championship match

Walker's international was the Wales v England match of March 1890. He was a member of the SFA Committee, representing Renfrewshire (the club he was connected to is not recorded), for three seasons from 1886-87. The international appears to be the only match he refereed, which seems rather unusual given that officials of that time generally refereed some prominent domestic matches.

John Wallace
Born: 1847
Died: 25th February 1888 aged 41
1A International; 3 Inter-Association matches
2 Scottish Cup Finals

Wallace was a prominent official of the late 1870's and early 1880's. His club was Beith and he became the Ayrshire FA President. He represented that association on the SFA Committee and rose to become Vice-President for season 1881-82. In that capacity, he was selected as the referee of the home match against England in 1882. He was also chosen to be Scotland's umpire in the home international against Wales that season. To cap a busy season, he was chosen as the referee for the Scottish Cup Final between Queen's Park and Dumbarton, a game which went to a replay. The Final was Wallace's second as he had handled the 1879 match.

Wallace was well used as a match official in his period of involvement with the game, refereeing three Inter-Association matches, one involving Ayrshire and two with Glasgow, and acting as an umpire for Glasgow in a home match against London and an away match against Sheffield.

Referees - 1890-2025

Andrew Allan
No of seasons on List: 20 (1909-10 to 1928-29)
1 League International; 2 Inter-Association matches
5 Old Firm matches; 5 Junior Internationals

Serving 20 seasons on the List, Allan was one of the leading referees of his era. He took charge of the Scottish League's International against the Irish League in 1922, and refereed the Glasgow v Sheffield Inter-Association matches of 1920 and 1922. He officiated at the Scottish Cup Semi-Final between Falkirk and Airdrieonians in 1924 and was the Reserve Referee for the 1922 and 1924 Finals. His five Old Firm matches were all played between 1915 and 1917. Of his five Junior Internationals, played between 1920 and 1928, one was Scotland's away match in Wales in 1925. In 1916 he refereed a match between Rangers and the Rest of Glasgow in aid of the Glasgow Corporation Belgian Relief Fund.

Hugh Alexander
Date of Birth: 13th March 1936
Died: 20th March 2017 aged 81
Admitted to SFA List: 1967-68
No. of seasons at Class 1: 13 (1973-74 to 1985-86)
No. of seasons as a FIFA Referee: 6 (1976-77 to 1977-78, 1981-82 to 1983-84 and 1985-86)
3 A International matches; 1 British International Championship match
UEFA: U18 Championships (1984); 1 UEFA Women's Competition Qualifier; 5 UEFA Club Competition matches (1 ECWC, 4 UC)
1 Scottish Cup Final

Kilmarnock's loss of a regular spectator in 1963 was refereeing's gain. Hugh Alexander decided that he no longer wanted to watch the team after forward Andy Kerr was transferred to Sunderland in March. So he decided to take up refereeing.

He progressed to the List four years later and his abilities were recognised by the Scottish Junior FA in 1970 when he was appointed to the Junior Cup Semi-Final between Ardrossan Winton Rovers and Blantyre Victoria. His performance was rewarded by being selected for the Final where Blantyre Victoria faced Penicuik Athletic. Another Junior Cup Semi-Final came his way in 1972-73 prior to promotion to Class 1.

His extremely consistent performances over the next three seasons propelled him to the FIFA List for season 1976-77. His first A International appointment was very early that season when he was appointed to take charge of the friendly between England and the Republic of Ireland in September 1976. His other two internationals were friendlies in the Republic of Ireland and Iceland in April and June 1978, respectively.

During his second spell on the FIFA List, Alexander refereed Northern Ireland v Wales in the British International Championship and was selected for the 1984 UEFA U18 Championships played in the Soviet Union.

Domestic performances returned him to FIFA status for his final season on the SFA List. His appointments that season however were only as a linesman in World Cup Qualifiers (In total, he ran the line in 11 international appointments). His sterling contribution as a referee was recognised with his appointment to the 1986 Scottish Cup Final, Aberdeen v Heart of Midlothian, a match which brought his refereeing career to a close.

The SFA appointed Alexander as the Referee Supervisor for Ayrshire RA in October 1988 and he served in that role until he retired at the end of season 1999-00.

Bill Anderson
Date of Birth: 11th June 1930
Died: March 2016 aged 86
Admitted to SFA List: 1960-61
No. of seasons at Class 1: 16 (1965-66 to 1980-81)
No. of years as a FIFA Referee: 4 (1968-69 to 1970-71 and 1977-78)
3 A Internationals; 1 League International; 2 Amateur Internationals

FIFA: 1 World Cup Qualifier
UEFA: 1 Youth Tournament Qualifier; 3 Club Competition matches (1 ECCC, 1 ECWC, 1 ICFC)
1 Scottish Cup Final; 1 League Cup Final; 1 Glasgow Cup Final; 5 Old Firm matches; 1 Junior International

Bill Anderson, a sales engineer, marked himself out as a top referee in the early stages of his career. After receiving line appointments to three ties in the UEFA Club Competitions in 1961 and 1963 and being a linesman in the 1963 League Cup Final, he was appointed as referee to a Junior International in his last season at Class 2. That was followed by selection for two internationals in the British Amateur Championship in 1966-67 – England matches against Northern Ireland and Wales. His performances brought him to the FIFA List after just two seasons at Class 1 and earned him the 1968 Scottish Cup Final, Dunfermline Athletic v Heart of Midlothian. In an era when such appointments were hard to come by, he did well to receive a World Cup Qualifier, Bulgaria v Netherlands, in October 1968.
After losing his FIFA status after 1970-71, Anderson returned to the FIFA List for 1977-78.
All his three A Internationals were in Iceland – Bermuda (1969), France (1970) and Sweden (1977).
Anderson was the referee of the Ibrox Disaster match between Rangers and Celtic in 1971. In the aftermath, a match between a Rangers/Celtic Select and a SFA XI was held to raise funds for the victims' families and Anderson refereed the game. He has the distinction of refereeing finals of two UK Inter-League cup competitions – the Texaco Cup Final 1st Leg, Airdrieonians v Derby County, in 1972, and the Anglo-Scottish Cup Final 2nd Leg, St. Mirren v Bristol City, in 1980.
His League Cup Final in 1976 was an Old Firm match. His five Old Firm matches, and five Semi-Finals in the League Cup, provide an indication of his standing in the game.
An appointment to the 1981 Glasgow Cup Final brought his time on the List to an end after which Anderson became a scout for Dundee United before emigrating to Australia.

John Baillie
Born: 1893
Died: 15th August 1958 aged 65
No. of seasons on List: 17 (1924-25 to 1939-40)
1 League International

Baillie had a lifelong involvement in refereeing. In the early part of his career during the 1920's, he was a committee member of the Mid-Lanark Referees' Association. He refereed the Scottish League's international against the Irish League at Ibrox Park in 1936. During the 1930's, his name had been put forward for consideration for other such matches, which gives an indication of the standard of his performances. Domestically, his highest honour was being appointed to a Scottish Cup Semi-Final, Kilmarnock v Rangers, in 1938. A Motherwell man, he refereed at Fir Park once a season – the club's annual public practice match at the start of each season.
He stopped refereeing in 1942-43 due to a knee injury after which he represented Douglas Water Thistle on the Lanarkshire Junior League Committee. He returned to refereeing in October 1948 when he was appointed as the Referee Supervisor for Lanarkshire RA and he served as the Vice-Chairman of the Referee Supervisors' Committee for three seasons from 1950-51. He worked his whole career in the railway industry, and at the time of his death was a Supervisor for three Glasgow goods stations.

Jimmy Barclay
Date of Birth: 26th July 1920
Died: 2nd July 2015 aged 94
Admitted to SFA List: 1949-50
No. of seasons at Class 1: 14 (1952-53 to 1954-55 and 1956-5 to 1966-67)
No. of years as a FIFA Referee: 5 (1953-54, 1958-59 to 1959-60 and 1961-62 to 1962-63)
1 British International Championship match; 2 British Amateur International Championship matches; 1 British Youth International Championship match; 2 U23 International matches
FIFA: 1 Olympic Qualifier

UEFA: 1 Club Competition match (1 ECCC)

Jimmy Barclay had quite a career, managing to achieve the rare feats of "comebacks" at domestic and international levels. After just one season at Class 1, during which he received his Youth International appointment, Scotland v Wales, he became a FIFA referee, albeit that he was in the Deputy category. He then suffered a demotion to Class 2 after season 1954-55. A contributory factor to his demotion may have been due to his speaking to the press following a Heart of Midlothian v Celtic match in February. There had been a hotly disputed goal in the game, with the Celtic goalkeeper having been charged over the line. Contrary to Scottish League rules, Barclay spoke to the press after the game to explain the circumstances. The League severely censured Barclay.

He bounced back to Class 1 after one season and progressed so well domestically that he returned to the FIFA List again for season 1958-59 and, with the exception of 1960-61, he stayed there until 1962-63. His British International Championship match was in that last season – Northern Ireland v England. He refereed two England U23 matches – against Turkey and Yugoslavia in 1962 and 1963, respectively. Iceland v Norway was his Olympic Qualifier in 1958 and he had a trip to Northern Ireland in 1962 to referee Linfield v Esbjerg fB in the European Champion Clubs' Cup.

In the summer of 1964, information emerged in the press that Barclay was one of five referees whose performances were to be closely monitored in the first half of the new season. He survived the scrutiny. Barclay tendered his resignation from the List in November 1966.

John Beaton
Date of Birth: 9th January 1982
Admitted to SFA List: 2005-06
No. of seasons at Class 1: 15 (2009-10 to 2024-25)
No. of years as a FIFA Referee: 14 (2012 to 2025)
No. of years as a FIFA Video Match Official: 1 (2025)
1 A International; 1 U21 International
FIFA: 5 World Cup Qualifiers

UEFA: 3 European Championship Qualifiers; 3 Nations League matches; 2 U21 Championship Qualifiers; 8 U19 Championship Qualifiers; 2 U17 Championship Qualifiers; 48 Club Competition matches (5 UCL, 31 (UEL (2 PO, 17 G, 4 LP), 11 UECL (4 PO, 3 G, 1 LP, 1 R16)
2 Scottish Cup Finals; 3 League Cup Finals; 1 Challenge Cup Final; 1 Youth Cup Final; 1 Junior Cup Final

John Beaton, a communications officer, has had a very solid career as a FIFA referee. He progressed to Category 1 after four seasons on the List, refereeing the 2009 Junior Cup Final in his last season at Category 2. His early performances quickly identified him as a future FIFA referee and he made the FIFA List in 2012. In his early years as a FIFA referee, Beaton served the standard UEFA apprenticeship by officiating at various Youth Championship mini-tournaments in countries such as Serbia, Croatia, Poland and Hungary. His U21 international was a friendly between England and Northern Ireland at the end of 2012 and the following year he refereed Arsenal v SSC Napoli in the UEFA Youth League.
By the middle of the decade, Beaton started to receive regular appointments to matches in the UEFA Club Competitions and he soon became established at that level, particularly in the Europa League. He has built up an impressive record. He has handled six Play-Off ties between the Europa League and the Conference League and 17 Group matches in the Europa League (with games such as Eintracht Frankfurt v Olympique de Marseille, Real Sociedad v AZ Alkmaar and FK Crvena Zvedva v SC Braga). Beaton had an excellent 2024-25 season in the new style League Phase of the Europa League, where he was appointed to four matches, Real Sociedad featuring again in a match against PAOK. His performances were rewarded with a Round of 16 assignment in the Conference League when he took charge of AC Fiorentina against Panathinaikos.
Beaton refereed Denmark and Chile in his international friendly in 2018, and he has handled two Estonia v Belgium internationals, one each in World Cup and European Championship Qualifiers.

During the period when Additional Assistant Referees were used in football, Beaton received 46 such appointments. He was part of the team which operated with William Collum and officiated at many matches in the Champions League and international matches, most notably at the European Championships in 2016.

Beaton's six national Cup Finals is an excellent achievement, more than reflecting his position as one of the country's top referees. The 2024 League Cup Final was an Old Firm match, one of eight Beaton has handled.

Beaton is also categorised as a VAR official in the FIFA List for 2025.

Willie Bell
Born: 1888
Died: 5th April 1970 aged 82
No. of seasons on List: 23 (1913-14 to 1935-36)
3 British International Championship matches; 4 League Internationals; 1 Amateur International
3 Scottish Cup Finals; 5 Glasgow Charity Cup Finals; 8 Old Firm matches; 2 Junior Internationals

Bell was undoubtedly one of the pre-eminent referees of the 1920's, and was recognised early in his career as "one of the most experienced and fairest referees in Scotland". His appointment to his third and last Scottish Cup Final, Rangers v Partick Thistle, in 1930, was reported as having "given entire satisfaction in both Ibrox and Firhill circles. He is a prime favourite with most First Division clubs." His name was regularly in the mix when it came to the selection of referees for the Scottish Cup Semi-Finals and Finals. In addition to refereeing four Semi-Finals, he was also Reserve Referee on four occasions for these matches. He was never selected in that role for the Final.

Bell handled the Scottish League's home internationals against the Football League in 1920, 1924 and 1929 and was appointed to the Irish League's match against the Football League in 1926.

He has the distinction of being the referee of the revered "Wembley Wizards" England v Scotland International in 1928. Other than a captioned portrait photograph of him being used, he is not mentioned once in the Sunday Post's very lengthy match report. He refereed England in each of his three Internationals, home and away matches against Wales in 1927 and 1929, respectively, being the other games. Given the manner by which appointments were made in that era, his appointments to these matches reflect the regard in which he was held by the English. Bell was also a linesman in the Wales v Scotland British International Championship matches of 1931 and 1933.

Of his Old Firm matches, one was the 1928 Scottish Cup Final, two were the Glasgow Charity Cup Finals of 1929 and 1930 and one in the Charity Cup Semi-Final of 1927.

He was closely involved with the Mid-Lanark RA, serving as its President in the mid-1920's. When he retired from refereeing, he became a scout for Sheffield Wednesday, having been offered a scouting role by some other English clubs.

Bert Benzie
Born: 1903
Died: 6th September 1971 aged 67
Admitted to List: 1934-35
No. of seasons at Class 1: 11 (1938-39 to 1948-49)
No. of years as a FIFA Referee: 1 (1948-49)
1 League International; 1 Wartime Representative match
1 Scottish Cup Final; 2 Glasgow Charity Cup Finals; 1 Old Firm match; 2 Junior Internationals; 1 Junior Cup Final

Bert Benzie played Junior football as a goalkeeper for Kilwinning Eglinton before taking up refereeing. He soon came to the fore in the Juniors and, once he reached the List, quickly became recognised as one of the country's best referees.

A fish merchant in Irvine, he was six feet tall, lankily built, and known for his sense of humour and smiling his way through matches. It was said of him: "Sometimes his smile is consoling to the players and sometimes annoying to the crowd. But he keeps on smiling just the same."

In an interview with a local paper in 1965, Benzie recounted: "There was nothing like a touch of humour for breaking the tension. A wisecrack and a laugh can do much to relax players. In my days as a referee, there was a lot of good natured chaff between players on opposing sides and between players and referees and it went a long way to keeping play clean without lessening ability, keen rivalry and the will to win. Cracks with players were given and taken good humouredly and without rancour and they in no way reduced the referee's authority. In fact they sometimes led to greater respect for them. I was friendly with many players and often mixed with them socially, but let them misbehave on the field and my liking for them as men and my admiration for their playing abilities in no way softened my attitude to them as an official. If their conduct meriting a booking or sending-off I took the necessary action and I didn't have to do it very often. There was less of the "wee black book" in my day because I maintained there was more goodwill on the field than there is now."

His Junior Internationals were Scotland against Wales and Ireland in the late 1930's. He had a top spell in the spring of 1940 as within a few weeks he refereed a Representative Match between an SFA XI and the Army, the Junior Cup Final between Maryhill and Morton Juniors and the Glasgow Charity Cup Final between Rangers and Clyde. His second Glasgow Charity Cup Final was in 1947 and was his one Old Firm match. In 1948, he was in charge of the Scottish League's international against the Irish League. His career was capped by refereeing the 1949 Scottish Cup Final, another Rangers v Clyde tie. Benzie resigned from the List that summer on doctor's orders due to an ankle injury. He applied to rejoin the List in 1950 but his application was declined.

The SFA appointed Benzie as the Referee Supervisor for Ayrshire RA when it introduced its refereeing structure in 1945 and he held the post until June 1950.

Benzie died as a consequence of a tragic accident. His car went down a quayside slipway into the water at Irvine harbour and started to sink. He was rescued, given artificial respiration and regained consciousness. Taken to Kilmarnock Infirmary, he died later that evening.

John Bissett
Born: 1915
Died: 24th April 1960 aged 44
Admitted to SFA List: 1949-50
No. of seasons at Class 1: 8 (1952-53 to 1959-60)
No. of seasons as a FIFA Referee: 3 (1953-54 to 1954-55 and 1958-59)
1 British Youth International Championship match; 1 British Amateur International Championship match; 1 Representative match

Bissett's performances in his first season at Class 1 earned him a place on the FIFA List in the Deputy category and he served two seasons at that level. He returned to the List as a full FIFA referee for season 1958-59.

His Youth International was a home Scotland match against England in Aberdeen in 1957, when he became the first Edinburgh referee to referee a match, played directly under the SFA's auspices, between the two associations. Bissett was chosen to referee the Representative match between an SFA XI and the Army in Edinburgh in 1958-59. His last international was the Amateur match between Wales and England in November 1959.

Bissett was tragically killed in a road accident in April 1960 on the way home to Edinburgh after attending Glasgow RA's Dinner Dance. His wife was seriously injured in the accident. His last match had been that afternoon, Alloa Athletic against Albion Rovers.

He had been closely involved with the work of Edinburgh & District RA, acting as a training instructor and as its appointment secretary during the 1950's. His commitment to refereeing was exemplified by his turning down a promotion to an executive role with the confectionary company he worked for, thinking that it would harm the time available to him for refereeing. Football rallied round the Bissett family after his death. In April 1961, a testimonial match was held for Mrs. Bissett when a match was played between an East of Scotland League Select and an East Junior League Select.

Gibby Bowman
Born: 1918
Died: 1985 aged 67
Admitted to SFA List: 1948-49
No. of seasons at Class 1: 12 (1953-54 to 1964-65)
No. of seasons as a FIFA Referee: 3 (1957-58 and 1960-61 to 1961-62)
1 A International; 1 British Youth International Championship match; 3 British Amateur International Championship matches; 3 U23 International matches
UEFA: 1 European Championship Qualifier; 1 Club Competition match (1 ECWC)
1 Old Firm match

Given the relatively short time he spent on the FIFA List - just three seasons over two spells – it is fair to say that Gibby Bowman achieved a lot. Having taken up refereeing during 1947-48, he was admitted to the SFA List the following season. During his first season at Class 1, his talent was identified by his selection to handle Scotland's Youth International against Ireland. The Amateur internationals he officiated all came consecutively between 1957 and 1960, all of the games being between Northern Ireland and England.

He was selected to referee the International friendly, Republic of Ireland v Norway, in 1960, and was in charge of Norway again two years later in its European Championship Qualifier against Sweden.

Bowman's U23 matches all featured Wales as the visitors – one match was in England and two in Northern Ireland. He returned to Northern Ireland for a tie in the European Cup Winners' Cup when he was appointed to referee Glenavon v Leicester City in 1961.

Bowman's standing as a referee in domestic football in Scotland is reflected in his selection for four Semi-Finals in the Scottish Cup and one in the League Cup, all these appointments coming between 1958 and 1961. His Old Firm match was in 1960.

Bowman retired from the List at just as season 1964-65 was about to start due to the pressures of business. He ran a Post-Office.

Iain Brines
Date of Birth: 22nd July 1967
Admitted to SFA List: 1994-95
No. of seasons at Class 1: 14 (2000-01 to 2013-14)
No. of years as a FIFA Referee: 6 (2003 to 2008)
3 A Internationals; 2 U21 Internationals; 1 Women's A International
UEFA: 4 U21 Championship Qualifiers; 3 U19 Championship Qualifiers; 2 U17 Championship Qualifiers; 12 Club Competition matches (8 UC (2 G), 2 UEL, 2 UIC)
1 Old Firm match; 1 Junior Cup Final

Brines emerged as a referee in the Highland League when he was serving in the RAF in Moray. Returning to Renfrewshire in the mid-1990's after leaving the RAF to join the police, he made steady progress through the ranks, refereeing the 2000 Junior Cup Final in the season prior to reaching Class 1.
Once at that category, his performances identified him as a prospect for international football and he achieved FIFA status in 2003. He had a busy first half of 2003 – handling a Scotland Women's international friendly against China, officiating at a UEFA U19 Championship Elite Round tournament in Portugal and two U21 Internationals – Belgium v Poland and England v Serbia & Montenegro.
Experience was gained at the Nordic U16 Cup in the Faroe Islands in the summer of 2003. Two of his three A Internationals came early in season 2004-05 – the Republic of Ireland v Bulgaria and the Netherlands v Liechtenstein. His third was Ghana v Nigeria, a match played in London in 2007. Brines' four UEFA U21 Championship Qualifiers all came in the year from October 2004, with appointments in Portugal, Georgia Spain and Ukraine.
Of his UEFA Club Competition matches, Brines had eight appointments in the UEFA Cup, generally in the opening rounds, and handled matches at Odense BK, SC Braga and

CSKA Moskva. He had two Group matches, the most notable being Paris Saint-Germain v FC Twente in 2008. Also in 2008, Brines officiated at the Toulon U21 Tournament at which he refereed Italy and Japan.

A tall, commanding figure and very street-wise, Brines was a prominent referee during his career. He was appointed to one Old Firm match, in 2011, and acted as Fourth Official at nine other games, a reflection of his ability to control the occupants of the technical areas and be a totally reliable backup for the referee.

The SFA appointed Brines as a Referee Observer the season after he retired and as a member of the Referee Committee in 2015. He became a member of the SFA Referee Operations staff for a brief period from 2019 and returned to the Referee Committee from 2020 for a couple of seasons.

Willie Brittle
Born: 1916
Died: 2002 aged 86
Admitted to SFA List: 1948-49
No. of seasons at Class 1: 14 (1951-52 to 1964-65)
No. of seasons as a FIFA Referee: 10 (1953-54 to 1964-65)
1 A International; 2 British International Championship matches; 1 British Amateur International Championship match; 1 Amateur International; 1 U23 Match; 1 Representative match
UEFA: 1 Club Competition match (1 ECCC (1 Q-F))
4 Glasgow Cup Finals; 2 Glasgow Charity Cup Finals; 7 Old Firm matches

Willie Brittle's ten seasons of unbroken service on the FIFA List is testament to his high standards and consistency in domestic football over that period. Having passed the refereeing examination in during season 1947-48, he was admitted to the SFA List the following season and reached Class 1 four seasons later. He was given an early taste of international football in the season prior to becoming a FIFA referee when he was chosen to officiate a Representative match between an SFA XI and the Army. His amateur international in 1954, a home Scottish match against the Republic in Ireland, was followed by refereeing an U23 friendly between Wales and England. England and Wales were the two associations in his British Amateur Championship match in 1960.

A Probation Officer, Brittle's international career blossomed in the 1960's. He went to Iceland to referee its friendly against Norway in 1962 and he handled England's British International Championship matches against Wales and Northern Ireland in 1963 and 1964, respectively. His most significant appointment was at club level, being selected to referee the 2nd Leg of the European Champions' Club Cup Quarter-Final, BV Borussia Dortmund v FK Dukla Praha in March 1964. It was his only appointment in European club competitions.

Although Brittle never landed either of Finals of the two national Cups (he did do four semi-finals between 1953 and 1960), he was compensated to some degree by being appointed to six Finals of the two Glasgow FA Cups and seven Old Firm matches. Two of the latter matches were Semi-Finals in each of the two Glasgow Cups. Semi-Finals are never the easiest of matches for referees at times and that Brittle was entrusted to do them signifies his abilities.

Brittle had played Junior football in the 1930's for Bridgeton Waverley and Vale of Clyde before taking up refereeing. In 1954, he played in an annual Charity match against Queen's Park, and was described as a "dazzling dribbler and played a storming game". He did miss a penalty though.

Willie Brown
Born: 1909
Died: Not known
Admitted to SFA List: 1939-40
No. of seasons at Class 1: 10 (1941-42 to 1951-52)
No. of seasons as a FIFA Referee: 2 (1950-51 to 1951-52)
4 Old Firm matches

Despite being on the FIFA List for two seasons, there is no record of Brown receiving an international appointment during this period. Having emerged as a referee during the Second World War, Brown was selected as a linesman for the Scotland v Wales Victory International in November 1945. A couple of months previously, he took charge of his first Old Firm match. At the end of that season, he was appointed to a Semi-Final tie between the two clubs in the Glasgow Charity Cup. His other Old Firm matches were League games in each of the following two seasons.

Brown, an engineer to trade, took up the chance to go to Argentina with John Cox and Jimmy Provan in the spring of 1948 along with five English referees. They were there until December and during that time Brown officiated at 30 games in the Argentine Primera Division, with one of his last matches being the famous River Plate v Boca Juniors derby.

Brown refereed at least one match in the Irish League (in 1950). The reason he came off the SFA List in 1952 is not known but Brown maintained a long involvement with refereeing, becoming Vice-President of Lanarkshire RA in 1965. He had been the Secretary of the Lanarkshire Section of the Scottish Football Referees' Association in the early 1940's.

Bobby Calder
Born: 1900
Died: 8th December 1983 aged 83
Admitted to List: 1938-39
No. of seasons at Class 1: 5 (1942-43 to 1947-48)
No. of seasons as a FIFA Referee: 1 (1947-48)
3 Wartime Representative matches
1 Scottish Cup Final; 1 League Cup Final; 2 Glasgow Cup Finals; 4 Glasgow Charity Cup Finals; 2 Summer Cup Finals; 1 Southern League Cup Final; 6 Old Firm matches

Bobby Calder may only have had a very short stint as a FIFA referee, resigning from the SFA List less than two months into the season he was on the FIFA List, but there is a story to be told about him. Calder was a football man through and through, and had a lifetime of involvement in the game – as a player, referee, Referee Supervisor, youth coach, manager and scout.

Small in stature, he was a winger with Rutherglen Glencairn, Pollok and Darvel in Junior football in the 1920's and early 1930's before taking up refereeing around 1933. He came to prominence in season 1939-40 when he refereed a Junior Cup

Semi-Final and ran the line in the Final. His career then really took off and he was a dominant figure in refereeing during the 1940's. His wartime representative matches were SFA XI's against the Football Association XI (twice) and the RAF XI. For the first match with the FA XI, Calder was presented with an inscribed whistle. At club level, it is astonishing that he refereed 11 Finals between May 1943 and September 1946. Two of these were Old Firm matches. The 1942 New Year's fixture in the Southern League had been his first Old Firm match, evidence that his abilities as a referee had been quickly recognised.

Calder had the honour of refereeing the first League Cup Final in April 1947 between Rangers and Aberdeen. A fortnight later, he was back at Hampden Park to referee the Scottish Cup Final, Aberdeen v Hibernian.

Calder was a linesman in the famous friendly match between Rangers and FC Dynamo Moskva in November 1945. In the match, a penalty was awarded to Rangers as a result of a signal made by him, standing with his flag raised while play surged to the other end of the field. The English referee, Tommy Thomson, heard the crowd's roars, went to consult Calder and then awarded the penalty. The following year, Calder refereed another Rangers friendly against continental opposition, AC Sparta Praha.

When the SFA introduced its refereeing structure in August 1945, Calder was appointed as one of the Referee Supervisors for the large Glasgow, Lanarkshire, Dunbartonshire and Renfrewshire RA. Calder threw himself into the role with gusto. During the season, on top of his supervisory role, he lectured on the Laws of the Game on countless occasions at youth clubs, guilds and old men's clubs all over the country. He regularly held football Quiz Nights. At Easter 1947, the SFA organised a Schoolboys' Coaching Course at Hampden Park and Calder attended throughout the week giving lectures on the Laws of the Game. Between giving these lectures during the day and refereeing a midweek match he was on night shift in his job as a railway signalman. All during this period, Calder also ran boys' teams in Rutherglen, something he was committed to for many years.

By late 1946, rumours were emerging in the game that Calder was being talked about as becoming a club manager. Nothing materialised until the summer of 1947 when he was interviewed by St. Johnstone and was also a candidate for Kilmarnock. In September, Calder accepted an offer from Dunfermline Athletic to become its manager. He resigned from the List and as a Referee Supervisor to take the post, with his last match as a referee being a Glasgow Cup Semi-Final Replay, Rangers v Queen's Park.

Calder threw himself into the role. Signings were made and a new style of training was introduced: gym work, Turkish baths and sun ray treatment were enjoyed by the players at Dunfermline Baths. He did not forget referees either - a hot water geyser, a bath and a heater were installed in the referees' dressing room at East End Park.

Things did not work however and Calder resigned in February 1948, citing concerns for his wife's health as the reason. He returned to his old job as a railway signalman and pondered his options. He re-applied to re-join the List but decided to take up the offer of a job in Canada in May, working for the Vancouver FA, supervising refereeing, coaching officials and lecturing at schools. Calder spent several months in Canada but had to return home as his wife, who had gone with him, took ill. The chance to go to referee in Argentina arose and he spent November and December there. He handled four matches and became another Scot who refereed the River Pate v Boca Juniors derby.

On his return to Scotland, he again submitted an application to the SFA to be reinstated to the List. The SFA required Calder to submit his birth certificate and refused his application as he was deemed to be too old, which created some criticism in the press. Quite remarkably, Calder refereed a friendly match in January 1949 between Celtic and Aston Villa whilst not being on the List.

It was after that match that Calder embarked on the greatest chapter of his football life and which superseded all that went before. He accepted an offer from Aberdeen to become its Chief Scout. Over the next 32 years he brought a multitude of players to Aberdeen. By the mid-1970's, it was estimated that Aberdeen had earned transfer fees in excess of £1,500,000 for selling players Calder had signed for the club. His fame in football was UK-wide and English newspapers carried features on his exploits. He was considered to be the best scout in the UK. Calder was a modest character, often setting out that "it was one thing to find a player, and quite another to develop him".

He retired as Chief Scout in August 1981 and as a token of gratitude for his outstanding contribution to the club's success over the years, Aberdeen took him in its official party for its European Cup Winners' Cup Final against Real Madrid CF in 1983.

Recognition of his achievements and standing within the game came to him in a variety of ways – the Scottish Players' Union gave Calder a Merit Award for his special services to football in 1980 and there were numerous youth competitions played for a Bobby Calder Cup. He was profiled in a radio programme. Following his death, Aberdeen instituted a Bobby Calder Award for the youth player deemed to have made the most progress over a season and Aberdeen City Council named a sports facility after him as a lasting tribute.

Jimmy Callaghan
Born: 1926
Died: 16th March 2005 aged 79
Admitted to SFA List: 1958-59
No. of seasons at Class 1: 12 (1963-64 to 1974-75)
No. of seasons as a FIFA Referee: 5 (1968-69 to 1972-73)
1 A International; 1 League International; 1 British Youth International Championship match; 3 U23 Internationals
UEFA: 1 Club Competition match (1 ICFC)
1 Scottish Cup Final; 1 Glasgow Cup Final; 3 Old Firm matches

Having qualified as a referee in the spring of 1957, Jimmy Callaghan took only one season to be admitted to the SFA List. He reached Class 1 five seasons later and, during that initial season, he refereed the Youth international between Northern Ireland and England. Callaghan's star was in the ascendancy once he reached the FIFA List in 1968-69. During that season, he had an Inter-Cities Fairs Cup tie in Belgium, an U23

International, England v Netherlands and a return trip to England to referee the international against Romania in January. His season was crowned when he refereed the Old Firm Scottish Cup Final. Another Old Firm match at the start of the following season, however, resulted in Callaghan being suspended by the SFA for a two-month period from mid-September 1969. Rangers had complained to the SFA that the Celtic player John Hughes, who had earlier been cautioned, should have been sent off for violent conduct. After a hearing, the SFA Referee Committee decided that Callaghan had failed in his duty as a referee and had committed a major error in failing to order off Hughes. The SFA went to the length of issuing reasons for the decision. As he was a Class 1 and a FIFA referee, more was expected of him by showing an example to younger colleagues. The committee also felt that there was a fear of laxity creeping into refereeing and causing a malaise and a reduction in discipline. More altruistically, it was thought that referees "should be desirably perfect in the atmosphere of a Celtic-Rangers match".

On the night of the meeting, Callaghan had a match at Stenhousemuir and that attracted press interest. It was reported that he was "apparently unperturbed about being the man in the middle of a major controversy." A few days later, to cap an eventful week for Callaghan, and with great coincidental timing, Glasgow RA presented him with an award for having refereed the Cup Final.

The SFA was at pains to set out that the suspension would not impact on his career, and this was the case. He maintained his place on the FIFA List and in the following seasons officiated at the Scottish League's International against the Irish League in 1970 and two Wales v England U23 matches.

After retiring, Callaghan maintained his membership with Glasgow RA. For many years, he attended the annual Referees' Conference as an ordinary member, going about his business in that quiet, imperturbable manner which the press had picked up on the day he received his suspension.

Bob Carruthers
Born: 1903
Died: 1960 aged 57
Admitted to List: 1934-35
No. of seasons at Class 1: 12 (1938-39 to 1947-48)
No. of seasons as a FIFA Referee: 1 (1947-48)
1 War-time Representative match

Carruthers started to make his mark in refereeing from the mid-1930's when he ran in the line in Scotland's Amateur International against Ireland in 1935 and did so again three years later in the British International Championship match against England. It was reported that his Second Division match between Raith Rovers and East Fife on New Year's Day in 1938 was the first in that Division to have neutral linesman. He was based in England whilst serving as a sergeant in the Army during the Second World War but the SFA retained his name on the List to make use of him when he was available. His representative match was in April 1940 when he refereed an SFA XI against the Empire Army XI at Tynecastle Park.
He had to call-off from a Heart of Midlothian v Rangers match in August 1940 as he was involved in a car crash and hospitalised in London. Rather amusingly, the then Lanarkshire RA had earlier that year fined Carruthers for being absent from meetings, quite overlooking the fact that he was away on army service.
He had another outing as a linesman in the Scotland v England Victory International in April 1946.
Carruthers was appointed by the SFA as a Referee Supervisor for Lanarkshire RA in December 1945, once it became an association in its own right following the introduction of the SFA refereeing structure at the start of that season.
He was invited to lecture on refereeing to the Irish FA's referees in October 1947. The talk covered the many aspects of a referee's duties – deportment, intelligence and appearance and a review of the Laws of the Game.
He resigned from the SFA List in November 1947 to concentrate on his Supervisor's role. His time as a FIFA referee naturally ended too, after just a few months. He was Chairman

of the Referee Supervisors' Committee for season 1949-50 but resigned as a Supervisor in April 1952.

Kevin Clancy
Date of Birth: 23rd November 1983
Admitted to SFA List: 2005-06
No. of seasons at Category 1: 16 (2009-10 to 2024-25)
No. of years as a FIFA Referee: 12 (2012 to 2023)
No. of years as a FIFA Video Match Official: 1 (2025)
1 A International; 3 U21 Internationals
FIFA: 2 World Cup Qualifiers
UEFA: 1 European Championship Qualifier; 1 Nations League match; 9 U21 Championship Qualifiers; U19 Championships (2014); 6 U19 Championship Qualifiers; 4 U17 Championship Qualifiers; 39 Club Competition matches (3 UCL, 19 UEL (5 G), 6 UECL (1 PO, 2 G), 11 UYL (3 R16)
1 Scottish Cup Final; 1 League Cup Final; 1 Challenge Cup Final; 4 Old Firm matches

Kevin Clancy announced himself early in his career as a fine prospect for the future and he quickly progressed to Category 1 once admitted to the SFA List. Tall and lean, Clancy continued to develop, and was given the opportunity to officiate at the 2011 Nordic U17 Cup in Finland. He became a FIFA referee in 2012 and made his debut in a UEFA U17 Championship Elite Round tournament in Germany in March. That was quickly followed up by an U21 international between the Republic of Ireland and Denmark.

Clancy was selected for the UEFA U19 Championships held in Hungary in 2014, where he refereed two Group matches and a Semi-Final, Germany v Austria.

His first UEFA Club Competition appointment was in a Europa League Qualifying Round tie in 2013, with a trip to Azerbaijan for an Inter Baku match. It was the first of 19 matches in the Europa League – 14 in the Qualifying Rounds and five Group matches. His Group matches featured teams such as FC Shakhtar Donetsk, RSC Anderlecht, Sevilla, Sporting Clube de Portugal and PSV Eindhoven. Clancy was also well used in the UEFA Youth League, receiving 11 appointments, refereeing clubs such as Real Madrid CF, Manchester United, Club Atletico de Madrid and Manchester City. He was assigned to three Round of 16 ties, with matches at Chelsea, Olympique Lyonnais and FC Porto.

The U21 Championship Qualifiers were a regular feature of Clancy's deployment by UEFA. He had nine such matches, with his assignments taking him to countries such as Sweden, Turkey, Hungary, Poland and Spain. In 2019, he handled an U21 friendly between France and Spain.

Clancy's two World Cup Qualifiers featured Liechtenstein in both games – his first in 2013 a home match against Latvia, the second an away game against Italy in 2017. He handled Latvia again in his European Championship match, a home match against Slovenia in 2019.

Clancy had 26 appointments as a Fourth Official and 41 as an Additional Assistant Referee across the range of international competitions.

A lawyer, Clancy has officiated at each of the three national domestic Cup Finals and has had charge of four Old Firm matches. He returned to the FIFA List in 2025 as a VAR official.

Kenny Clark
Date of Birth: 1st November 1961
Admitted to SFA List: 1986-87
No. of seasons at Category 1: 17 (1991-92 to 2007-08)
No. of years as a FIFA Referee: 13 (1993-2005)
No. of years as a FIFA Linesman: 1 (1992)
7 A Internationals; 2 U21 Internationals
FIFA: 1 World Cup Qualifier; Olympics (1992 (Linesman))
UEFA: 1 European Championship Qualifier; U21 Championship Final (linesman); 5 U21 Qualifiers; U16 Championships (1995); 22 Club Competition matches (1 ECWC, 16 UC (2 G), 3 UCL, 2 UIC)
3 Scottish Cup Finals; 3 League Cup Finals; 2 Challenge Cup Finals; 1 Youth Cup Final; 13 Old Firm matches

Kenny Clark played for Duntocher Boys' Club and Glasgow University before turning to refereeing after a leg injury curtailed any hopes of continuing to play. He was identified as a talent and was promoted to Class 1 midway through season 1991-92 and, over his career, fully justified the expectations that had been held for him. He served a year as a FIFA Assistant Referee in 1992 and in that role was selected for the Olympics in Barcelona, where he officiated in eight matches, culminating in the Bronze Medal match, Ghana v Australia, played in the Nou Camp. Prior to the Olympics, he ran the line to Brian McGinlay in the 2nd Leg of the UEFA U21 Championship Final, Sweden v Italy.

Progressing to the FIFA Referee List in 1993, he maintained his status for 13 seasons and received many significant appointments. That said, his international career did not reach the heights that his talents deserved. A criminal defence lawyer, his court commitments impacted greatly on his availability at times and UEFA held back from making greater use of his services. Had he been as available as other referees, there is little doubt that he would have been viewed as one of Europe's top referees.

UEFA selected Clark as one of the referees for the U16 Championships in Belgium in 1995 (which compensated for his having to decline selection the previous year for the U18 Championships due to family holiday plans). UEFA made frequent use of Clark in the UEFA Cup and, along with appointments in other competitions, he was often deployed to eastern Europe, so much so that he jokingly referred to himself as "UEFA's Eastern European Correspondent".

In domestic football, Clark was in the very top echelon of the referees of his generation. He recovered extremely well from the scrutiny placed on him when he missed the infamous head butt by Duncan Ferguson in a Rangers v Raith Rovers match in 1994, an incident which ended in Ferguson serving a prison sentence. As his career developed he became a great exponent of all the necessary skills required by referees to control and manage matches to the best effect. A total of six Finals in the Scottish Cup and League Cup together with 13 Old Firm matches reflect the qualities he had as a referee and the standing in which he was held. Three of his Old Firm matches were in the League Cup – a Quarter-Final, a Semi-Final and a Final (in 2003).

After a period away from refereeing once he retired, during which time he contributed a regular column for a newspaper, Clark was appointed as a Referee Observer by the SFA in 2016 and became a member of the Referee Committee the following year. An accomplished after dinner speaker, he is now also a Referee Observer for UEFA.

William Collum
Date of Birth: 18th January 1979
Admitted to SFA List: 2000-01
No. of seasons at Category 1: 20 (2004-05 to 2023-24)
No. of years as a FIFA Referee: 19 (2006 to 2024)
No. of years as a FIFA Video Match Official: 1 (2022)
16 A Internationals; 4 U21 Internationals
FIFA: 2 U20 World Cups (2011 and 2017 (VAR)); 9 World Cup Qualifiers
UEFA: European Championships (2016); 14 European Championship Qualifiers; 5 Nations League matches; 3 U21 Qualifiers; U19 Championships (2008 (F)); 4 U19 Championship Qualifiers; 102 Club Competition matches (5 UC (1 G, 1 R32), 49 UCL (6 PO, 30 G, 5 R16, 2 Q-F), 8 PO, 14 G, 5 R32, 5 R16, 6 Q-F, 1 S-F), 5 UECL (1 PO, 1 G, 1 KO PO, 2 R16), 2 UIC, 1 SC)
4 Scottish Cup Finals; 2 League Cup Finals; 1 Youth Cup Final; 10 Old Firm matches; 1 Junior Cup Final

William Collum ranks as one of the best ever Scottish referees, having a stellar career. He qualified as a referee in December 1993 when he was 14, at a time when the SFA had reduced for a short period the entry age into refereeing by two years. Five years later, aged 19, he refereed the 1998 Scottish Amateur Cup Final, a match in which he sent off three players, and in 2004 he refereed the Junior Cup Final. These two appointments were an indicator of his talent being recognised by the respective Amateur and Junior National Associations and what lay in store for Collum. His abilities were, naturally, identified also by the SFA and he was an early beneficiary of the Referee Academy launched by the SFA in 2000 to nurture and develop talented referees.

Promoted to Class 1 in 2004, he became a FIFA referee two years later and was quickly included in UEFA's Talent and Mentors Programme. Selected for the UEFA U19 Championships in the Czech Republic in 2008, he refereed the Final between Germany and Italy. His performances in UEFA's competitions enabled him to move through its referee categories and he reached the Elite Category in January 2013. Along the way, Collum had also caught the eye of FIFA and he officiated at the FIFA U20 World Cup in Colombia in 2011, where he handled the Group matches Cameroon v New Zealand and Saudi Arabia v Guatemala.

His inclusion in UEFA's Elite category opened up the door for Collum to become one of Europe's top referees over the next few years, handling many of the major European national and club teams. He controlled 30 Group matches in the Champions League and 15 in the Europa League. He had 14 Play-off ties in the two competitions. In the knock-out stages, he refereed 26 matches, including two Quarter-Finals in the Champions League and six in the Europa League. He had a Semi-Final in the Europa League in 2018 between Olympique de Marseille and FC Salzburg. The top match he had at club level was his appointment to the 2015 UEFA Super Cup Final between the two Spanish sides, FC Barcelona and Sevilla, in Tblisi, Georgia. The match was played in 40 degrees heat and Collum suffered severely from dehydration for a couple of days after the match.

Collum was chosen for the 2016 European Championships in France where he refereed the host country in its match against Albania. Czech Republic v Turkey was his other appointment in the Finals.

Collum was selected for a second FIFA U20 World Cup in 2017, held in South Korea. On this occasion, his role was as a VAR official and he had six appointments during the competition, one of which was a Quarter-Final between Venezuela and the USA.

In domestic football, Collum, in addition to refereeing four Scottish Cup and two League Cup Finals, handled 11 Semi-Finals in the two competitions. That figure should have been 12 but he had the severe misfortunate to pull a calf muscle in his warm up before the 2023 Scottish Cup Semi-Final between Rangers and Celtic. Don Robertson, the Fourth Official, stepped in to replace him. He refereed the Old Firm in the 2017 Scottish Cup Semi-Final and the 2019 League Cup Final, two of the 10 Old Firm matches he was in charge of.

Collum's steadfast approach was much-maligned, very unfairly, by participants in Scottish football but he was an excellent referee throughout his career, with great strength of character. He finished his career in the summer of 2024 when he became the SFA's Head of Refereeing. The combination of his professional background as a schoolteacher and his vast experience as a referee are the ideal attributes to make a real success of the job and to further the development of Scottish refereeing. He joined the ranks of UEFA's Referee Observers in 2025 and will undoubtedly make great use of his knowledge for the benefit of European refereeing.

Alistair Coutts
Date of Birth: 21st December 1950
Admitted to SFA List: 1989-90
No. of seasons at Class 3A/3: 6 (1989-90 to 1993-94)
No. of seasons as a FIFA Referee: 2 (1986-87 and 1987)
FIFA: 1 Olympic Qualifier

Alistair Coutts served a year and a half as a FIFA referee through the Hong Kong FA, that odd figure being a consequence of FIFA changing the International List from a seasonal basis to the calendar year from 1987.

He qualified as a referee in Aberdeen in 1976 after playing amateur football. A job move took him to Hong Kong in 1978 and, continuing to referee, he progressed to the Hong Kong FA's Class 1 List of Referees by 1981. His performances continued to impress and he made the FIFA List in 1986.

His one known appointment as a FIFA referee is the Olympic Qualifier, China v Thailand, in 1987.

Work took him back to Scotland to Perth and Coutts applied to be admitted to the SFA's List for season 1989-90. His application was given careful consideration. 38 at the time,

Coutts was over what was regarded to be the maximum age of 35 for admission to the List. The traditional approach was to decline such applications but the SFA decided to make an exception (and also by disregarding the standard requirement for a referee to have served at least two seasons in Junior football before being able to apply) and to include him at Class 3A rather than directly at Class 1 as Coutts had tried, leaning on his FIFA status achieved in Hong Kong. Coutts served six seasons at Class 3A and Class 3, refereeing in the Tayside Juniors and running the line in the Scottish League. He received one international appointment during his time on the SFA List – a European Championship Qualifier, Faroe Islands v Denmark, in September 1991 as an assistant to Jim McCluskey. He was also a linesman in a Challenge Cup Semi-Final in 1992. He came off the List at the end of season 1993-94 due to the retiral age conditions.

John Cox
Born: 1910
Died: Not Known
Admitted to List: 1938-39
No. of seasons at Class 1: 10 (1942-43 to 1945-46 and 1947-48 to 1953-54)
No. of seasons as a FIFA Referee: 1 (1950-51)
1 Wartime Representative match
1 League Cup Final; 1 Southern League Cup Final; 1 Glasgow Cup Final; 7 Old Firm matches

John Cox played Junior football for Maryhill and Burnbank Athletic as an inside-left from the mid-1920's and was capped twice for Junior Scotland in 1930, playing against England and Wales. He took up refereeing in 1937 and made the List the following year. He was officiating in the First Division within a couple of seasons and received his first major appointment in 1942 when he handled the Glasgow Cup Final, Rangers v Third Lanark. He ran the line to Peter Craigmyle in the SFA XI v FA XI Representative match at Hampden in 1943. Cox's standing in the game was confirmed when he refereed five Old Firm matches in a two year period from 1943 and the 1944 Southern

League Cup Final, Rangers v Hibernian. His growing status was confirmed when he was selected to referee the Wartime Representative match between an SFA XI v an FA XI in April 1945, effectively a full international.

His career took some interesting turns in the post-war period. He was absent from the List in season 1946-47. When the SFA introduced its refereeing structure in 1945, Cox was unwilling to comply with the SFA's conditions and he did not transfer from the Scottish Football Referees' Association to the SFA's set-up. In September 1946 the Scottish League suggested to the SFA that his name should be added to the Class 1 list. Given the level of matches he had refereed, it was an understandable request with the League being keen to use his services. The SFA Referee Committee responded by indicating that it was prepared to ask the Referee Supervisors' Committee to "reconsider the position of this referee if and when he comes into line with the other referees on the Official List, undertakes to sit his refresher examination, and complies with the arrangements for training made by the Supervisor in his area." Cox was eventually admitted to the List as a Class 1 referee in December 1947. Another twist in his story occurred. Early in 1948, Cox signed a contract to referee in Argentina and he travelled there in March with two other Scots, Willie Brown and Jimmy Provan, and five English referees. He was there through to December and refereed 31 matches in the Primera Division.

After returning from Argentina, Cox, a car mechanic, successfully applied to the SFA to be reinstated to the List, and was appointed to a League Cup Semi-Final in October 1949. His performances were such that he was a FIFA referee for season 1950-51. Another twist in his story happened in January 1951 when he was removed as a Class 1 referee, having failed the Refresher Examination that all Listed officials had been required to take to demonstrate their up-to-date knowledge of the Laws of the Game. He did eventually pass the examination and returned to the List the following season. Cox's capabilities were again confirmed when the Scottish League appointed him to the 1953 League Cup Final between East Fife and Partick

Thistle. A few weeks previously, he had refereed the Old Firm in a Glasgow Cup Semi-Final (and the replay).

Cox officiated regularly in Northern Ireland from 1950 to 1953 and was highly regarded there. He certainly made a quick impression as just a few months after his first game, he was appointed to the 1950 Irish Cup Final, Linfield v Distillery.

Cox resigned from the List in February 1954 to become a scout for Aberdeen, citing that he thought it was "the right time to go, when I'm probably at my best". Cox lived in Rutherglen, the same town as Bobby Calder, the former referee who had become Aberdeen's Chief Scout, so it is easy to imagine how the opportunity for Cox came about.

Peter Craigmyle
Date of Birth: 1st January 1894
Died: 21st November 1979 aged 85
No. of seasons on List: 29 (1920-21 to 1948-49)
No. of seasons as a FIFA Referee: 1 (1947-48)
3 British International Championship matches; 1 Amateur International; 6 League Internationals; 9 Representative matches; 4 Wartime Representative matches; 2 Victory Internationals
3 Scottish Cup Finals; 1 League Cup Final; 1 Summer Cup Final; 2 Southern League Cup Finals; 3 Glasgow Cup Finals; 2 Glasgow Charity Cup Finals; 7 Old Firm matches; 2 Junior Internationals; 3 Irish Cup Finals; 1 Irish Gold Cup Final

Peter Craigmyle is without doubt one of the most significant figures in Scottish refereeing. He was a top referee for 31 years and achieved a level of fame in Scotland and elsewhere which was staggering. Refereeing was but one string to his bow as he was well-known for singing, organising concerts, appearing on radio programmes and giving talks on various subjects beyond refereeing. He became extremely well known by many and was popular and well-liked in football (not that common for a referee!). In an era well before the modern levels of mass communication, Craigmyle's name was carried extremely regularly in newspapers through his entire career. Newspapers soon get to know the source of a good story and Craigmyle was adept at providing stories to many contacts in the newspaper world. He was certainly a showman. His popularity, reflected by often being referred to just by his first-name, stemmed from the personality he displayed when refereeing. He became famous for his many gestures and mannerisms in his refereeing style – the outstretched arm, with finger pointing to the penalty spot, the little trot to the centre from the pavilion, the hearty handshake, sweeping gestures with his arm and the knocking together of two erring players' heads. When he retired in 1949, Craigmyle wrote an autobiography, in which he recounted tales from his refereeing days. The book had forewords from George Graham and Stanley Rous, Secretaries of the SFA and the Football Association, respectively, which reflects the esteem in which Craigmyle was held. In 2023, a book was published on Craigmyle which was comprised of newspaper stories in which he featured and which confirms the giant character that he was.

And yet, it was by chance that Craigmyle became a referee. In 1916, he broke both his legs in an accident in the naval dockyard in Invergordon. At the time, he was playing as a goalkeeper for Linksfield in Aberdeen, and also played water polo and cricket for clubs in the city. Early in 1918, after over a year walking with crutches and returning to some semblance of mobility, he was encouraged to take up refereeing by the manager of Aberdeen, Jimmy Phillip. Very much on the basis of wishing to strengthen his legs and regaining fitness, he accepted the suggestion. He refereed in amateur football for a year and, in April 1919, handled a number of friendly matches Aberdeen played against other League clubs. He made the SFA and Scottish League Lists for the following season and never looked back.

Once he made the List, he decided to take things seriously and applied himself. His fitness had returned and he realised that complete fitness was vital if he were to make a name for himself. He made arrangements with Aberdeen to train daily with their players and he did this throughout his career. Craigmyle was renowned for his fitness and for the amount of running he did in matches. As part of his fitness regime, for 20 years or so, he employed a masseur to treat him at matches.

Major appointments soon came his way. 1922 was a breakthrough year for him – his first Old Firm match on New Year's Day, a Scottish Cup Semi-Final, Partick Thistle v Rangers in March, a Junior International, Scotland v England at Aberdeen in April, and the Glasgow Cup Final, Rangers v Clyde, in September. His first international was England v Ireland in October 1924, a match flanked on either side by appointments to League Internationals.

Given the length of his career and his standing as a referee, it is remarkable to think that Craigmyle only had three appointments in the British International Championship. His second was Ireland v Wales in 1926 and after a 14-year gap, he refereed England v Ireland again in 1938.

A similar thought could be entertained regarding his having only refereed three Scottish Cup Finals – 1926, 1931 and 1932. He did do 11 Semi-Finals in the Scottish Cup. The competition between referees for the major appointments is always fierce and it certainly was throughout Craigmyle's career. When the voting system for these appointments at the SFA Council meetings is factored in, the view might be reached that there were other referees just as popular, if not more so, than Craigmyle when votes were being cast. He missed out a few times certainly, as his selection as the Reserve Referee on seven occasions during the 1920's would indicate. There is a famous tale from the 1931 Cup Final between Celtic and Motherwell. To all and sundry at the match, it appeared that Craigmyle was chased by two Celtic players behind the goals after refusing a penalty claim by Celtic. Newspaper photographs appear to give the impression that this was the case. In his autobiography, Craigmyle told his version of events, claiming to be running to take up a position for a corner kick and being unaware of any players behind him.

The 1920's was a golden period in Craigmyle's career. Beyond his international appointment he was selected for six Finals in the Glasgow FA's two cup competitions in a four year period, one Final being between the Old Firm.

His fortunes dipped for a few seasons after the 1932 Scottish Cup Final but they revived again for the last decade of his career. The 1940's saw him favoured with many prestigious appointments such as the Wartime Representative matches between the SFA and FA XI's, which were essentially unofficial Scotland v England internationals. Craigmyle was appointed to such a match in April 1941 which delighted him as it was the one fixture he had had always wanted to referee. He was selected for the same game two years later and, given that he had been confined to bed the day before by his doctor, it was miraculous that he somehow defied the doctor and managed to do the game – with a temperature of 100 degrees. After the match, he fainted in his dressing room. Also in 1943, Craigmyle was appointed to referee Irish FA XI and Irish League XI representative matches against the British Army XI.

He completed a hat-trick of Scotland v England matches when he refereed the Victory International in 1946. Craigmyle was a linesman in the Britain v Rest of Europe Select match played at Hampden Park in 1947. His last major domestic honour came later that year when he was appointed to the League Cup Final, East Fife v Falkirk.

Craigmyle made his mark in Irish football during his career. He frequently refereed there, predominantly between 1928 and 1933. He was appointed to the Gold Cup Final, Distillery v Bangor, in 1930 and his first Irish Cup Final, Cliftonville v Linfield, followed in 1933. Staying in Aberdeen, travelling to Northern Ireland would have been quite an undertaking. For a match at Derry City in 1930, Craigmyle took an overnight boat from Glasgow to Londonderry on the Friday and travelled back from Belfast on an overnight boat to Glasgow. On the Sunday afternoon, in typical style, Craigmyle stopped off in Arbroath to speak at a meeting. In 1938, he refereed a friendly Glentoran played against Luton Town, with his name used in a newspaper advert publicising the match. It must have thought that he might add a few spectators on to the gate.

Craigmyle's popularity in Orkney and Shetland knew no bounds, as the football associations of the islands regularly invited him to referee their annual match. He made headlines (in Northern Ireland surprisingly) on one occasion by flying from Inverness to Kirkwall to do one match. The islanders always made the most of visits as he was always asked to lecture on the Laws of the Game. In 1931, he donated a Cup (in his name) to the Orkney FA for competition between the local clubs. Craigmyle ventured also to the Faroe Islands on a five day trip in July 1936 to referee a series of five matches between the locals and a Norwegian team.

Craigmyle spent a month in Malta in December 1947 following an invitation to referee and to lecture on the Laws of the Game. The year before, he had accepted an invitation to become the Honorary President of the Malta Referees' Association. An Aberdonian in Malta who had taken a referees' course under Craigmyle back home had been instrumental in the invitation being made. Whilst there, he refereed matches between Maltese Representative and club teams against SK Rapid of Austria.

Craigmyle announced that he was retiring from the SFA List at the end of season 1948-49. The SFA recognised his lengthy service by presenting him with an inscribed gold medallion. His last League match was Rangers v Queen of the South on 2nd April 1949. The two clubs made a joint presentation of a gold watch to mark his service. After thanking the clubs for their gift, Craigmyle, being Craigmyle, sang a song. Additionally, the Rangers Supporters' Clubs presented him with a silver whistle. His refereeing career did not finish there, though. From Glasgow, he headed to Belfast where he refereed the replay of the Irish Cup Semi-Final between Glentoran and Portadown on the Monday. He returned to Northern Ireland two weeks later to referee Glentoran against Derry City in the Final. He had also refereed the previous season's Irish Cup Final.

The Irish Cup Final was not exactly his last match though. At a function in Fraserburgh in early May, Craigmyle said he had refereed 19 games in 24 days. He was back in action again in December 1949 when he returned to Malta, responding to an emergency call from the island's football association due to a dispute with the local referees. He spent a month there, officiating at many League matches and helped resolve the dispute. He felt obliged in the circumstances to resign from the position of Honorary President. Despite retiring at the end of the previous season, he had maintained fitness by training twice a week at Pittodrie Stadium.

Craigmyle ran a tobacconist and sports shop in Aberdeen and for a period supplied the club's kit. Rumours often emerged at various times that he was to become a Club Director. This never materialised but he was a shareholder for many years.

Given his standing in the game, it was inevitable that Craigmyle would be appointed as a Referee Supervisor when it introduced its refereeing system in 1945. Craigmyle was responsible for Aberdeen and the North of Scotland, a huge geographical area, and he approached the role with his customary vigour. He served as the Chairman of the Referee Supervisors' Committee for a total of 11 seasons and played a pivotal role in the setting of the foundations of the operation of SFA's system. He resigned as a Referee Supervisor in April 1959.

Craigmyle had had a remarkable career as a referee and as the Referee Supervisors' Committee Chairman he continued to contribute to Scottish refereeing. He was a great personality both on and off the field. It was said of him that "he is not merely a good referee. He is not merely a good speaker. He is an orator able to hold and enthrall a gathering by the sheer power and fascination of his eloquence." Humorous tales of Craigmyle in action in football matches abound – like the instance he dashed off the field to get a new pair of shorts for a player and when he apprehended an intruder on the pitch by grabbing him by the scruff of the neck and escorting to the touchline. There cannot be too many referees who received an ovation from both sets of supporters after an Old Firm game, as happened to him after what was his last match between Celtic and Rangers in 1947.

Willie Crawford
Born: 1911
Died: Not Known
Admitted to SFA List: 1938-39
No. of seasons at Class 1: 3 (1944-45 to 1946-47)
FIFA: 1 World Cup Qualifier
Panamerican Championships (1952); Central American and Caribbean Championships (1953); Central American Games (1954)

Crawford had a quite remarkable career – managing to referee a World Cup Qualifier, Mexico v Haiti, in 1953 without ever being a FIFA referee. He also refereed 16 other A International matches, all in Central American and South American Championships.

He followed in the footsteps of the three Scots, Willie Brown, John Cox and Jimmy Provan, who had gone to Argentina in the spring of 1948 along with five English referees. He decided to take up the offer of going to Argentina in March 1949. He refereed 36 matches in the Primera Division between April and December in 1949, one of the matches being the famous derby, Boca Juniors v River Plate.

Crawford had been admitted to the SFA List in 1938 and it took him six seasons to reach the top level. He served just three seasons at Class 1, with his only significant appointment of note being a Glasgow Cup Semi-Final, Clyde v Rangers, in 1945. He was demoted to Class 3 for his final season.

It is not known why his time on the List came to an end after season 1947-48 – did he choose to resign or was he deleted? But regardless of the circumstances, the opportunity to go to Argentina soon materialised and it was obviously very attractive to him. Put simply, his career from that point on went into overdrive and the level of football he found himself officiating over the next few years would surely have been beyond his wildest dreams.

On his return to Scotland after his stint in Argentina, he was in demand and he accepted contracts to referee in Chile (1950 to 1953), Mexico (1953 to 1955) and Costa Rica (1957 to 1958), making a successful career out of it. It is incredible to think that despite never being a FIFA referee he officiated at so many International matches in major competitions. That is no doubt a reflection of how football was in that part of the world in that era (particularly on how the "local" referees were viewed) and that FIFA was quite happy to turn a blind eye to its own rules to allow referees such as Willie Crawford to handle international matches.

Bill Crombie
Date of Birth: 12th May 1947
Died: October 2023 aged 76
Admitted to SFA List: 1977-78

No. of seasons at Class 1: 14 (1983-84 to 1996-97)
No. of seasons/years as a FIFA Referee: 7 (1986-87 to 1990 and 1992 to 1993)
1 A International;
FIFA: Futsal World Cup (1989 (F))
UEFA: 2 Club Competition matches (1 ECWC, 1 UCL); 1 Women's European Championship Qualifier; 1 U21 Championship Qualifier; 3 U18 Championship Qualifiers; U16 Championships (1987)
1 Youth Cup Final; 1 Old Firm match; 1 Junior Cup Final

Bill Crombie took up refereeing aged 22 after deciding he could do better than the referees of the amateur games in which he had been playing. Eight years later he made the List. He had a big end to season 1980-81 when he ran the line in the Scottish Cup Final between Rangers and Dundee United and the following Saturday he returned to Hampden Park to complete a unique double of sorts when he was a linesman in the Junior Cup Final.

Class 1 status was reached in 1983-84 after refereeing the 1983 Junior Cup Final and his domestic performances over the next three seasons were such that he graduated to the FIFA List. After refereeing a Scotland v England Qualifier in the UEFA Women's Championship in 1986, Crombie was selected for the UEFA U16 Championships in France in 1987. His greatest appointment as a FIFA referee was his selection to FIFA's first-ever World Futsal Championships which were held in the Netherlands in 1989. He crowned his selection by refereeing the Final between Brazil and the host nation.

After losing his place on the FIFA List for 1991, he did well to return for a further two seasons in 1992. Typical of the era, the majority of his refereeing appointments came in the UEFA U18 and U21 Championship Qualifiers. Crombie was regularly used as a linesman during his time as a FIFA referee. In this role his appointments included two A Internationals, three Olympic Qualifiers, one European Championship Qualifier and one World Cup Qualifier. He considered his most memorable appointment to have been one he received prior to becoming a FIFA referee – running the line on a European Champion

Clubs' Cup match between the Italian clubs, Hellas Verona and Juventus in 1985. Bob Valentine was the referee and the other linesman was Les Mottram. The match was played behind closed doors.

Crombie's latter years on the FIFA List coincided with the formal introduction of the Fourth Official and he was selected for a World Cup Qualifier in that role.

In domestic football, Crombie was the referee of six semi-finals in the major Cup Competitions between 1987 and 1995, and the Fourth Official for the 1994 Scottish Cup Final.

Injury problems had a serious impact on his final season of his career and, despite his best efforts to see it through to the end, he had to admit defeat in his battle and resigned from the SFA List in February 1997.

Crombie was committed to refereeing and he continued to officiate in youth football in Edinburgh for a number of years. He had done so through his entire career, exemplified by running the line on an U13 Final at Tynecastle Park in 1991 and officiating at the Aberdeen International Youth Festival three years in a row from 1992. He had a connection to the Tynecastle Boys' Club in Edinburgh and served the club in voluntary capacity once he hung up his whistle.

Frank Crossley
Born: 1917
Died: 16th March 2008 aged 91
Admitted to SFA List: 1948-49
No. of seasons at Class 1: 11 (1952-53 to 1962-63)
No. of seasons as a FIFA Referee: 2 (1955-56 and 1960-61)
2 British Amateur International Championship matches; 2 British Youth International Championship matches
UEFA: 1 Club Competition match (1 ICFC (1 Q-F))

Frank Crossley gave sterling service to refereeing and to the SFA throughout his entire career. His 11 season stint as a Class 1 referee saw him handling countless top league matches, though he did not gain selection for any Semi-Final or Final appointments to the two major Cups. His consistent performances did secure two seasons as a FIFA referee, five seasons apart. His first season was in the Deputy category.

His major appointments were to two British Amateur International Championship matches, Scotland v Wales in 1954 and Wales v England in 1958. He handled a home Scottish Youth international against Northern Ireland in 1958 and refereed England v Wales in the same Championship two seasons later. His one club international appointment was Birmingham City's Inter-Cities Fairs Cup tie against Boldklub Kobenhavn in 1960.

Crossley was often appointed to major club friendlies in Scotland and one such match was Motherwell against the Brazilian club, Flamengo, in 1960, a match he always looked back on with fond memory. Motherwell won the match 9-2 with Ian St. John scoring six goals. Playing for Flamengo was the future World Cup Winner, Gerson.

Crossley was the Secretary of Lanarkshire RA for 12 seasons from 1950-51 and represented the SFA at a Referee Instructors' Course organised by the Football Association in 1961. This involvement with the SFA was a harbinger of what was to follow, as he chose to retire from refereeing at the end of season 1962-63 when the SFA invited him to become the Referee Supervisor for Lanarkshire RA, a position he held for 33 years. He served as the Vice-Chairman of the Referee Supervisors' Committee for nine seasons from 1966-67 and was a member of its Executive Committee for 30 seasons.

Crossley was a quiet, unassuming man and had a great understanding of the workings of the refereeing world. He was much respected and was influential in the careers of many referees. He had a very canny eye when it came to the assessment of referees and was a master in the phrasing his reports. He operated as a Referee Observer for UEFA for a number of years.

Refereeing was not his only interest as he was also deeply connected to cricket. He was once a reserve for the Scottish International cricket team for a match against the Army and acted as an umpire for many years in the Western Cricket Union.

Arthur Crossman
Born: 1919
Died: 1993 aged 74
Admitted to SFA List: 1948-49
No. of seasons at Class 1: 9 (1956-57 to 1964-65)
No. of seasons as a FIFA Referee: 1 (1961-62)
1 British Amateur International Championship match
UEFA: 1 Club Competition match (1 ICFC)

Crossman had an early taste of international football when he was appointed as a linesman to the British International Championship match, Northern Ireland v England, in 1952 when he was at Class 3A. His progress at Class 1 was rewarded with an appointment to the British Amateur International Championship match, Wales v Northern Ireland, in January 1961, before making the FIFA List for the following season. His one appointment that season was to an Inter Cities' Fairs Cup match, Sheffield Wednesday v. Olympique Lyonnais.

Crossman was occasionally referred to in press reports of matches for wearing an eyeshade. At one match one wag shouted to him that he should "deal the cards"!

After retiring at the end of season 1964-65, Crossman tarnished his reputation somewhat a few months later by being suspended by Edinburgh & District RA, at the instigation of the SFA, for having made critical comments of the refereeing set-up in Scotland in newspaper articles. Crossman was at the time the association's main training class instructor. He had also put forward a proposal at the start of that season to the East of Scotland Junior FA that he and other ex-Class 1 referees should be allowed to act as unpaid linesmen in Junior games where younger referees were officiating. The idea was undoubtedly from a selfish perspective, given that there would be few other former referees around, but it reflected a commitment to the refereeing movement and a willingness to support younger officials. Evidence of this commitment had been displayed at Edinburgh & District RA's annual dinner in 1961 when, after thanking the Edinburgh press for their co-operation, he appealed to the press as a whole to help referees in their work by educating the public in the Laws of the Game (which shows how long that drum has been beaten).

Matthew Dale
Born: 1896
Died: 25th April 1954 aged 58
No. of seasons on List: 15 (1933-34 to 1947-48)
1 A International
4 Old Firm matches

Dale made a mark early in his career when he was appointed as a linesman to Willie Webb for the 1934 Scotland v Wales Amateur International. Promoted by the Scottish League to its List of First Division referees in 1938, he quickly settled into the top level. After losing at Celtic in December that year to a disputed "offside" goal, Hibernian issued a statement saying that the club considered that "Dale had handled the game well" and that "his exhibition promised well for the future". That seemed to be the case as his first Old Firm match was in April 1940. His major appointments came in the latter part of his career, when he refereed the Scotland v Wales Victory International in November 1945 and the Victory Cup Semi-Final, Celtic v Rangers in June 1946, which went to a replay. He was selected for the 1947 Scottish Cup Semi-Final, Arbroath v Aberdeen.

Andrew Dallas
Date of Birth: 1st February 1983
Admitted to SFA List: 2007-08
No. of years as a Category 1: 11 seasons (2012-13 to 2022-23)
No. of seasons as a FIFA Referee: 5 (2015 to 2019)
No. of years as a FIFA Video Match Official: 1 (2025)
2 A Internationals
FIFA: 1 World Cup Qualifier
UEFA: 1 European Championship Qualifier; 1 Nations League match; 2 U21 Championship Qualifiers; U19 Championships (2018); 4 U19 Championship Qualifiers; 2 U17 Championship Qualifiers; 17 Club Competition matches (2 UCL, 9 UEL (4 G), 6 UYL (1 R16)

1 League Cup Final; 1 Challenge Cup Final

After his father Hugh suggested to him that he should consider taking up refereeing, Andrew Dallas ended up following in his footsteps by becoming a FIFA referee. Being the son of a famous father in the same field is never the easiest of paths to follow and what he achieved in refereeing is to his credit.

Once at Category 1, Dallas reached FIFA status in his third season. His first year was a busy one – a UEFA U17 Championship tournament in Azerbaijan, a Europa League Qualifier in Iceland, a UEFA U21 Championship match in Latvia, a Youth League match between Manchester City and Juventus and an U19 Championship tournament in Cyprus.

His A Internationals were matches between Estonia and Norway in 2016 and the Republic of Ireland and the USA in 2018. He took charge of Norway again in 2017 in a World Cup Qualifier in San Marino and handled Malta v Spain in a European Championship Qualifier in 2019.

Dallas was selected for the 2018 UEFA U19 Championships in Finland, where he refereed two Group matches. He forged a fair record in the UEFA Youth League, refereeing six matches including a Round of 16 tie in 2018 between Club Atletico de Madrid and FC Basel 1893 and a Quarter-Final between FC Porto and Midtjylland in 2019. In the Europa League, Dallas had four Group match appointments over his last two years on the FIFA List.

Dallas decided to resign from the FIFA List at the end of season 2018-19, citing the increasing difficulties in arranging time away from work in view of a promotion with the construction company he worked for. On top his own appointments, he had acted as a Fourth Official and as an Additional Assistant Referee on 48 occasions.

Injuries began to plague Dallas over the next few seasons he chose to retire from active refereeing at the end of season 2022-23. A new path opened up with the introduction of VAR in Scotland in the autumn of 2022 and Dallas has operated as a VAR official since then and returned to the FIFA List in that capacity in 2025.

Hugh Dallas
Date of Birth: 26th October 1957
Admitted to SFA List: 1986-87
No. of seasons at Class 1: 14 (1991-92 to 2004-05)
No. of years as a FIFA Referee: 10 (1993 to 2002)
No. of years as a FIFA Linesman: 1 (1992)
9 A Internationals
FIFA: 2 World Cups (1998 and 2002); 8 World Cup Qualifiers; Confederations Cup (2001); Olympics (1996)
UEFA: European Championships (2000); 4 European Championship Qualifiers; 1 U21 Championship Qualifier; U18 Championships (1994); 3 U18 Qualifiers; 47 Club Competition matches (4 ECWC (2 Q-F), 10 UC (2 S-F, 1 F), 31 UCL (24 G, 2 Q-F, 1 S-F) 1 UIC, 1 SC); 1 Women's Championship Qualifier
4 Scottish Cup Finals; 4 League Cup Finals; 15 Old Firm matches

Hugh Dallas was the most famous Scottish referee of his generation and was one of the best officials in the world at the height of his career. Selection for two World Cups, a Confederations Cup, one European Championships and an Olympics is testament to his standing in world football.
After playing juvenile and amateur football, Dallas' path into refereeing started when he was encouraged to be a linesman in a charity match in 1980. He refereed his first amateur match the following year, sending off three players and cautioned five others, and wondered what he had let himself in for. However, the refereeing bug took hold and he never looked back. He progressed into Junior football and got on to the SFA List for season 1986-87. Five seasons later, he became a Class 1 referee and made the FIFA List as an Assistant Referee in 1992. During that year, he ran the line to Brian McGinlay in the 2nd Leg of the UEFA U21 Championship Final, Sweden v Italy.
Dallas became a FIFA referee in 1993. His first experience in that role came when he got the chance to referee in the Toulon U21 Tournament in France that year and was selected for the Final between England and France. Season 1993-94 ended by being chosen as the Fourth Official when Jim McCluskey was

appointed to referee the 2nd leg of the UEFA Cup Final, refereeing his first A International, Belgium v Zambia, and selection for the UEFA U18 Championships.

The upward trajectory of his career continued in 1996 when he was Les Mottram's Fourth Official for the 2nd Leg of the UEFA Super Cup and the European Championships and by being one of three European referees selected for that year's Olympics in Atlanta, where he refereed three Group matches. He was now starting to make a name for himself in international football and he was invited to referee the Netherlands v Brazil international in August 1996, the opening match of the Amsterdam Arena.

A pinnacle was reached in 1998 when he was chosen for the World Cup, one of 15 UEFA referees. He handled one Group match, Belgium v Mexico, when he sent off two players and cautioned three others, before being appointed to the high-profile Quarter-Final tie between the host nation France and Italy. By this stage, he was one eight referees left in the Finals and considered to be in the running for a further appointment but this did not materialise.

He was now firmly established as one of Europe's and the world's top referees and selection for the 2000 European Championships followed automatically. His standing was now such that he and the Italian referee Pierluigi Collina, with whom he became a great friend, were members of a UEFA panel which drew up the refereeing guidelines for the Finals. He handled two Group matches at the Championships and was Fourth Official in the Quarter-Final between Spain and France and France's Semi-Final against Portugal.

Being selected for the FIFA Confederations Cup in Japan/Korea in 2001 was a pre-cursor to being involved in the following year's World Cup in the same two countries. In the Qualifiers, he had been specifically selected by FIFA to referee Uruguay v Brazil in July 2001. He was now at the peak of his career and at the Finals, he refereed another Quarter-Final, Germany v USA, before landing the honour of being Fourth Official for the Final, Germany v Brazil, refereed by Collina.

Given his established status at national level, Dallas's career ran along very complementary lines in club competitions. He had two major appointments – the 1999 UEFA Cup Final, Parma

AC v Olympique de Marseille, and the 2003 UEFA Super Cup Final, Real Madrid CF v Feyenoord. In the UEFA Champions League, he officiated in 24 Group matches, two Quarter-Finals and one Semi-Final. He handled two Semi-Finals in the UEFA Cup and two Quarter-Finals in the European Cup Winners' Cup.

In domestic football, Dallas became a main figure in refereeing from the early stages of his Class 1 career. His first Old Firm match was in November 1995. A League match between the clubs in May 1999 had a profound bearing on him. Whilst he had become well-known in football by this time, the impact of what happened to him in this match firmly established his name into the consciousness of the wider public. The game was tense and ill-tempered. The Celtic player Stephane Mahe was sent off and the player's reactions towards Dallas provoked supporters. Crowd trouble spilled on to the pitch four times, a Rangers fan tried to attack Dallas, a Celtic supporter fell 40 feet from a stand and then Dallas was stuck by coins, causing blood to flow from his head for which he needed stitches. Images of him kneeling on the ground in a stunned state went round the world. Within minutes of play resuming, Dallas awarded Rangers a penalty which added further to the chaotic scenes within the ground. That night, windows at his house were smashed by stones. Police protection was required over the next few weeks.

The events of the match gave him a media profile and in the years that followed he was often prevailed upon to give comment on various matters involving referees and football.

Prior to the game, Dallas had already been announced as the referee for the Scottish Cup Final between the two clubs three weeks later. There was never any question of him withdrawing from the appointment or being replaced despite the external pressures. The Final thankfully passed off without any issues. Dallas handled another Old Firm Scottish Cup Final in 2002. His first national Cup Final had been the Scottish Cup Final of 1996 between Rangers and Heart of Midlothian. Being appointed to eight Cup Finals in a nine year period was a terrific achievement. In addition, he was Fourth Official in two League Cup Finals and also handled nine semi-finals in the Scottish Cup and League Cup.

Dallas chose to retire at the end of season 2004-05, one season before the then mandatory retirement age limit. He was immediately appointed as a member of the SFA Referee Committee and to the UEFA Referees' Committee, acting as a Referee Observer for both associations. UEFA also made him a mentor for its referee development programme. In September 2006, he stepped down from the SFA Referee Committee when he was appointed to the staff as Referee Development Officer. He succeeded Donald McVicar as Head of Referee Development in 2009. Dallas' time in the position was short-lived as he was dismissed by the SFA in late 2010 as a consequence of getting caught up, along with a few other members of staff, in the sending on of an offensive email. He continued on the UEFA Referees' Committee, serving a season as Deputy Chairman before a change with UEFA's structure saw him becoming one of its full-time Refereeing Officers. Working alongside the Chief Referee Officer, Pierluigi Collina, he had major responsibility dealing with the appointment of referees to UEFA's competitions. In this role, he played an influential role in the progress of Scotland's FIFA referees at UEFA level for the next decade before a regime change within UEFA saw him leave his position. Thereafter, he took up positions at various times with the Greek FA and the Turkish FA in refereeing roles and in 2024 was working as an adviser with the Professional Game Match Officials body in England. He continues to act as a Referee Observer for UEFA.

Dallas was certainly a world class referee, with his management of matches and control of players being his strong points, gaining him respect. His facial gestures and shrugging of his shoulders became something of a trademark and have been much imitated by other referees to assist in their control of match incidents.

Bobby Davidson
Date of Birth: 19th July 1928
Died: 22nd December 1992 aged 64
Admitted to SFA List: 1950-51
No. of seasons at Class 1: 23 (1953-54 to 1975-76)
No of seasons as a FIFA Referee: 22 (1954-55 to 1975-1976)

13 A Internationals; 8 British International Championship matches; 1 Amateur International; 1 British Amateur Championship International; 1 British Youth International Championship match; 3 League Internationals; 1 U23 International

FIFA: 3 World Cups (1962, 1970 and 1974); 4 World Cup Qualifiers

UEFA: 3 European Championship Qualifiers; 24 Club Competition matches (8 ECCC (1 Q-F), 4 ECWC (1 Q-F, 1 F), 6 UC (1 S-F), 6 ICFC)

4 Scottish Cup Finals; 5 League Cup Finals; 7 Old Firm matches

If it is difficult comparing players to try to decide who the best player is, the same applies to comparing referees. That said, Bobby Davidson has a strong claim in any such debate to be considered the best referee Scotland has ever produced. His 22 consecutive seasons as a FIFA referee and selection for three World Cups is unlikely to ever be surpassed.

He took up refereeing aged 15 to help out his school and then took the SFA course. He did so in the company of his close friend Alistair MacKenzie who went on to become a FIFA referee himself. They attended the same school in Coatbridge and started their refereeing careers in the Airdrie & Coatbridge Amateur League. Davidson was refereeing in Junior football whilst still a teenager. He got on to the List aged 22 and was Class 1 at 25. After one season he was on the FIFA List, with that first season being in the Deputy category. His first international appointment was at the end of season 1954-55, when he refereed England against Wales in the British Amateur Championship. He had quickly made an impression in domestic football as he was appointed to the Aberdeen v Clyde Semi-Final in the Scottish Cup that same season. His first full international was the British International Championship match, Wales v Northern Ireland, in 1956.

Within a couple of seasons, he had firmly established himself in the Scottish game and was considered to be amongst the best in the country. By 1958, there was speculation that, along with Jack Mowat and Willie Brittle, he might be in the running for selection for that year's World Cup. His career was taking off with appointments to World Cup Qualifiers and he had the honour of refereeing the Final of a pre-season club tournament in Cadiz between Real Madrid CF and Athletic Club Bilbao in 1960. The following year, he was appointed to the 1st Leg of the Inter-Cities Fairs Cup Final, Birmingham City v AS Roma, a match which was his first in European club competition.

Over the next 15 years, he would handle many important club competition matches, such as Real Madrid CF v AFC Ajax and AFC Ajax v SL Benfica in the European Champion Clubs' Cup in 1967 and 1969 respectively, the latter being a Quarter-Final. He had another Quarter-Final appointment in the European Cup Winners' Cup in 1972, SC Dynamo Berlin v. Atvidabergs FF and a UEFA Cup Semi-Final, Club Brugge KV v Hamburger SV, in 1976.

Given the fierce competition which existed amongst referees for such appointments, to have refereed eight matches in the British International Championship demonstrates the standing Davidson had in the game. He refereed England in five of these matches and handled a further three England friendly matches at Wembley Stadium. Furthermore, he was the referee of the Football Association's Centenary match against the Rest of the World Select in 1963.

His fame was such that in 1964 he was invited to Bermuda to run a six week football course and to lecture on refereeing and the tactical side of the game. In 1966 he was invited to referee some tour games in Canada.

In domestic football, Davidson was appointed to four Scottish Cup Finals and five League Cup Finals over a 20 season period. He also had 17 appointments to Semi-Finals in the two competitions.

Being chosen for the World Cup would be the pinnacle of any referee's ambition. Davidson was selected three times, an outstanding achievement. The first of his three World Cups was Chile in 1962 where he refereed two Group matches and was appointed to the Final as a linesman. In the 1970 Finals in Mexico, Davidson handled one Group match and had two outings as a linesman. His third Finals, in West Germany in 1974, started with great hope on his part but ended in bitter disappointment. He refereed the Second Round Group match between the Netherlands and Argentina and ran the line in three other matches. Davidson had been led to believe that he was being appointed to the Final only for the FIFA Referees' Committee to select the English referee, Jack Taylor instead. Davidson returned to Scotland in anger and in a very emotional state at not getting the Final and threatened to quit refereeing. He did, however, carry on and was rewarded by being appointed to the European Cup Winners' Cup Final, FC Dynamo Kyiv v Ferencvárosi TC, in 1975. His last domestic Cup Final, the Scottish Cup Final between Rangers and Heart of Midlothian, followed in 1976.

Season 1975-76 turned out to be his last as a referee as he submitted his resignation from the SFA List in early July 1976, having been included in it for the forthcoming season. He had actually started his pre-season training in the standard way he had followed for many years. Davidson preferred training on his own or with players at Airdrieonians, rather than with a group of referees. His regime consisted of road runs to build stamina, a series of 200 metres and shorter sprints. As he got older, he would start his pre-season training earlier as it took him longer to reach peak fitness.

The receipt of his letter coincided with an SFA Council meeting and his resignation was announced by the Referee Committee Chairman, David Will. The members were surprised, which probably reflected the place of Davidson within the game and his constant presence for 25 years. His name had to be hurriedly withdrawn from the FIFA List nominations. When he was asked to comment on his resignation, Davidson said he felt that he had been around long enough as a referee and that it was time to make way for younger referees.

Davidson, who operated a painting and decorating firm in Airdrie, was recognised as a firm and fair referee and won respect for his authority. At the 1970 World Cup, a former World Cup referee described Davidson as a "tough man as well as a superb referee," adding "There are no tricks that can fool him. He knows what refereeing is all about and heaven help anyone who gets nasty with him". In a 1974 newspaper poll of Scottish players he was rated the best in the country. A certain

Alex Ferguson, then a player with Ayr United, was quoted as saying "Bobby Davidson is easily the best. He tries to be fair and he's not afraid. There are players who try to run games. I've tried it myself. But there is no way you can do this when he is in charge". He was most certainly a strong referee and had an extremely determined nature. That unshakeable attitude tended to give an impression of arrogance which maybe rubbed club people up the wrong way. Reputations did not influence him and he certainly stood up against Jock Stein, the Celtic manager and the dominant figure in Scottish football in the 1960's and 1970's. There were a few run-ins between the pair over the years. In the way of Scottish football, it can take little to build up resentment towards a referee. Davidson once had to get a police escort from Celtic Park after having sent Jimmy Johnstone off in a cup tie against Aberdeen.

The following text from an article by the esteemed journalist John Rafferty in the Scotsman in 1972 encapsulates the hysteria which can often surround a referee (and by reproducing the text, it is intended to show that modern day hysteria is not entirely new): "When the appointment (to a two-legged League Cup Quarter-Final Celtic v Dundee, which went to a third match) was announced, he had absolutely no chance of having a good game – as far as the crowds were concerned. He was put under tremendous stress because, immediately his name was bandied about among players and spectators and there were all sorts of sinister prognostications about what he would do to Celtic. The crowd waited for him and assailed him, even before he had blown his whistle. And in that hysteria which is peculiar to football grounds, the little mistakes which are to be expected from any referee, are magnified to bias and bigotry. In fact, Davidson had a fair game each time in the three matches and that is extraordinary given the pressure he was under. It had been a long time since had refereed a Celtic match."

Within a couple of months of retiring as a referee, Davidson joined the Board of Airdrieonians and served as Chairman from 1985 to 1989. He was on the SFA Council from 1984-85 to 1990-91 and 1992-93, representing the Scottish League, serving firstly on the Appeals Committee and then the Disciplinary & Referee Committee. For season 1989-90 he was the Chairman of the Appeals Committee and a member of the Executive & General Purposes Committee. In 1992-93, he was the Scottish League's Vice-President and served once more on the Executive & General Purposes Committee. He died suddenly in December 1992. The SFA Council stood in silence as a mark of respect at its meeting in January.

Willie Davidson
Born: 1903
Died: 1991 aged 88
Admitted to SFA List: 1941-42
No. of seasons at Class 1: 9 (1943-44 to 1951-52)
No. of seasons as a FIFA Referee: 2 (1948-49 and 1950-51)
3 British Youth Championship Internationals
1 Glasgow Charity Cup Final; 4 Old Firm matches

Willie Davidson emerged as a referee in the early 1940's and established himself in the top flight within a couple of seasons. He performed well enough to earn his first match between the Old Firm in 1943, in which he sent off two Celtic players with Rangers running out convincing 8-1 winners. Three more such matches were to follow over the next seven years, culminating in his officiating at the Glasgow Charity Cup Final between the clubs in 1949-50. Earlier that season, he also refereed the Old Firm Semi-Final tie in the Glasgow Cup.
His international appointments were limited to refereeing three home Scotland matches in the British Youth International Championships against each of the other British associations in 1951 and 1952.
After retiring as a referee, Davidson acted for a period as a commentator for the blind at matches.

William Dawson
No of seasons on List: 8(1926-27 to 1933-34)
1 Amateur International
1 Junior International

Dawson had a relatively short career and, given the competition with the other referees of the era, can be considered to have done well to receive his international appointments, both of which came in his last two seasons on the List – the Amateur International between Scotland and Ireland in 1933 and the Junior International, Scotland v Wales in 1934. He also ran the line in the British International Championship match, Scotland v Wales, in September 1933. A month later, he refereed a fairly unusual friendly match for its time – Heart of Midlothian v a Chile-Peru Select.

David Dickinson
Date of Birth: 16th February 1990
Admitted to SFA List: 2011-12
No. of seasons at Class 1: 7 (2018-19 to 2025)
No. of years as a FIFA Referee: 3 (2023 to 2025)
1 A International
UEFA: 2 U21 Championship Qualifiers; 6 U17 Championship Qualifiers; 2 U19 Championship Qualifiers; 8 Club Competition matches (1 UEL, 5 UECL (2 LP), 2 UYL)
1 Junior Cup Final

Having attained FIFA status in 2023, David Dickinson exemplifies the success of the SFA's referee development programmes. His potential for the future was identified early and he has been nurtured along the referee pathway. Tall and athletic, Dickinson is progressing nicely at UEFA level in his third year.

His first year started off in the fairly standard way, being selected for an UEFA U17 Championship qualifying tournament held in Albania. By the end of the year he had been appointed to a 1st Round Europa Conference League qualifying tie in Slovakia, two U21 Championship Qualifiers, Sweden v North Macedonia and Bulgaria v Estonia, a Youth League match between BV Borussia Dortmund and AC Milan, and another U17 Championship qualifying tournament in Liechtenstein.

After further qualification matches in the Europa and Conference Leagues at the start of season 2024-25, Dickinson received two League Phase appointments in the Conference League at FC Lugano in Switzerland and FK Mlada Boleslav in the Czech Republic. Another U21 Championship Qualifier, Romania v Montenegro, was also fulfilled.

Dickinson has also had a variety of appointments as a Fourth Official in his time as a FIFA referee.

He received his debut A International appointment in a friendly between Poland and Moldova in June 2025.

Stuart Dougal
Date of Birth: 6th November 1962
Admitted to SFA List: 1989-90
No. of seasons at Class 1/Category 1: 16 (1993-94 to 2008-09)
No. of years as a FIFA Referee: 12 (1996 to 2007)
No. of years as a FIFA Linesman: 2 (1993 to 1994)
6 A Internationals; 1 U21 International
FIFA: 4 World Cup Qualifiers; as Linesman: 2 World Cup Qualifiers
UEFA: 5 European Championship Qualifiers; 4 U21 Championship Qualifiers; U16 Championships (1996); 44 Club Competition matches (3 ECWC, 20 UC (4 G, 2 R32), 17 UCL (11 G); as Linesman: 6 Club Competition matches (2 ECWC Q-F); As Fourth Official: European Championships (2004 (1Q-F))
2 Scottish Cup Finals; 1 League Cup Final; 1 Challenge Cup Final; 11 Old Firm matches

Stuart Dougal was one of Scotland's leading referees for over 10 years from the mid-1990's. He had a tough, no-nonsense approach to refereeing and was not afraid of disciplining players, something which in all likelihood helped to make his name.

It had all started for him in 1985 when he had the misfortune to break his back in a work accident which put paid to playing football. He was encouraged to take up refereeing by a friend of his father, Joe Kelly, a Class 1 referee in the 1960's. Dougal was admitted to the SFA List in 1989 and four seasons later was a Class 1 referee. Identified as a future prospect, he was a FIFA linesman in 1992 and served two years in that capacity. During that spell, he was a linesman in two Quarter-Finals in the European Cup Winners' Cup.

He became a FIFA referee in 1996 and during the following 12 years enjoyed a fine career in international football. Selection for the UEFA U16 Championships in Austria came his way in his first year. At club level, he garnered 44 UEFA Club competition matches as a referee, his pinnacle being selected for UEFA Intertoto Cup Finals in 2003 and 2005. In the UEFA Champions League, he was in charge of 11 Group matches. No respecter of reputation, Dougal made headlines in 2000 when he sent off the Juventus players Zinedine Zidane and Edgar Davids in a home match against Hamburger SV. In the UEFA Cup he was appointed to two ties in the Round of 32. Dougal was Fourth Official to Hugh Dallas in the 2002 UEFA Super Cup Final, Real Madrid CF v Feyenoord.

Dougal regularly received appointments in the World Cup and European Championship Qualifiers but it was as a Fourth Official that his greatest honour was received, being selected in that role for the 2004 European Championships in Portugal. He had four Group matches and was chosen for a Quarter-Final, France v Greece.

Amongst his A Internationals, there were two notable appointments –the Republic of Ireland v Argentina in 1998 and Norway v Brazil in 2006.

In 1998, Dougal officiated at two Play-Off matches in the Bosnia & Herzegovina League and, the following year, at three matches in the USA's Major Soccer League.

Dougal was twice appointed to the Scottish Cup Final (2004 and 2008) and once to the League Cup Final, in 2005. He also refereed the 2005 Challenge Cup Final. Additionally, he handled six Semi-Finals in these cup competitions between 2000 and 2006. These appointments, together with his 11 Old Firm matches over a 10 year period, confirm his standing as amongst the top group of referees in Scotland during his career.

He had a setback in 2004 when he was caught by a television camera swearing at a Rangers player during a match at Partick Thistle, which resulted in him being fined £200 by the Referee Committee.

Whilst Dougal, an accountant who works in insolvency, did not maintain a direct involvement in the refereeing movement once he retired, he played a notable part for refereeing by assisting

BBC Scotland in commenting on VAR decisions in Scottish football through a regular programme on its football website following the introduction of VAR during season 2022-23. The knowledgeable and sensible approach taken by Dougal was an excellent means of communicating interpretations on the Laws of the Game to the football public and to enable a better understanding of refereeing decisions being gained.

Tom Dougray
Born: 1879
Died: 16th November 1964 aged 85
No. of seasons on List: 34 (1900-01 to 1933-34)
7 British International Championship matches; 5 League Internationals; 3 Amateur Internationals; 1 Inter-Association match
11 Scottish Cup Finals; 4 Glasgow Cup Finals; 3 Glasgow Charity Cup Finals; 10 Old Firm matches; 3 Junior Internationals; 3 Junior Cup Finals

Tom Dougray is one of the greats of not just Scottish but British refereeing. He has an outstanding record of achievement and had a high reputation throughout his career.
A player for Nitshill Levern Victoria, an injury put paid to a playing career. He took up refereeing, no doubt influenced by his older brother James who was a Scottish League referee in the early 1900's. (Another brother, John, was on the League's List during the 1920's.)
His first big appointment was in 1909 when he was appointed to the Scottish Cup Semi-Final, Celtic v Clyde. It was the start of a quite amazing period of dominance in the Cup over the following 21 seasons (interrupted for five seasons because of the Cup was not played due to the First World War). His first Final was in 1910 and he refereed the following two. He beat that "hat trick" when he refereed four consecutive Finals from 1922. His last Final was in 1933. His 11 Finals surpassed Tom Robertson's record of ten and it is unlikely ever to be beaten. Over this period of 21 seasons, he was selected as the Reserve Referee for the Final five times, he had 14 Cup Semi-Final appointments and was the Reserve Referee for another four

Semi-Finals. There were only two seasons in which his name did not feature in any way for the Semi-Finals and Finals (1929-30 and 1933-34) and only two seasons where he was selected just as a Reserve Referee (1927-28 and 1931-32). His record is made all the more remarkable as the appointments to the Cup Semi-Finals and Finals were done by the SFA Council members casting votes on the appointments. It is surely evidence of club officials having a high regard for Dougray's capabilities as a referee.

Regard for his ability was also held in the other British countries and is reflected in the appointments he received. He refereed four consecutive England v Scotland matches from 1922 and refereed England in his other three British International Championship matches.

Three of his five League Internationals featured the Football League and his three Amateur internationals each involved England. His first Amateur International in 1912 was England v the Netherlands, the first instance of a Scottish referee taking charge of an international match which featured a non-British team.

Dougray, who worked as a wholesale butcher, was not a tall man, standing only 5 foot 5 inches, and was described as having a "loping gait" and being of a "quiet demeanour". After an Ireland v England international, an Irish newspaper was very praiseworthy of him, conveying that he was "In the forefront of the top referees" and that "He is impartial, prompt, fair and decisive and knows nothing of "fear, favour, affection or ill-will"" In his last season, a Scottish newspaper described him as an "aristocratic and autocratic knight of the whistle".

In season 1911-12, Dougray set a record when he became the first referee to officiate the Finals of the Scottish Cup, the Glasgow Cup and the Glasgow Charity Cup in the same season. Dougray served as President of the Scottish Football Referees' Association in the late 1920's, thus maintaining a family connection with the association as his brother James was one of its founders in 1903.

There was unfortunately a touch of sadness as to how Dougray's tremendous career came to an end. In January 1934, the SFA Referee Committee wrote to the Scottish League expressing the opinion that Dougray was no longer physically capable of officiating at important matches and that it had decided not to appoint him to any further Scottish Cup ties beyond the one he had been appointed to. It was suggested that the League take a similar approach and that he should not be assigned to any matches after his current set of appointments had been fulfilled, unless he resigned. The League did not agree to the suggestion. It was in a slight predicament in any case. By a coincidence of timing, at that same meeting, confirmation from the Football League was received on the acceptance of Dougray for the League International in Glasgow in February. That turned out to be Dougray's last major appointment.

The issue of his fitness capabilities was something that Dougray had become aware of in any case and, after some contemplation, he decided to retire at the end of the season. When he tendered his resignation to the League in early May, it recorded its "sincere appreciation of the long, valuable and distinguished service rendered by Dougray since he was admitted to the List at the beginning of season 1907-08 – 27 years ago." The news of Dougray's pending retirement became public knowledge towards the end of the season and, at his last senior match, a local cup-tie between Hibernian and Heart of Midlothian, the crowd cheered him off the pitch at the end of the game, which he appreciated very much.

He refereed a Schoolboys' International, Scotland v Wales at Cowdenbeath a few days later and was again cheered off the field by the teams through a guard of honour. His final match was in June when he refereed the annual Orkney v Shetland match. In a speech after the game, Dougray said that he never thought for a moment that his long career would end in Lerwick.

In September 1934, the Scottish Football Referees' Association held a well attended dinner in Glasgow to mark Dougray's retirement.

In 1937, Dougray was invited to become honorary president of the Anti-Gambling League.

Douglas Downie
Date of Birth: 9th February 1937
Died: 13th July 2025 aged 88
Admitted to SFA List: 1969-70
No. of seasons at Class 1: 12 (1974-75 to 1985-86)
No. of seasons as a FIFA Referee: 2 (1979-80 to 1980-81)
UEFA: 1 Youth Tournament Qualifier; 1 U18 Championship Qualifier

Before being promoted to Class 1, Douglas Downie refereed Junior Cup Semi-Finals in 1972 and 1974. His steady progress and development once at Class 1 saw him rewarded with a place on the FIFA List for two seasons from 1979-80. He had just two appointments as a FIFA referee, both in Qualifiers for the UEFA U18 Championship, in Iceland and in Wales. During his time as a FIFA referee he had two appointments as a linesman, to Qualifiers in the European Championships and the Olympics.

Prior to achieving FIFA status, he had five line international appointments, his first being in his first season on the List – a World Cup Qualifier between the Republic of Ireland and Denmark – and the major one being appointed to the 2nd Leg of the 1976 UEFA Cup Semi-Final, Club Brugge KV v Hamburger SV, refereed by Bobby Davidson. He received other line appointments post-FIFA List.

Downie's top appointments in domestic football were to the Scottish Cup Semi-Final between Rangers and Aberdeen in 1980, and the 1st Leg of a League Cup Semi-Final in 1981, St. Mirren v Rangers. These appointments were a reflection of the good period he was then enjoying.

He was committed to refereeing, being a training class instructor with Edinburgh & District RA for many years. That commitment saw him finish his refereeing career a season earlier than the mandatory retiral age as, in the summer of 1986, the SFA appointed him as a Referee Supervisor for Edinburgh & District RA, with responsibility for the West Lothian training area. He served in the role until July 1999 when he moved to Fife RA as its Referee Supervisor and then its Association Manager. Downie had an energetic and diligent style and put much into being a Referee Supervisor. On top of the onerous duties of being a Supervisor, he had a very busy professional life as he and his wife ran a children's care home in Edinburgh. Downie stepped down from his Association Manager's role in 2006 due to health reasons.

Jimmy Duncan
Date of Birth: 24th February 1947
Admitted to SFA List: 1975-76
No. of seasons at Class 1: 11 (1980-81 to 1991-92)
No. of seasons/years as a FIFA Referee: 3 (1986-87 to 1988)
UEFA: 2 Club Competition matches (2 UC); 1 U16 Championship Qualifier
1 Old Firm match

Jimmy Duncan played in the East of Scotland League as a forward with Vale of Leithen, Gala Fairydean and Hawick Royal Albert before injury brought his playing days to an end. He took up refereeing because he wanted to keep involved in the game. Once he made the List, he was picked as a linesman for the 1978 Scottish Cup Final, Rangers v Aberdeen, in what was his last season at Class 3A.
After five seasons at Class 1, his consistent performances brought him to the FIFA list for season 1986-87. His club competition matches were both in the early rounds of the UEFA Cup, with matches in Poland and Sweden. In the UEFA U16 Qualifiers, he refereed Northern Ireland v. Republic of Ireland in 1987. He had charge of Northern Ireland's U16s again a month afterwards in a friendly against Canada, played at Rugby Park, Kilmarnock. Canada featured again when he refereed them in a home Scotland U20 friendly later that year.
Duncan's star had been in the ascendancy in domestic football during the mid-1980's, highlighted firstly by his appointment to the 2nd Leg of the League Cup Semi-Final between Hibernian and Rangers in 1985, and then to an Old Firm match in October 1987. This turned out to be a match which unfortunately impacted on his career. He had to deal with an outbreak of player indiscipline during the game and sent off three players in one incident. Due to the furore created within the stadium by

the players, the Glasgow Procurator Fiscal ordered the police to investigate with the upshot being that four players were charged with breach of the peace by conducting themselves in a disorderly manner with the matter ending up in court. During the trial, Duncan, not unreasonably, said that he "never expected to be in court after sending the players off" and that if police intervention in football became a habit, he would have to seriously consider whether he should continue to referee. Although not at fault for what happened in the match (a report said that a fourth player could easily have been sent off), Duncan was affected by all the events surrounding it and his star waned. Injury problems affected him in his last season or two and he was forced to resign as a Class 1 referee in October 1991.

He was not lost to the refereeing movement and he became the trainer for the Borders section of Edinburgh & District RA for many years, travelling weekly from his home in Gorebridge to Galashiels, having also been a training class instructor for the Borders area during the 1980's.

Charlie Faultless
Date of Birth: 5th March 1908
Died: 27th November 1998 aged 90
Admitted to List: 1935-36
No. of seasons at Class 1: 16 (1938-39 to 1945-46 and 1947-48 to 1954-55)
No. of seasons as a FIFA Referee: 4 (1951-52 to 1954-55)
2 British International Championship matches; 1 British Amateur Championship match; 1 Amateur International; 1 League International
FIFA: World Cup (1954)
2 Scottish Cup Finals; 1 Old Firm match; 1 Irish Cup Final

Faultless was a man with an impeccable name for a referee as he could justifiably say that had given a faultless performance in every match. He started in football as a goalkeeper, playing for Motherwell, Morton and Brechin City before turning to refereeing. Faultless' first taste of international football was in 1937 when he was a linesman in Scotland's British

International Championship match in Wales. He also ran the line in the SFA XI v FA XI Wartime Representative match in 1941.

The Second World War interrupted his career to a great extent as he served in the Armed Forces and he spent a season or so at Class 2 when he returned to civilian life (in which he was a director of a ladies clothes-making company). His career took off from the late 1940's once he returned to Class 1 in January 1948. In 1949 he was nominated by the SFA as one of its candidates for the World Cup as a replacement for Willie Webb following Webb's resignation. That same year, the Scottish League replaced him as referee on an Aberdeen v Morton fixture once it had come to its notice that he was a former Morton player. He did referee at Pittodrie Stadium in 1949 when he took charge of the Scotland v Ireland Amateur international.

Another Amateur International followed in 1952 when he refereed the friendly between England and France at Norwich. Seasons 1953-54 and 1954-54 were the best of his career. During this period, he refereed four British International Championship matches, two home Scottish League Internationals, two Scottish Cup Finals, one Old Firm match and officiated at the 1954 World Cup in Switzerland. At the World Cup, he handled a Group match between Brazil and Yugoslavia, a Quarter-Final, Austria v Switzerland, and was a linesman for the Semi-Final, Hungary against Uruguay.

Faultless was a linesman once more later in 1954 for the England v West Germany friendly international. The referee was Vicenzo Orlandini (Italy) and the other linesman was Mervyn Griffiths (Wales), both of whom had also been at the World Cup.

During season 1949-50, Faultless refereed regularly in the Irish League and occasionally in the following seasons. His commitment to refereeing in Northern Ireland was rewarded in 1953 when he was appointed to the Irish Cup Final, Linfield v Coleraine.

Faultless chose to retire at the end of season 1954-55, going out at the top after refereeing the Scottish Cup Final between Clyde and Celtic. For the next 20 years he reported on football matches for the Sunday Express. He made a refereeing comeback of sorts in 1958 when he and Jack Mowat refereed a televised Schools' 5-a-side competition in Glasgow's Kelvin Hall.

Alan Ferguson
Date of Birth: 4th April 1938
Admitted to SFA List: 1971-72
No. of seasons at Class 1: 13 (1975-76 to 1987-88)
No. of seasons as a FIFA Referee: 6 (1981-82 to 1986-87)
1 A International;
UEFA: 1 European Championship Qualifier; 2 Club Competition matches (2 ECCC); U18 Championships (1983); 2 U18 Championship Qualifiers; 2 U16 Championship Qualifiers; 3 Women's Championship Qualifiers;
1 Glasgow Cup Final; 3 Old Firm matches

One of Scotland's leading referees during the 1980's, Alan Ferguson's six consecutive seasons as a FIFA referee is testament to the consistency of his performances. An early achievement had been an appointment as a linesman in the 1974 Junior Cup Final. He reached Class 1 after four seasons on the List.
Ferguson's UEFA debut as a referee was in an U18 Championship Qualifier, West Germany v Switzerland, in December 1982 and he finished that season by being selected for the Finals in England.
His A International was a friendly between Iceland and Norway in 1984 and he returned to Iceland two years later for a European Championship Qualifier against France. The European Champion Clubs' Cup provided his two club competition matches - in 1983 (another trip to Iceland) and in 1985 (in the Republic of Ireland). In both matches, the visiting clubs were Hungarian.
International Women's football began to gain traction in the 1980's and Ferguson received three appointments to Qualifiers in the UEFA Women's Championship in a four year period from 1982 to 1986. All were home matches for Scotland with

the opponents being the Republic of Ireland (twice) and Northern Ireland.

Ferguson had 11 appointments as a linesman in various international competitions, the major one being to the 2nd Leg of the 1986 UEFA Cup Final, 1.FC Koln v Real Madrid CF, refereed by Bob Valentine.

Ferguson was appointed to two Scottish Cup and two League Cup Semi-Finals between 1983 and 1984. One of his three Old Firm matches was the Glasgow Cup Final of 1983-84.

He took umbrage at having to retire due to the age limit of 50 at the end of season 1987-88, when he was quoted in a newspaper report as "being totally incensed at having to give up". At that time the SFA reviewed the possibility of relaxing the retiral age but decided against doing so. Ferguson felt that there would be a lack of experienced referees the next season. In taking his stance, he accepted that fitness test conditions would have to be applied stringently but he was very confident that he would comply with them. He had always been very fit and with his slim build, grey hair and moustache, he cut something of a suave figure on the field of play.

In the couple of years after retiring, Ferguson made a few appearances on Scotland's football shows, Sportscene and Scotsport, talking about refereeing incidents in matches and any current talking points.

Any grievance he felt at having to retire did not linger for long as he maintained a close connection with refereeing through his association, Glasgow RA, where he acted as a fitness trainer for many years and served as the association's first Coaching Co-ordinator at monthly meetings when the SFA introduced the role in the early 1990's.

Peter Fitzpatrick
Born: 1912
Died: 1986 aged 74
Admitted to SFA List: 1944-45
No. of seasons at Class 1: 13 (1947-48 to 1959-60)
No. of seasons as a FIFA Referee: 2 (1955-56 and 1958-59)
1 British International Championship match; 1 Amateur International match

2 Glasgow Charity Cup Finals; 1 Old Firm match

A blacksmith, Peter Fitzpatrick played for a number of Junior clubs – Croy Celtic, Lanark United, Auchinleck Talbot and Morton Juniors. He took up refereeing after a referee failed to show up for a match. Although he was admitted to the List in 1944-45, he did not officiate in any games as he was called up to serve in the Royal Engineers. After being demobbed, he took only a couple seasons to make it to Class 1 for season 1947-48, He then had a very meteoric rise in his career as he was appointed to referee England against Ireland in the British International Championship that October. By that point, he had had only refereed nine League matches: six in B Division and three in A Division. Fitzpatrick is the only referee in the post-war period to have officiated in the British Home International Championship when not holding FIFA status.

That match was the high point of his career, notwithstanding becoming a FIFA referee twice during the 1950's. He had also been nominated by the SFA to the Football Association as one of three possible referees for the England's 1951 International against Wales (Jack Mowat and Doug Gerrard being the other two). In his second season as a FIFA referee, he returned to England to referee the Amateur international friendly against Finland.

England was again the destination for his only other international match, an appointment as a linesman to Jack Mowat in the international friendly against Austria in 1951.

In domestic football, Fitzpatrick refereed two Glasgow Charity Cup Finals, the first at the end of season 1947-48 being between the Old Firm. His second Final was 10 years later – Rangers v Clyde.

For two seasons from 1949-50, Fitzpatrick refereed a number of games in Northern Irish football. A dip in his performance levels must have happened during season 1949-50 as he was reclassified to Class 2 at the end of the season. However, he quickly bounced back to Class 1 in January 1951. In his half season back at Class 2, Fitzpatrick refereed a friendly between Celtic and SS Lazio in September 1950. He had originally been appointed as a linesman to the match but replaced George

Mitchell as the referee as Mitchell withdrew late due to illness. Prior to Scotland's World Cup team heading off to Sweden in 1958, Fitzpatrick refereed the squad's last training match at Girvan.

His career closed with an appointment to referee the Renfrewshire Cup Final between Morton and St. Mirren in May 1960, a match which went to a replay. Fitzpatrick was a training class instructor with Glasgow RA from 1946 to 1962 and, in that role, was responsible for guiding many referees, including future FIFA ones, through the Laws of the Game examination.

Ian Foote
Date of Birth: 16th November 1930
Died: 13th December 1995 aged 65
Admitted to SFA List: 1962-63
No. of seasons at Class 1: 16 (1965-66 to 1980-81)
No. of seasons as a FIFA Referee: 8 (1973-74 to 1980-81)
1 A International; 2 British International Championship matches; 1 British Youth International Championship match
FIFA: 4 World Cup Qualifiers; 1 Olympic Qualifier
UEFA: 1 European Championship Qualifier; 2 Youth Tournament Qualifiers; 16 Club Competition matches (1 ECCC, 4 ECWC (1 Q-F), 11 UC (1 Q-F, 1 F)
3 Scottish Cup Finals; 1 League Cup Final; 2 Glasgow Cup Finals; 8 Old Firm matches

Ian Foote developed an exceptionally strong record over his eight seasons as a FIFA referee and can stake a claim to be regarded as one of the leading European referees of his era. He quickly established himself at international level, receiving four World Cup Qualifiers and one European Championship Qualifier during his career. He handled three World Cup Qualifiers for the 1978 Finals, with one match being South Korea against Iran in July 1977. He had a first class record in the UEFA Club Competition appointments and in the UEFA Cup in particular, in which he had 11 matches. These included a Quarter-Final 1st Leg tie between FK Dukla Praha and Hertha BSC Berlin in 1978-79 and the 1st Leg of the Final itself that same season: FK Crvena zvezda v VfL Borussia

Monchengladbach. He received another Quarter-Final appointment in the European Champion Clubs' Cup in 1979-80 when he refereed the 1st Leg of the Hamburger SV and HNK Hadjuk Split tie.

Foote was as a goalkeeper with Petershill and Bo'ness United before joining Eaglesham Amateurs with which club he reached the 1959 Scottish Amateur Cup Final.

In his second season on the List, he officiated as a linesman in a Scottish Cup Semi-Final, Kilmarnock v Dundee. Foote blossomed as a referee from the early 1970's, earning FIFA status in 1973-74. For the remainder of his career he was one of the top referees in Scotland. His first Scottish Cup Final was Celtic v Airdrieonians in 1975. He handled the League Cup Final between Rangers and Aberdeen four seasons later and at the end of the season he fell heir to the 2nd Replay of the Rangers v Hibernian Scottish Cup Final, replacing Brian McGinlay who had gone to referee in Japan.

He was in charge of eight Old Firm matches in a four year period from 1975, two of the matches being Finals of the Glasgow Cup in 1975 and 1976.

Foote's final season on the List, 1980-81, got underway by refereeing the Drybrough Cup Final between Aberdeen and St. Mirren. He had also refereed the Final of this pre-season competition between Aberdeen and Celtic in 1971. He brought the curtain down on his career by officiating at the Scottish Cup Final between Rangers and Dundee United. He got an extra last game out of it as the Final went to a replay.

Foote, a wholesale grocer, served as Ayrshire RA's Referee Supervisor for seven seasons from 1982-83 before being switched to become a Supervisor for Glasgow RA early in season 1988-89. He resigned from the position the following summer.

Alan Freeland
Date of Birth: 22nd January 1961
Admitted to SFA List: 1984-85
No. of seasons at Class 1: 15 (1993-94 to 2007-08)
No. of years as a FIFA Referee: 5 (1997-1999 and 2001-2002)
1 U21 International

UEFA: 2 U21 Championship Qualifiers; 1 U19 Championship Qualifier; 6 U18 Championship Qualifiers; 2 U16 Championship Qualifiers; 8 Club Competition matches (5 UC, 3 UIC)

After playing schools' football, Alan Freeland took up refereeing at 16 years of age, and was awarded the Peter Craigmyle Trophy by Aberdeen & District RA for gaining the top mark in the Entrance Examination. He then served his apprenticeship in juvenile and junior football before making the List in 1984-85.

He received his first international appointment in November 1987 as a linesman to George Smith in a UEFA Cup tie at Sporting Clube de Portugal. As can invariably happen in refereeing from time to time, the appointment created a major dilemma for Freeland. His wife was due to give birth to their first child a day or so after the match date. After the required discussion with his wife, permission was granted to accept the appointment. Not for the first time in refereeing, football won the day.

Selected to be a linesman in the 1996 League Cup Final, Freeland's steady progress once he reached Class 1 brought him to the FIFA List in 1999. He served two spells on the FIFA List through to 2002, missing out in 2000. In 1997, Freeland had been given the opportunity to gain experience at international level by officiating at the Toulon U21 Tournament.

At club level, UEFA deployed Freeland in the Qualifying and First Rounds of the UEFA and Intertoto Cups. His most significant appointment was as referee of Parma AC v HJK Helsinki in the UEFA Cup in 2001. Freeland received regular appointments to the UEFA Championships at the Under Age levels and handled Georgia v Romania and Ukraine v Norway in UEFA U21 Championship Qualifiers.

His U21 International was a friendly between Germany and Sweden in 2001.

Over his career, Freeland frequently acted as a Fourth Official, numbering 20 such appointments, eight of them being Group matches in the UEFA Champions League. He was Fourth Official to Stuart Dougal in an Intertoto Cup Final in 2003 and fulfilled the role in international friendlies played in Norway and Northern Ireland in 1998 and 1999. In domestic football, he was Fourth Official in the 2008 Scottish Cup Final, his last appointment before retiring.

Freeland became an SFA Referee Observer during season 2008-09 and the following season was appointed to the Referee Committee. He stepped down from these positions at the end of season 2020-21 for family reasons. Freeland was a Referee Observer for UEFA for a few seasons.

David Galloway
Born: 1941
Admitted to SFA List: 1974-75
No. of seasons at Class 1: 5 (1980-81 to 1984-85)
No. of seasons as a FIFA Referee: 4 (1969-70 to 1972-73)
FIFA: 1 World Cup Qualifier
1 Junior International; 1 Junior Cup Final

David Galloway became a FIFA referee through the Zambian FA when he lived in the country in the 1960's. His one known international appointment as a FIFA referee was the World Cup Qualifier, Mauritius v Kenya, in 1972.

On his return to Scotland, his FIFA status counted for nothing in regard to the operation of the SFA's refereeing structure and he had to start on the SFA List at Class 3A. It took him six seasons to reach Class 1. He had two major line appointments during his time at Class 3A - an international friendly, England v Republic of Ireland, in 1976 and a Scottish Cup Semi-Final, Rangers v Heart of Midlothian, in 1977. By his final season at Class 2 he had firmly established himself in Junior football and refereed the 1980 Junior Cup Final, Baillieston v Benburb, and a home international against Northern Ireland.

Once at Class 1, he fulfilled line appointments on a European Cup Winners' Cup tie in 1980, a British International Championship match, Wales v Northern Ireland in 1982, and a home Scotland Women's European Championship Qualifier, also in 1982.

Galloway never quite established himself at Class 1 and, given his previous FIFA status, he slowly grew disenchanted with the lack of opportunities given to him being of the belief that he should have been receiving better quality appointments. Eventually, he resigned from the List in March 1985.

Doug Gerrard
Born: 10th March 1913
Died: 13th March 1970 aged 57
Admitted to List: 1938-39
No. of seasons at Class 1: 15 (1941-42 to 1946-47 and 1949-50 to 1957-58)
No. of seasons as a FIFA Referee: 6 (1951-52 to 1956-57)
1 A international; 4 British International Championship matches; 1 British Youth International Championship match; 1 League International
2 Old Firm matches

An Aberdonian, Gerrard played for the Junior club Hall Russell United and was good enough to be nominated for selection for the Scotland Junior team for the match against England in 1933, though ultimately he was not capped.
He took up refereeing in the following years and made the List for season 1938-39 and was refereeing League matches three seasons later. His career dipped in February 1947 when he was re-classified to Class 2. Whilst at this Class, however, he was chosen to referee Scotland's British Youth International Championship game against England in October 1948, a match played in Aberdeen.
He buckled down, recovered and returned to Class 1 for season 1949-50. His career took off once he was back at Class 1 and he became a FIFA referee two seasons later.
1951 to 1953 was a golden period for him. From October 1951 Gerrard refereed three British International Championship matches within a year, with the games being in Wales, Northern Ireland and England. He was a linesman to Jack Mowat for England's international friendly against Austria in December 1951. In April 1952, he refereed Scotland's international against the USA. This gives him the distinction of being the last Scottish referee to referee a home Scotland International. He was in charge of the Scottish League's International against the

Football League in 1953. In domestic football, Gerrard refereed Scottish Cup Semi-Finals in 1951 and 1952, the latter tie between Motherwell and Heart of Midlothian going to three games. His two Old Firm matches were during this great period for him.

His final British International Championship match was Northern Ireland v Wales in 1957.

Gerrard's career came to an ignominious end in February 1958 when he was deleted from the SFA List as a result of goings-on at the St. Johnstone v Dundee match which he had refereed on New Year's Day. He had taken a little too much to drink on the train from Aberdeen and, at the toss of the coin before kick-off, he bent down to pick up the coin and keeled over, worse for wear. Newspaper reports indicated that during the game he dropped his whistle several times and controlled play from a kneeling position for several minutes.

Naturally, the affair created headlines and the SFA launched an investigation. Gerrard, a foreman baker, strenuously denied the allegations when the press made enquiries of him but his time was up.

John Gordon
Date of Birth: 10th February 1930
Died: 21st November 2000 aged 70
Admitted to SFA List: 1957-58
No. of seasons at Class 1: 19 (1960-61 to 1978-79)
No. of seasons as a FIFA Referee: 9 (1967-68 and 1971-72 to 1978-79)
4 A Internationals; 3 British International Championship matches
FIFA: World Cup (1978); 3 World Cup Qualifiers; 1 Olympic Qualifier
UEFA: 1 European Championship Qualifier; U23 Competition Final 1st Leg (1976); 16 Club Competition matches (3 ECCC (1 Q-F), 4 ECWC, 9 UC)
1 Scottish Cup Final; 1 League Cup Final; 6 Old Firm matches

It took John Gordon just three seasons to reach Class 1 after getting on to the List. He had come to prominence in Junior football, handling the 1959 Junior Cup Final between Irvine Meadow XI and Shettleston and a Semi-Final the following season.

An early indication of what was to lie ahead was his appointment to a British Youth International Championship match, England v Northern Ireland, at Old Trafford in 1961. After refereeing a Scottish Cup Semi-Final in 1967, he graduated to the FIFA List for one season in 1967-68 when he was appointed to Wales v England in the British International Championship and to FC Barcelona v FC Zurich in the Inter-Cities Fairs Cup. Gordon returned to the FIFA List in 1971-72 and maintained his place on it for the next eight seasons. During this period he came into his own, becoming firmly established in international football in the mid-1970's, and received many important appointments, culminating in his selection for the 1978 World Cup in Argentina.

He officiated at three World Cup Qualifiers in 1977, with one trip to Africa to referee Zambia against Egypt. His Olympic Qualifier was in 1975 when he was in charge of Iceland and the USSR. Over his career, he had five appointments to games in Iceland, the first four of them all being in 1973 – a UEFA Youth Tournament Qualifier against Luxembourg and three A Internationals, all against East Germany. UEFA appointed him to the 1st Leg of its U23 Competition Final, Hungary v USSR in 1976. In the build up to the World Cup, Gordon officiated at the international friendly between West Germany and the USSR.

At club level, he was regularly given good assignments with his biggest appointment being the European Champion Clubs' Cup Quarter-Final 1st Leg, SL Benfica v FC Bayern Munchen in 1976.

At the World Cup, Gordon was appointed to Tunisia v Mexico in the Group Stage and to Austria v Netherlands in the 2nd Group Stage. He ran the line in the Italy v Hungary Group match.

Gordon refereed six Old Firm matches between 1973 and 1977, with the first being the 1973 Scottish Cup Final. His League Cup Final was in 1974 when Celtic played Hibernian. Gordon handled seven Semi-Final matches in the two Cups over his career.

Returning from the World Cup, Gordon was keen to carry on for as long as possible – the retiral age of 50 had not yet been introduced – despite the criticism and bad publicity which he seemed to attract. Season 1978-79 started well, with an appointment to the European Championship Qualifier, Sweden v Czechoslovakia, in October and a UEFA Cup appointment, AC Milan v Levski Sofia in November. His world came crashing down, however, after the match in Milan. The SFA got wind that Gordon and his linesmen had accepted excessive gifts from AC Milan before the match and launched an investigation. Despite repeated warnings given to them during their interviews as to the consequences, Gordon and his linesmen were uncooperative. Whilst the impartiality of the officials during the match was unquestioned, they were considered to have been foolhardy in allowing themselves to be put in a position whereby their impartiality could be prejudiced. They were found to be in gross breach of UEFA regulations governing hospitality by accepting an excessive amount of gifts well beyond permitted limits and deleted from the SFA's List. Gordon's name was automatically removed from the FIFA List. It was a sad end to what had been a fine career. Gordon, a cashier with a Dundee confectionary company, had developed a reputation for strong discipline. A cheerful outgoing personality, he was viewed as a flamboyant character with press reports describing him as having a "strutting style and accompanying histrionics". He was certainly dedicated. In a talk he gave in 1968 he offered the following comments on his preparation for every match: "I never referee any match without my kit being fully laundered, down to the laces on my boots. My laces are scrubbed, washed and ironed before they go on, for a very good reason. When you go into the players' dressing room, it would not do if your boots are dirty. You are trying to get a sense of respect as soon as you see them." He no doubt followed that pre-match procedure when he refereed a charity match at Tannadice Park between teams of ministers and butchers in April 1979.

George Hamilton
No. of seasons on List: 15 (1908-09 to 1921-22)
1 League International
1 Glasgow Cup Final; 4 Glasgow Charity Cup Finals; 6 Old Firm matches

Hamilton's career peaked in his last few seasons on the List with all his major appointments coming between 1918 and 1922. He refereed the Scottish League's international against the Football League in 1919. Handling six Old Firm matches in four years from 1918 to 1922 was quite an achievement, with two of the games being Finals in the Glasgow Cup and the Glasgow Charity Cup. Two of his other matches were Semi-Finals in these Cups. He was also appointed as the referee for the Final of the Victory Cup, Heart of Midlothian v St. Mirren, in 1919, a one-off competition organised by the Scottish League to mark the end of the First World War. Hamilton continued to referee after his time on the List came to an end. He was registered by the Ayrshire FA, after having moved from Motherwell to Kilbirnie in 1919.

Ross Hardie
Date of Birth: 19th April 1995
Admitted to SFA List: 2013-14
No. of seasons at Class 1: 4 (2021-22 to 2024-25)
No. of years as a FIFA Referee: 1 (2025)

Ross Hardie was admitted to the SFA List midway through season 2013-14 aged 19 and, nurtured through the pathway system, was promoted to Category 1 for season 2021-22. Regarded as a future prospect, he was appointed to a match between Iceland and Croatia in a UEFA U16 Development Tournament hosted by the SFA in 2017. Once at Category 1, progress steadily continued and he reached the FIFA List in 2025.
In his time at Category 1, Hardie has acted as a Fourth Official at two home UEFA Youth League matches played by Rangers and Hamilton Academical and at four Europa Conference League Phase matches in the autumn of 2024. These

appointments will have helped prepare Hardie for what lies ahead in his career as a FIFA referee.

Willie Harvie
Admitted to SFA List: 1949-50
No. of seasons at Class 1: 8 (1952-53 to 1959-60)
No. of seasons as a FIFA Referee: 2 (1955-56 to 1956-57)
2 British Amateur Championship matches; 1 League International
1 Old Firm match; 1 Junior International

Harvie's two seasons on the FIFA List were in the Deputy category. In his first season he was appointed to referee the Wales v England match in the British Amateur Championship. His other international appointments came in the two seasons after he came off the FIFA List, handling the Scottish League's international against the Irish League in 1957 and another Amateur Championship match between England and Wales in 1958.
Harvie's abilities as a referee were recognised by his appointment to an Old Firm League match in 1958.
From Dalry, Harvie had performed well in Junior football when he was at Class 2, being appointed to a Scotland international against Ireland in February 1949 and to a Junior Cup Semi-Final the following season between Blantyre Victoria and Stoneyburn, a tie which went to three games.

Bob Henderson
Born: 1932
Died: January 1987 aged 55
Admitted to SFA List: 1958-59
No. of seasons at Class 1: 11 (1964-65 to 1974-75)
No. of seasons as a FIFA Referee: 2 (1966-67 to 1967-68)
1 A International; 1 U23 International
UEFA: 1 Club Competition match (1 ICFC)

When Bob Henderson was promoted to Class 1 for season 1964-65, he found himself placed in a real dilemma. A policeman in Dundee, he was told by his Chief Constable that he did not have permission to officiate as he had broken police rules, in that he could not have any other employment. Given that he wished to continue refereeing, Henderson decided to quit the police. He accepted that people would think he was being crazy for doing so and for giving up the security of a police job but, as a single man, said he was prepared to take the risk and find another job, which he did.

Henderson's bold decision was vindicated as he reached the FIFA List two seasons later. In his first season as a FIFA referee, he refereed an U23 international between Northern Ireland and Wales, an international friendly, Iceland v East Germany and ran the line to Tom Wharton in the England v Wales British International Championship match. The following season saw him take charge of St. Patrick's Athletic v Girondins de Bordeaux in the Inter-Cities Fairs Cup. His first international appointment had been in 1961-62 when he was a linesman in a European Championship Qualifier between Norway and Sweden.

Henderson lost his Class 1 status at the end of season 1974-75 and decided to emigrate to Melbourne in Australia to join his brother. He continued to referee and in 1976 was in charge of a friendly between the Victoria State Select and Tottenham Hotspur. Henderson had been a training class instructor for Angus & Perthshire RA and he maintained an involvement in the coaching of referees in Victoria.

Abbie Hendry
Date of Birth: 16th February 1999
Admitted to SFA List: 2020-21
No. of seasons at Category 3: 4 (2021-22 to 2024-25)
No. of years as a FIFA Referee: 1 (2025)
UEFA: 1 Women's Nations League match

Abbie Hendry is in her first year as a FIFA referee and gained her place by her promising performances, having been identified early as a prospect to follow in the path of Morag Pirie and Lorraine Watson. By taking up refereeing, she followed in the footsteps of her mother, Kelly Kyle, who operated as an assistant in the Tayside area of the East Region Junior FA for many seasons.

To help her development, she was appointed by the SFA to officiate at several Scotland Women's international friendlies at U16, U17 and U23 levels in 2023 and 2024 against countries such as Switzerland, Hungary and the Czech Republic. These matches will have provided an excellent platform for her career development.

Since 2019, she also has built up a bank of experience as a Fourth Official in 15 matches in a variety of women's competitions, including World Cup Qualifiers, European Championship Qualifiers, A Internationals, the UEFA Champions League matches and the UEFA U17 Championship.

She received her first UEFA appointment when she refereed the Women's Nations League match between Liechtenstein and Armenia in June 2025.

Hendry was appointed as the Fourth Official to the 2025 Scottish Women's Cup Final between Glasgow City and Rangers.

William Holburn
No. of seasons on List: 12 (1924-25 to 1935-36)
1 Amateur International
2 Old Firm matches

Holburn refereed Wales v England in his Amateur International in 1932. At that point he was starting to make a name for himself but he never quite achieved a full breakthrough into the top group of referees of the time. He was one of three referees put forward by the Scottish League to the Irish League for the League international in 1932, but was not selected. Being appointed to two Old Firm matches, however, is an indication of his standing at the time. His first match was in January 1930 and his second, in September 1931, was the game in which the Celtic goalkeeper John Thomson tragically died after an accidental collision with the Rangers player Sam English. Holburn wrote a heartfelt letter to Thomson's parents, expressing sympathy for their son's death. The letter was published in newspapers. He attended Thomson's funeral along with representatives of the Scottish Football Referees' Association. As a sign perhaps of the place in society that referees held at the time, Holburn's marriage in 1934 made the newspapers as did occasions when he sang or read lessons at church services in Glasgow.

Douglas Hope

Date of Birth: 25th October 1944
Admitted to SFA List: 1976-77
No. of seasons at Class 1: 12 (1982-83 to 1993-94)
No. of years as a FIFA Referee: 3 (1989 to 1991)
1 A International; 2 U21 Internationals
UEFA: 2 U16 Championship Qualifiers; 1 Women's Championship Qualifier; 2 Club Competition matches (2 UC)
2 Scottish Cup Finals; 1 League Cup Final; 1 Challenge Cup Final; 2 Glasgow Cup Finals; 8 Old Firm matches

A player in amateur and junior football, Douglas Hope accepted that he was not renowned as a "clean player". When playing for Drumchapel Amateurs, he was cautioned in a match by his brother Kenny, who also became a FIFA referee. Qualifying as a referee in December 1967, Hope served a lengthy apprenticeship to get to Class 1. During this period, he refereed a Junior Cup Semi-Final in 1981.

Hope progressed steadily during his time at Class 1 and received his first big appointment when selected for an Old Firm Glasgow Cup Final at the end of season 1985-86, the first match between the clubs following the arrival of Graeme Souness as the Rangers manager and with the usual pre-match hype going into over-drive as a consequence. He refereed the clubs again in the following season's Final.

His steady climb culminated in 1989 when he reached FIFA status. Over his three years at that level, he refereed the A International, Sweden v Denmark, in 1990, two home England U21 Internationals against Wales and West Germany and a UEFA Women's Championship Qualifier between Northern Ireland and the Republic of Ireland. UEFA Cup appointments took him to the Republic of Ireland and Finland. Over the duration of his career, Hope had 15 international appointments as a linesman across the range of major competitions.

When asked once why he could enjoy refereeing, Hope said that he would not referee if he did not enjoy it, adding that there was pressure, but a different type to that which he got at work, in which he also had to make quick decisions. A Reporter to the Children's Panel, he was once attacked by a woman who kicked him and punched in the face during a hearing. Given that example, handling footballers was a relative walk in the park for him and his calm, unflustered demeanour stood him in great stead in controlling matches and diffusing on-field situations.

He undoubtedly came into his own in the latter part of his career, as evidenced by his appointment to the 1992 and 1994 Scottish Cup Finals, the 1993 League Cup Final and the 1994 Challenge Cup Final. He refereed the Old Firm League Cup Semi-Final in season 1993-94, his third successive Old Firm match.

On retiring as a referee, Hope served as a Referee Supervisor for Glasgow RA and Renfrewshire RA until 2005-06 and thereafter as a Referee Observer until season 2021-22. He was a member of the Referee Committee for two seasons from 2004-05.

Kenny Hope
Date of Birth: 7th June 1941
Died: 10th December 2021 aged 80
Admitted to SFA List: 1966-67
No. of seasons at Class 1: 17 (1974-75 to 1990-91)
No. of seasons/years as a FIFA Referee: 12 (1978-79, 1980-81 to 1990)
2 A Internationals; 1 B International
FIFA: U16 World Cup (1987); 2 World Cup Qualifiers; Olympics (1988); 3 Olympic Qualifiers
UEFA: U18 Championships (1982); 2 U18 Championship Qualifiers; 13 Club Competition matches (5 ECWC, 8 UC)
1 Scottish Cup Final; 1 League Cup Final; 1 Challenge Cup Final; 1 Glasgow Cup Final; 1 Junior International

Having qualified as a referee during 1961-62, Kenny Hope did exceptionally well to enjoy an excellent career after recovering from a serious illness soon after reaching Class 1 in 1974. His determination to succeed was rewarded by breaking through to the FIFA List for season 1978-79, during which he refereed his first international friendly, Iceland against West Germany. After missing out for the following season, he then regained his place and served with distinction throughout the 1980's.

Hope was selected for the UEFA U18 Championships in Finland in 1982 and, five years later, was chosen for the FIFA U16 World Cup in Canada. At the competition, he refereed two Group matches (USSR matches against Mexico and Bolivia) and, after running the line in a Quarter-Final and a Semi-Final, was picked as a linesman for the Final between Nigeria and the USSR.

After handling three Qualifiers, Hope was chosen for the Olympics in Seoul in 1988, where he took charge of a Group match between Tunisia and West Germany and ran the line in two others.

Hope's other international friendly was Republic of Ireland Wales v in 1986; his appointments in the World Cup Qualifiers were in Iceland and the USSR in 1981 and 1989, respectively. A trip to Israel in 1987 saw him handle a B International against West Germany.

In the UEFA Club Competitions, Hope was predominantly used in the early rounds of the UEFA Cup, receiving appointments to matches at SV Werder Bremen, Athletic Club Bilbao, Bayer 04 Leverkusen, Sporting Clube de Portugal and AS Monaco. A home FC Barcelona tie was amongst his appointments in the European Cup Winners' Cup.

During his career, Hope received numerous appointments as a linesman, the first being to a tie in the European Cup Winners' Cup in 1969. He ran the line to John Paterson in the European Cup Winners' Cup Quarter-Final, SL Benfica v PSV Eindhoven, in his first season at Class 1.

Two of Hope's seven Old Firm matches were Cup Finals and were both in 1982 – the Glasgow Cup and the League Cup. His Scottish Cup Final was St. Mirren's win over Dundee United in

1987. He refereed the Scottish League's first Challenge Cup Final, Ayr United v Dundee, in 1990.

Hope was a very popular referee amongst players in Scottish football due to his approachability and application of commonsense in handling matches. He was a character who liked to have a bit of banter with players during matches but equally he could stamp his authority over them when required. Due to retire at the end of season 1990-91, his career came to a premature end in the last few months of that season due to an Achilles injury.

Hope was quickly appointed by the SFA as a Referee Supervisor for Glasgow RA and served on the Supervisors' Executive Committee for 11 seasons and then the Referee Committee for six seasons until 2008-09. He was a Referee Observer until season 2010-11 and continued his service to refereeing for few years thereafter as a Referee Development Adviser, continuing to give the benefit of his long experience to referees in Junior football.

Jimmy Hudson
No. of seasons on List: 17 (1921-22 to 1937-38)
1 League International
1 Glasgow Charity Cup Final

Hudson's best year was in 1931, four seasons after being admitted to the Scottish League's List. He refereed the Glasgow Charity Cup Final between Rangers and Queen's Park in May and in November was appointed the Scottish League's International against the Football League. His performances brought him into consideration for the Scottish Cup Semi-Finals. He was the Reserve Referee for the Hamilton Academical v Partick Thistle Semi-Final of 1930, losing out in the voting to Peter Craigmyle.

Throughout his time on the List in the 1930's, Hudson was one of the core group of referees used in the First Division. As was the case with many other referees of that era, he refereed in other grades of Scottish football when free of a senior appointment, officiating in the Scottish Secondary Juvenile FA Cup Final, Port Glasgow Rangers v Hamilton Social in 1935.

After ending his refereeing career, he acted as a scout for Wallsall FC.

Mungo Hutton
Born: 31st July 1894
Died: 6th January 1977 aged 82
No. of seasons on List: 16 (1926-27 to 1941-42)
1 British International Championship match; 4 Amateur Internationals; 3 League Internationals; 1 Inter-Association match
2 Scottish Cup Finals; 5 Glasgow Cup Finals; 2 Glasgow Charity Cup Finals; 11 Old Firm matches; 2 Junior Internationals; 3 Junior Cup Finals

A Scottish Schools' cricket internationalist, Hutton was severely wounded in the First World War whilst serving in the Gordon Highlanders and was the recipient of the Croix de Guerre from France. Hutton played for Aberdeen before taking up refereeing. He was from a football family – his father Peter had played for Stenhousemuir and became a club director and President for many years, representing Stirlingshire FA on the SFA Council. Early in his career Hutton requested the Scottish League not to appoint him to any Stenhousemuir matches and Aberdeen made a similar request due to his past connection to the club.

Hutton regularly gained plaudits in press reports for his handling of matches. The main headline of "Well played Mungo Hutton!" was used in one report of an Arbroath v Celtic match in 1936. The report referred to his "eagle eye and fairness in the conduct of the match" and that he had been "judicious in his judgements – not stopping play unnecessarily but being definite when penalising a deliberate offender – the referee showed how a game could be handled."

Such was the regard in which he was held, he was favoured with many Old Firm appointments, refereeing seven out of 15 such games in the four year period between September 1934 and September 1938. Two of the 15 matches were Finals of the Glasgow Cup and the Glasgow Charity Cup.

Given his place amongst Scottish referees during the 1930's, and allowing for the competition which existed for such appointments, it is none the less surprising that Hutton was only selected once to referee a match in the British International Championship - the Wales v England match of 1933. His four Amateur Internationals all followed in the next four years, home Scotland matches against England, Ireland and Wales (twice).

In addition to his two Scottish Cup Finals of 1934 and 1937, he handled Semi-Final ties in four consecutive seasons from 1934.

Hutton officiated regularly in Northern Ireland in the early 1930's, with over 25 appointments in a four season period.

By 1939, he had to dispel rumours of his retirement, although he started to restrict his availability for midweek appointments outside league and cup competitions. The outbreak of the Second World War extended his career by a couple of seasons and he eventually retired at the end of season 1941-42. After the War ended, he became a scout for Chelsea. He worked 40 years with White Horse Distillers in Glasgow and in later life he moved to England to live near his son.

Alex Jackson
Date of Birth: 20th January 1876
Died: 6th February 1942 aged 66
No. of seasons on List: 29 (1896-97 to 1923-24)
2 A Internationals; 12 British International Championship matches; 6 League Internationals; 1 Amateur International
1 Scottish Cup Final; 4 Glasgow Cup Finals; 1 Glasgow Charity Cup Final; I Junior International (1910)

Jackson had a remarkably long career and is one of the early greats of Scottish referees. At one time the Scottish Half-Mile Champion, he started refereeing in his early 20's and his ability was quickly recognised by being appointed to the 1898 Renfrewshire Cup Final. All his major appointments came from 1909-10 onwards. His 12 appointments in a 13 year period from 1910 in the British International Championship is a remarkable tally, the second highest of the Scottish referees after Tom Robertson. England featured in all of these matches – he refereed five Ireland v England games, three England v Ireland games, two England v Wales matches, one Wales v England and England v Scotland in 1913.

His two A Internationals were both in the spring of 1919 when he was appointed to referee Scotland's home matches against Ireland and England. Three of his League internationals were matches between the Football League and the Irish League.

The absence of appointments to Old Firm matches can be explained by an association he had with Rangers in his younger days as he was starting out in refereeing, his appointments generally being listed at A. Jackson (Rangers). He did not referee Rangers in any of his various Finals, though Celtic featured in five of them. His Scottish Cup Final came early in his career – the 1901 match between Heart of Midlothian and Celtic.

Jackson refereed frequently in Northern Ireland for a period and became a firm favourite there with the standard of his performances. His popularity is further demonstrated by having refereed five Ireland v England Amateur internationals and an Irish Amateur international against France in 1922.

On resigning from the List in August 1923, the Scottish League appointed him (and Alex Edward, another long-serving referee who resigned at the same time) as a Referee Inspector (a role the League had considered creating in 1911). In this position he made a significant contribution to Scottish refereeing, assessing referees and reporting on them to the League. The League effectively gave control to Jackson and Edward to compile its List of Referees each season. This lasted until 1930, when the League decided to discontinue their positions and introduced a system of clubs reporting on referees. The method of operation by the League in the 1920's was very much a forerunner of what the SFA introduced in 1945.

During 1930 Jackson became a Director of Ayr United FC and in 1937-38 he was elected as a member of the SFL Management Committee. Jackson had been heavily involved as a member of the Scottish Football Referees' Association from its inception in 1903 until he retired from the List and was its President for five seasons from 1910-11. He worked for the Glasgow Education Authority for 50 years, retiring in 1940.

Joe Jackson
Admitted to List: 1941-42
No of seasons at Class 1: 9 (1946-47 to 1954-55)
1 A International
1 Glasgow Charity Cup Final; 4 Old Firm matches

Jackson came to prominence by refereeing a Scottish Junior Cup Semi-Final in 1940 and running the line in that season's Final. Within a couple of seasons of getting on to the List, he was appointed to his first Old Firm match in September 1943. His international appointment was a friendly between Scotland and Belgium in January 1946. It can be supposed that he was under orders to get the game played as Hampden Park was under a few inches of snow and hard with frost. To add to the difficulties, the match was played in thick fog.

He was appointed to League Cup Semi-Finals in 1948, 1951 and 1952, the middle one being an Old Firm match. By this time, he had become well-established and, in his final season, his service was rewarded when he was appointed to referee the Glasgow Charity Cup Final, Rangers v Queen's Park.

In an article Tom Wharton contributed to Glasgow RA's 50th Anniversary Programme, he described Jackson as a real character, stating that his "words of advice to a young referee going on a tough assignment were always simple: if 22 players are too many, try 20, and if that is still too many, try 18." Wharton also added that, in the post-war period when clothing was rationed and coupon allowances were used to obtain kit, Jackson's referee's tunic was a pyjama jacket dyed black.

Proof of Jackson being a character was evident in 1967 when he entered a Sunday Post competition to win a day trip to watch Celtic in the European Cup Final in Lisbon. Entrants had to submit a letter on "My proudest memory of a Celtic player since the war". He was one of the six winners. His letter was: "In a game at Brockville, there was a clash in which former Celt Jimmy Delaney and the present Celtic Assistant manager, Sean Fallon, were involved. Jimmy was about to shoot when Sean tackled him, blocked the ball and in so doing, fractured his arm. He waved away attention from trainer Dowdalls with the words "As long it's not my leg, I'm okay". I was the referee of that game. Sean Fallon may not have been everybody's cup of tea as a great ball-player, but as a wholehearted fit-as-a-fiddle trier – and scrupulously clean – he would be difficult to equal." It's hard to imagine a referee putting their head above the parapet to enter such a competition – but Jackson did. He did live near Celtic Park for many years so that may just have played a part in things.

Rollo Kyle
Date of Birth: 1940
Died: 8th December 1979 aged 39
Admitted to SFA List: 1967-68
No. of seasons at Class 1: 8 (1971-72 to 1978-79)
No. of seasons as a FIFA Referee: 3 (1974-75 to 1976-77)
1 A International; 1 U23 International; 1 U21 International
UEFA: 1 Youth Tournament Qualifier

Rollo Kyle's performances brought him to FIFA status after just three seasons at Class 1, with his progress being reflected in his appointment to a Scottish Cup Semi-Final, Airdrieonians v Motherwell, in 1974-75.
Kyle commenced his FIFA career by officiating at an A International between Iceland and Finland in August 1974. He returned to Iceland a couple of months later to handle the UEFA Youth Tournament Qualifier against Northern Ireland. Later that same season he was appointed to referee the U23 international friendly, Wales v England. His last appointment was to referee Scotland's U21 friendly against Wales in February 1977.
As a linesman, he received five international appointments, three of them being World Cup Qualifiers with the first being Republic of Ireland v Denmark in 1968 when he was at Class 3A. He accompanied John Gordon to a Qualifier in Zambia in 1977 and was appointed with Gordon again in November 1978 to the UEFA Cup match, AC Milan v Levski Sofia.
Events surrounding this match brought his career to a close as all three officials were deleted from the SFA for a gross breach of UEFA regulations governing hospitality by accepting an excessive amount of gifts well beyond permitted limits. The

SFA investigation had been sparked off by a chance remark by Kyle to his father Donald, a Referee Supervisor for Glasgow RA. Kyle senior spoke to Jack Mowat, the Referee Supervisors' Committee Chairman about the matter and Mowat felt obliged to report it to the SFA.
Part of the SFA's decision was that the officials would not be able to re-apply for inclusion on the List until 1981. Kyle, an art teacher, did not get the opportunity to do so as he tragically died of a brain haemorrhage in 1979.

Willie Laidlaw
Date of Birth: 13th June 1954
Admitted to SFA List: 1979-79
No. of seasons on List: 9 (1978-79 to 1986-87)
No. of seasons as a FIFA Referee: 7 (1993 to 1999)
FIFA Linesman: 1992
FIFA: 1 World Cup Qualifier; 4 Women's A Internationals
10 Canadian National Championship Finals (4 Men's Gold Medal Matches; 1 Women's Gold Medal match; 1 Youths Gold Medal match)

Little did Willie Laidlaw know what was to lie ahead of him on the refereeing front when he decided to emigrate to Canada in 1986 – becoming a FIFA referee a few years later would never have crossed his mind. At that time, Laidlaw, a medical laboratory technologist in Edinburgh, was in his second season at Class 3B, having been reclassified from Class 3A after seven seasons, and was essentially a rank and file referee on the List. Had he remained in Scotland, he would have expected to serve through to the retiral age of 48. His career in Scotland had been marked by line appointments in World Cup Qualifiers in Iceland and West Germany in 1981 and 1984, respectively, and appointments to two Old Firm League matches in 1981 and 1983.
Laidlaw caught the refereeing bug early, from his father, who referced in Edinburgh amateur football. He passed the referee examination in April 1968 aged 13, an achievement which made a national newspaper for being the youngest referee in

Scotland. In his early days, Laidlaw often acted as a linesman to his father at his matches.

There was to be a complete change of gear once in Canada. Laidlaw progressed so well that he was appointed as a FIFA linesman for 1992, and ran the line that year in a USA v Republic of Ireland international in Washington. He stepped up to FIFA referee status in 1993 and served seven seasons in that capacity. Laidlaw's World Cup Qualifier was a match between Guatemala and Trinidad & Tobago, played in Los Angeles, in 1996. He was Fourth Official in two other Qualifiers that year, Guatemala v Nicaragua, and St. Vincent & the Grenadines v Honduras, the latter match being played in Jamaica.

Laidlaw refereed Canada's Women's international team in matches against Sweden, Iceland and Norway. In 1998, he was appointed to referee the Women's Final of the Goodwill Games (an international sports competition created in the 1980's by the American media mogul Ted Turner in response to the political troubles surrounding the Olympics in the 1980's) between the USA and China in New York. Laidlaw picked up an Achilles injury during the first half, unfortunately, and had to be replaced for the second half. In 1993, he refereed Colorado Foxes v Fort Lauderdale Strikers in the American Professional Soccer League.

In Canadian football, Laidlaw officiated at 10 National Championship Finals, refereeing four men's Gold Medal Matches and the same match in the Women's and Youth Championship. Additionally, he refereed one Canada Games Gold Medal match, British Columbia v Quebec, and several provincial Cup Finals. He experienced a taste of Scottish football again in 1994 when he handled Aberdeen and Celtic in the Final of the Hamilton Cup tournament.

Laidlaw contributed hugely to Canadian refereeing and football after his own career came to a close. In addition to being a Board member of the Manitoba Soccer Association and a member of its Referee Committee for many years, he was a National Referee Assessor and provincial referee Instructor (2000 – 2014), Director of Officials for the Manitoba Soccer Association (2001-02) and the Winnipeg Youth Soccer Association (2002-2013).

His contribution to the game was recognised by the Canada Soccer Association in 2010 when he was the recipient of its Award of Merit. Previously, in 2001, he received an award for having shown the greatest progress at national and international levels as a referee. The Manitoba Referees' Association honoured him with an award in 2015 as part of its 50th anniversary celebrations. When he retired from work, Laidlaw moved to live in Indiana in the United States. He continues to be involved in refereeing, acting as a Referee Assessor from 2016 to 2018, and currently as a Referee Mentor. He still occasionally referees when needed.

Eddie Lennie
Date of Birth: 5th October 1959
Admitted to SFA List: 1983-84
No. of seasons on List: 9 (1983-84 to 1991-92)
No. of seasons as a FIFA Referee: 9 (1996 to 2004)
1 A International; 1 U23 International
FIFA: World Cup (1998); 5 World Cup Qualifiers; Olympics (1996); 3 Olympic Qualifiers
Oceania: Nations Cup (2000)
4 National Soccer League Grand Finals; 3 State Grand League Finals

Eddie Lennie's decision to emigrate to Perth, Australia in the autumn of 1991 was a life-changer in more ways than one - he became a FIFA referee just over four years later, in 1996. When he was still living in Scotland, would he have ever dreamed of refereeing at a World Cup and at the Olympics? That is exactly what happened, which is, in the context of his career in Scotland, a tremendous achievement and one which is greatly to his credit.

Having missed out on promotion to Class 1 following four seasons at Class 2 and reclassified to Class 3B in 1990, Lennie's career in Scotland was seemingly on the wane. The high points had been an appointment as a linesman to a World Cup Qualifier, Poland v Belgium, in 1985 and to a Scottish Cup Semi-Final in 1986. Refereeing was not high amongst his priorities when he emigrated but he became involved at grassroots level and then made extremely rapid progression through the ranks, being appointed to the Final of a State Cup two years in succession from 1993.

After a year as an assistant in the Australian National List he was promoted to the referees' list in 1994. He finished the 1994-95 season by refereeing the international friendly, Australia v Sweden, the National Soccer League Grand Final and the Western Australia Grand State Final. He was also voted the Australian Referee of the Year, an award he received again in 1996 and 2000. He was Western Australia's Referee of the Year five times.

In his first year as a FIFA referee in 1996, Lennie was selected for that year's Olympics in Atlanta. There, he refereed two Group matches in the Men's Competition, one of which was USA v Portugal, and one Group match in the Women's Competition, Norway v Germany. Having refereed three Qualifiers in places as diverse as Fiji and Kuwait, Lennie was chosen as one of the referees for the 1998 World Cup in France and in the Group matches refereed Italy v Cameroon and Romania v Tunisia, the latter match being played in the Stade de France.

In 2000, he was a referee in the Oceania Nations Cup played in Tahiti and, after handling three Group games, he refereed the Semi-Final between New Zealand and the Solomon Islands. His time as a FIFA referee was concluded by officiating at the 2004 Kirin Cup in Japan, where he took charge of the host nation's match against Serbia & Montenegro.

In the Australian National Soccer League, Lennie handled 195 matches over 11 years. After one fiery match between Melbourne Knights and South Melbourne in 1998 he left the stadium in the back of a police car after sending off two Knights players and the team's coach. Having been described earlier in his time in Australia as possessing a calm demeanour and a willingness to interact with players on the field, it would seem that did not count for much in that particular game. He refereed four National League Grand Finals, a record at the time of his last Final in 2000, and numerous State Finals in Western Australia.

After retiring from refereeing in late 2004, Lennie maintained an active role in the game, by immediately becoming an instructor and assessor. In Western Australia he was the football association's Referee Development Manager for 13 years and the State Director of Referees; in 2008, he was appointed as a Referee Instructor and Assessor for FIFA and the Asian Football Confederation and in 2019 he was appointed an Elite Referees' Coach with Football Australia (the national governing body).

His contribution to football and to refereeing in Australia has been recognised in various forms. He was inducted into the Hall of Fames of the Western Australia FA and Football Australia in 2005 and 2007, respectively. The Australian Government presented him the Centenary Medal in 2006 in recognition of his "contribution to Australian society" and, two years later, he was awarded the Medal of the Order of Australia. He received a Special Merit Award from Western Australia's Hall of Fame in 2019.

William McArthur
Born: 1859
Died: 8th December 1931 aged 72
No. of seasons on List: 10 (1897-98 to 1907-08)
1 League International

McArthur played for King's Park and Callander Rob Roy before taking up refereeing and becoming one of the top of referees of his generation. His League International appointment was in 1903 when he refereed the Football League against the Irish League in Bradford. He refereed two Scottish Cup Semi-Finals - in 1904, Rangers v Morton, and in 1906, Port Glasgow Athletic v Heart of Midlothian. He was also selected as a Reserve Referee for the other 1906 Semi-Final, St. Mirren v Third Lanark.

McArthur refereed occasionally in the Irish League in the mid-1900's.

On finishing as a referee, he served for a few years on the King's Park committee and as a director when the club became a company. Afterwards, he kept involved in football by acting as a scout for several Scottish and English clubs. He was a plumber to trade and worked with a Stirling company for over 50 years. He died suddenly whilst in Stirling Royal Infirmary.

Gordon McCabe
Date of Birth: 13th February 1983
Admitted to SFA List: 2014-15
No. of seasons at Category 3 Specialist Assistant Referee: 2 (2023-24 to 2024-25)
No. of years as a FIFA Futsal Referee: 8 (2018 to 2025)
2 Futsal Internationals; 3 Home Nations Futsal Championships
UEFA: Futsal Champions League (5 Q Groups)

Gordon McCabe is Scotland's first FIFA Futsal referee. Admitted to the SFA List midway through season 2014-15 at Category 4, ostensibly to help service Junior football in the Tayside area, he had a background in officiating in Futsal in his home town of Perth, one of the main centres of the game in Scotland. His appearance on the scene coincided with an SFA drive to develop Futsal. From the refereeing perspective the timing was good – it opened the door for the SFA to consider nominating an official for the FIFA Futsal Referee List. The opportunity was taken for 2018 and McCabe's nomination was accepted.
Prior to being admitted to the FIFA List, McCabe had refereed two Scotland Futsal Internationals against Gibraltar in 2015 and officiated at the 2017 Home Nations Futsal Championships. UEFA has regularly appointed him to Futsal Champions League Qualifying tournaments in countries such as Austria, Norway, Albania, Switzerland and Poland. At these tournaments, the officials take their turns at fulfilling all the roles at the matches – the main referee, the second referee, assistant referee and timekeeper.
McCabe has officiated regularly at the latter stages Scottish Futsal Cup. He has progressed within the SFA List, becoming a Specialist Assistant Referee for season 2023-24.

Alex McClintock
Date of Birth: 21st June 1919
Died: 6th February 2016 aged 96
Admitted to SFA List: 1950-51
No. of seasons at Class 1: 8 (1952-53 to 1959-60)
No. of seasons as a FIFA Referee: 1 (1956-57)
2 British Amateur Championship matches; 1 British Youth International Championship match
1 Glasgow Cup Final; 1 Old Firm match; 2 Junior Internationals

Alex McClintock took up refereeing whilst serving in North Africa as an aircraft technician during the Second World War, and handled matches between Navy, Army and RAF teams. At the end of his first season on the List, he refereed the Junior International, Scotland against Northern Ireland. It took him only two seasons to reach Class 1 and, four seasons later, his performances were rewarded with a place on the FIFA List, albeit in the Deputy category. His first Amateur international had been during season 1953-54 when he was appointed to the Scotland v Northern Ireland match. The following season saw him referee Scotland's home British Youth International Championship match against England. During his season on the FIFA List, he refereed England and Wales in his second British Amateur Championship match. Following the match, McClintock received a letter from Stanley Rous, the Football Association Secretary, thanking him for the way he had handled the match to the satisfaction of both managers.
McClintock refereed the 1956 Glasgow Cup Final between Rangers and Clyde, a match where he had to whistle for the police to come on to the field of play to assist him deal with the aftermath of an incident which resulted in a Clyde player being sent off. His Old Firm match was a Glasgow Charity Cup Semi-Final in 1958. After coming off the SFA List in 1960, he continued to referee for a couple of seasons. In 1961 he refereed the Junior International, Scotland v Northern Ireland.
After finishing refereeing, McClintock had a long association with youth sports through Bishopbriggs Sports Club (he was awarded the MBE in 2000 for services to youth sport), and worked as a sports reporter for Scottish Television. In the mid-

1960's, he formed Bishopbriggs Amateurs and had the future Rangers and Scotland manager Walter Smith as team captain. McClintock had a further Rangers connection as he discovered Ally McCoist when acting as a scout for St. Johnstone in the 1970's. He was also a scout at various times for Dundee United, Blackburn Rovers and Heart of Midlothian.

Jim McCluskey
Date of Birth: 1st November 1950
Died: 14th November 2013 aged 63
Admitted to SFA List: 1980-81
No. of seasons at Class 1: 16 (1984-85 to 1999-00)
No. of seasons/years as a FIFA Referee: 9 (1987-88 to 1995)
4 A Internationals; 1 B International
FIFA: 1 World Cup Qualifier; U16 World Cup (1989); Women's World Cup (1991)
UEFA: 6 European Championship Qualifiers; 3 U21 Championship Qualifiers; U16 Championships (1989); 3 U16 Championship Qualifiers; Women's Championships (1991 (F); 1 Women's Championship Qualifier; 19 Club Competition matches (2 ECCC, 2 ECWC (2 Q-F), 11 UC (1 F), 4 UCL (2 G) 2 Scottish Cup Finals; 4 League Cup Finals; 1 Challenge Cup Final; 2 Youth Cup Finals

Jim McCluskey was, without question, one of the best ever referees produced by Scotland. A quiet self-effacing man off the field, he found that being in charge of a game was his natural habitat. He exuded control and commanded games with his personality and by the players respecting his natural authority. In refereeing terms, he was the ultimate "safe pair of hands", able to deal comfortably with the most demanding situations in matches and was admired for the "feel" he had for a game. His excellent fitness allowed him to be always close to play and to quell any protests over his calls. McCluskey was hugely respected within Scottish refereeing and clubs had great regard for his abilities.

McCluskey, from Salsburgh, was a reserve player with Airdrieonians for three seasons from 1968 before joining Shotts Bon Accord. He took up refereeing when he was 26 after sustaining a knee injury. A quantity surveyor, work took him to Ayrshire and he eventually became the managing director of the construction company he worked for. He soon made his mark in refereeing once he got on to the SFA List in 1980. Season 1982-83 ended by being appointed to referee a Scotland Junior International against Northern Ireland and selection as a linesman for the Scottish Cup Final. He had just one season at Class 2 before promotion to Class 1, his talent having caught the eye of Jack Mowat, the Referee Supervisors' Committee Chairman. In his first season at Class 1, McCluskey was chosen as the referee of the first ever SFA Youth Cup Final. He made the FIFA List after three seasons at Class 1, establishing himself as one of the top referees in the country.

His first UEFA appointment was to a Women's European Championship Qualifier between Norway and Denmark and in 1989 he was selected for the UEFA U16 Championships in Denmark. Also that year, he enjoyed a piece of good fortune when FIFA chose him to replace the injured George Smith as a referee in the U16 World Cup held in Scotland. In the Group matches, he refereed Guinea v Portugal.

His international career then gathered momentum. His first A International was an England friendly against Denmark in 1990. He was to go on to referee a further two England friendlies over the next few seasons, with the opponents being Brazil and Greece. His B International was also an England game, against Switzerland. Refereeing a friendly between Germany and Italy in 1994 indicates the place he had reached in refereeing, as does the six European Championship Qualifiers he handled. McCluskey refereed Brazil for a second time in 1995 in its match against Japan in the Football Association's Umbro Cup tournament.

Women's football featured strongly in McCluskey's career. He refereed the Final between Germany and Norway in the 1991 UEFA Women's Championships held in Denmark and, later that year, FIFA selected him for the Women's World Cup in China. After handling two of Italy's games in the Group Stages (against Nigeria and Germany), McCluskey was a linesman in Italy's Quarter-Final against Norway and was then appointed to referee the Semi-Final between Sweden v Norway.

McCluskey developed a fine record in the UEFA Club Competitions, with appointments to matches involving many major European clubs. In the European Cup Winners' Cup, he received appointments to two Quarter-Finals - Club Atletico de Madrid v Olympiacos in 1993 and Bayer 04 Leverkusen v SL Benfica and 1994. UEFA deployed him regularly in the UEFA Cup and in 1994 he was appointed to referee the 2nd Leg of the Final between FC Internazionale Milano and Casino Salzburg. (His second Youth Cup Final appointment was used as a warm up match for him and his team for the Final). McCluskey certainly had an affinity with the UEFA Cup during his career. He had been a linesman to Bob Valentine for the 2nd Leg of the 1985 Final between 1.FC Koln and Real Madrid CF and in 1989 he was a linesman to David Syme in the 2nd Leg of the Semi-Final, FC Bayern Munchen v SSC Napoli.

In 1994-95, he refereed the UEFA Cup tie between Sporting Clube de Portugal and Real Madrid CF. His last international appointment in December 1995 before coming off the FIFA List due to the age limit featured Real Madrid CF again, in the club's away match against Grasshopper Club Zurich.

The one major disappointment McCluskey experienced in his international career was missing out on selection for the 1994 World Cup, with another Scot, Les Mottram, winning the day.

McCluskey's two Scottish Cup Finals were both Rangers and Aberdeen affairs in 1993 and 2000, the latter being the last match of his career. His tally of 15 Old Firm match represents an excellent reflection of his standing in the game. His second such match was the 1990 League Cup Final and he was in charge of the two clubs in three other Cup ties.

Before the 1990 League Cup Final, the Celtic Supporters Association, bizarrely, hired a private detective to look into McCluskey' background, hoping to discover an allegiance to Rangers. Celtic correctly distanced itself from their supporters' actions, but it was an example of the weird happenings which can occur in Scottish football.

In addition to refereeing his six Scottish and League Cup Finals, McCluskey was appointed on 12 occasions to referee Semi-Finals in these Cups, another indicator of the regard in which he was held.

When McCluskey retired, Ayrshire RA organised a dinner in his honour. Such dinners are common in refereeing but the gathering for McCluskey's was the biggest in memory with referees travelling from all over Scotland to attend, such was the esteem in which he was held. Football was well represented too, at the Dinner, with David Taylor (SFA Chief Executive) and Peter Donald (Scottish League Secretary) paying tribute to McCluskey in addresses.

The SFA appointed McCluskey as the Referee Supervisor for Ayrshire RA shortly after he retired and from 2003-04, he served as a member of the Referee Committee. UEFA made use of his services again in the role of Referee Observer. Very sadly, in 2011, McCluskey was struck down by a rare blood illness and succumbed to it two years later.

Michael McCurry
Date of Birth: 4th June 1964
Admitted to SFA List: 1991-92
No. of seasons at Class 1: 15 (1993-94 to 2008-09)
No. of years as a FIFA Referee: 9 (1996 to 2004)
6 A Internationals; 3 U21 Internationals
FIFA: U19 World Cup (2001); 1 World Cup Qualifier
UEFA: 2 European Championship Qualifiers; 3 U21 Championship Qualifiers; 3 U18 Championship Qualifiers; U16 Championships (1998 (F)); 2 U16 Championship Qualifiers; 21 Club Competition matches (2 ECWC, 9 UC (1 G), 5 UCL (4 G), 5 UIC (1 F))
1 League Cup Final; 1 Challenge Cup Final; 5 Old Firm matches

A supremely fit individual, Michael McCurry was identified as a future talent early in his career and he earned FIFA status in 1996 after three seasons at Class 1. The highlight of his early seasons on the FIFA List was selection for the UEFA U16 Championships hosted by Scotland in 1998. McCurry refereed the Quarter-Final between Greece and Spain and had the honour of being appointed to the Final, Italy v Republic of Ireland.

The first of his six A Internationals was Northern Ireland's match against Canada in 1999. Over the next five years, he refereed international friendlies in Norway, France, Denmark, Republic of Ireland and England.

A World Cup Qualifier in Malta in 2001 was followed by the high point in his career – selection for the FIFA U19 World Cup, held in Argentina, where he refereed the Group match encounter between Costa Rica and Ethiopia and the host nation's Round of 16 match against China.

In the UEFA Club Competitions, a variety of excellent appointments came McCurry's way. He refereed the 1st Leg of an Intertoto Cup Final between Paris Saint-Germain and Brescia Calcio in 2001 and the following year he handled a Semi-Final in the competition, Willem II Tilburg v Malaga CF. He received four Group match appointments in the UEFA Champions League, refereeing clubs such as PSV Eindhoven, SS Lazio, FC Barcelona, FC Lokomotiv Moskva and AEK Athens. In nine appointments in the UEFA Cup, his highest profile ties were SBV Vitesse v FC Internazionale Milano and BV Borussia Dortmund v FC Kobenhavn.

As a Fourth Official, McCurry was appointed to a Semi-Final in the UEFA Cup and to Quarter-Finals in the European Cup Winners' Cup and the UEFA Champions League.

European Championship Qualifiers in Cyprus and Belarus were fulfilled in 2003.

McCurry's League Cup Final was between Rangers and Motherwell in 2005. He was appointed to seven Semi-Finals in the Scottish Cup and League Cup between 2001 and 2008 and handled five Old Firm League matches between 2003 and 2007. He refereed the 2001 Challenge Cup Final.

As his career progressed, McCurry, an accountant who became a Baptist Minister for a Glasgow Church, became intellectually at odds with the diktats on instructions to referees on the application of the Laws, being of the view that it removed the element of discretion and skill which he felt was an important part of a referee's ability to control a match in the way he wanted to. McCurry considered that his enjoyment of the game was being affected as a result. A newspaper interview in 2006 conveyed his thoughts. His last season on the SFA List was 2008-09, with a number of factors contributing to his being removed from the List. It was a sad end to what had been a fine career.

Matthew MacDermid

Date of Birth: 28th April 1993
Admitted to SFA List: 2011-12
No. of seasons at Category 1: 5 (2021-22 to 2024-25)
No. of years as a FIFA Referee: 2 (2024 to 2025)
1 A International; 1 U21 International
UEFA: 2 U17 Championship Qualifiers; 4 Club Competition matches (2 UECL, 2 UYL)
1 Challenge Cup Final; 1 Youth Cup Final

In just two years on the FIFA List, Matthew MacDermid's appointments exemplify the opportunities which exist for referees in European football. A UEFA U17 Championship Elite Round tournament in Greece in March 2024 saw his international debut and that was followed by two Europa Conference League Qualifiers in Wales and Lithuania at the start of season 2024-25. In the autumn, Youth League appointments were fulfilled in Moldova and then Spain, where he refereed Real Betis Balompie v US Sassuolo Calcio.
In March 2025, MacDermid handled his first A International, a friendly between Sweden and Northern Ireland.
Since becoming a Category 1 referee, MacDermid has acted as a Fourth Official in 16 matches in various international competitions.
MacDermid is a prime example of someone taking up refereeing at a young age, demonstrating the talent and commitment to progress and benefitting from the SFA's development programmes. He refereed the Youth Cup Final in 2015, a match between the Old Firm, and the 2024 Challenge Cup Final between the New Saints (of Wales) and Airdrieonians. To give him an introduction to international football, he was appointed to a home Scotland U21 International against Northern Ireland in 2022.

Dougie McDonald
Date of Birth: 8th October 1965
Admitted to SFA List: 1992-93
No. of seasons at Class 1/Category 1: 13 (1997-98 to 2010-11)
No. of years as a FIFA Referee: 11 (2000 to 2010)
7 A Internationals; 3 U21 Internationals
FIFA: 2 World Cup Qualifiers
UEFA: 1 European Championship Qualifier; 3 U21 Championship Qualifiers; U19 Championships (2004); 3 U19 Youth Championship Qualifiers; 2 U18 Youth Championship Qualifiers; U16 Championships (2000); Regions Cup (1999); 34 Club Competition matches (17 UC (5 G), 7 UCL, 9 UEL (2 PO, 5 G), 1 UIC)
2 Scottish Cup Finals; 2 League Cup Finals; 1 Youth Cup Final; 5 Old Firm matches

In advance of gaining FIFA status, Dougie McDonald was given the chance to gain international experience in 1999 by officiating at a Qualifying Group tournament and in the Final Competition of the UEFA Regions Cup (played in Italy), a tournament for amateur players and with the referees being non-FIFA. In the first few months of being a FIFA referee, he was selected for the UEFA U16 Championships in Israel, where he officiated at three Group matches.

McDonald's career took off over the next few seasons, with appointments in UEFA's Under Age competitions, U21 Internationals in Greece, Northern Ireland and England and a World Cup Qualifier in 2001 between the Faroe Islands and Switzerland. Selection for the UEFA U19 Championships in Switzerland in 2004 completed a "double" in the Finals of these Under Age competitions.

The first of his seven A Internationals was a match between Northern Ireland and Finland in 2003, quickly followed by a Belgium v Poland friendly. He had a diverse range of international friendlies which included France v Bosnia & Herzegovina, Wales v Paraguay, South Korea v Ghana (a match played in Edinburgh) and Greece v Cyprus.

In the UEFA Club Competitions, McDonald handled six matches in the Qualifying Rounds of the Champions League and had six Group Stage appointments as a Fourth Official. He was predominantly used in the UEFA Cup and its successor, the Europa League. In these, he had five Group matches in each competition, taking charge of ties involving prominent clubs such as Zenit St. Petersburg v Sevilla, FC Basel 1893 v Feyenoord, Steaua București v Fenerbache SK and FC Porto v SK Rapid Wien. In the Europa League, he also received two appointments to ties in the Play-offs. Many of his appointments were in eastern Europe, with one trip to Ukraine in 2001 having to be aborted due to the impact of the 9/11 atrocity in New York.

McDonald, a transport planner, refereed the Scottish Cup Finals of 2006 and 2010 and the League Cup Finals of 2007 and 2009, the latter being one of his five Old Firm matches. Between the two Cups, he was the referee of six Semi-Finals.

McDonald's last year on the FIFA List was in 2010, due to the age limits, and that year brought his domestic career crashing to a regrettable end in November. The trigger point had occurred in a Dundee United v Celtic match in October when he rescinded a penalty he had awarded to Celtic and which led to his making an error of judgement by misleading the Referee Observer in a post-match discussion about that decision. This resulted in his being censured after an investigation by the SFA. In the outside football world, however, an almighty furore had broken out because of what had happened in the match. Much else had been focused on Scottish referees at that time, with personal abuse being a major theme and provoking a febrile atmosphere, and McDonald's incident attracted huge comment in the media and was a contributory factor in the referees declaring a "weekend of unavailability" at the end of November. As a consequence of the maelstrom which had developed, McDonald, after initially indicating that he would not resign, came to the view that his position had become a distraction and decided to retire. One ill-judged remark in a heat of the moment conversation with an assistant in the dressing-room after that match at Tannadice Park had brought what had been a very solid career to a premature end.

Brian McGinlay
Date of Birth: 24th August 1945
Admitted to SFA List: 1966-67
No. of seasons at Class 1: 18 (1973-74 to 1985-86 and 1988-89 to 1992-93)
No. of seasons/years as a FIFA Referee: 12 (1976-77 to 1985-86 and 1991 to 1992)
2 A Internationals; 3 British International Championship matches
FIFA: 6 World Cup Qualifiers; U19 World Cup (1983); Olympics (1984); 1 Olympic Qualifier
UEFA: European Championships (1980); 5 European Championship Qualifiers; U21 Championship Final 2nd Leg (1992); 1 U21 Championship Qualifier; 1 Youth Tournament Qualifier; 32 Club Competition matches (7 ECCC (1 Q-F), 4 ECWC (1 Q-F, 1 S-F), 21 UC (2 Q-F, 1 S-F)

Brian McGinlay is a giant of Scottish refereeing. At his peak, he was one of Europe's, if not the world's, best referees. A friendly, likeable character, he was well respected within the game. He was totally devoted to refereeing, undertaking the referee training class as soon as he could, aged 16, in 1961. He was admitted to the SFA List when he was 21, a remarkably young age for the time. McGinlay served a seven year apprenticeship before becoming a Class 1 referee for season 1973-74. He made an immediate impact, with the Sunday Post carrying a feature on him during the season. He was viewed as being different from other referees, being younger (28) than his fellow referees and having longish hair. He was also establishing a no-nonsense reputation as a strict disciplinarian, something which undoubtedly helped provide a solid foundation for him as his career developed and which he was able to use to his advantage in controlling matches.

His ambition to become a FIFA referee was achieved after three seasons at Class 1. His first A International came along quickly, Iceland v Luxembourg, in September 1976, and a World Cup Qualifier, Israel v South Korea, followed later in the season. Regular appointments in the UEFA Club Competitions started to come his way during 1977-78 and he began to establish his name in Europe.

He had a major European Championship Qualifier in 1979 when he was appointed to referee Spain and Yugoslavia in Valencia. It was a fiery match, with two sendings-off and three cautions, and there was huge crowd disorder which resulted in UEFA banning Spain from staging any internationals at the ground for two years. Despite Spain's narrow defeat in the match, McGinlay received fulsome praise in the Spanish press for his performance. Later in the season, McGinlay was appointed to the all-German affair between Eintracht Frankfurt and FC Bayern Munchen in the 2nd Leg of the UEFA Cup Semi-Final.

Selection for the 1980 European Championships in Italy, where he refereed West Germany and Greece in the Group Stages, established him in the top rank of European referees. In the three years from 1982, he refereed Quarter-Finals in each of the three UEFA Club Competitions. In 1983, FIFA selected him for the U19 World Cup in Mexico, at which he refereed Austria and Argentina in the Group matches and had two line appointments. Selection for the Olympics in Los Angeles in 1984 continued McGinlay's upward trajectory. After refereeing a Group match between Brazil and Saudi Arabia, he then handled a Quarter-Final between Italy and Chile and was selected to referee the Bronze Medal match, Italy v Yugoslavia. Prior to the Olympics, McGinlay was selected as a linesman to Bob Valentine in the European Championships in France.

With these appointments to the Finals of major Competitions, the portents for McGinlay to realise his ambition to referee at a World Cup were looking very good and he was duly rewarded by being chosen for the Mexico Finals in 1986. However, McGinlay's world totally collapsed in April when, later in the day after refereeing a Scottish Cup Semi-Final, he was arrested and charged under a section of the Criminal Justice (Scotland) Act 1980. The Glasgow Procurator Fiscal decided that there was no case to answer with the case being closed with no proceedings.

It was a difficult and delicate time and after initially believing that he would be able ride out the media storm which his arrest had created, McGinlay, after taking counsel from trusted voices in the game, decided to resign from the List. As a result, his World Cup dream was shattered and his ambition would not be realised. Having been in Mexico in 1983, he had been preparing very well for what lay ahead in terms of the fitness levels required to handle matches in heat and at altitude.

McGinlay pursued a complaint against the police in respect of his arrest in a fight to clear his name, which took until November 1987 to resolve when the Crown Office determined in his favour.

A very quick attempt to return to the following season's List failed, as did an application for season 1987-88. In the spring of 1988, the SFA Office Bearers gave the Referee Committee the go-ahead to consider another re-application. This time, he was successful. It would have been foolhardy for football to deny itself the services of a top-class referee.

McGinlay was welcomed back into the game and over the next couple of seasons, his performances returned him to the FIFA List for 1991 and 1992. UEFA made good use of him once more, as he was appointed to a Semi-Final of the European Cup Winners' Cup, AS Monaco v Feyenoord, in 1991 and the 2nd Leg of the UEFA U21 Championship Final between Sweden and Italy in 1992. He suffered a setback in February 1992 when he failed a UEFA Fitness Test and was taken off a European Champion Clubs' Cup Quarter-Final between SL Benfica and AC Sparta Praha. He redeemed himself by passing the Test the following month.

The failure of that UEFA Fitness Test was, however, an indication of McGinlay having issues with his fitness as he got older. These continued and resulted in his announcing his retirement in November 1992.

His had been a superb career, blighted by missing out on the 1986 World Cup. McGinlay had been a real personality in Scottish football. In the early part of his career, he had been the runner up in the McKinlay's Personality of the Month Award in April 1977, something extremely unusual for a referee. He had been held in high esteem by managers. Alex Ferguson once described him as "brilliant" after an Aberdeen v Celtic match. A sales manager for a Glasgow office equipment company,

McGinlay had been able to take time away from his job to accept several opportunities to referee abroad which came his way. In the spring of 1979, he refereed in the Major Soccer League in the United States. He officiated in 30 matches, in which he sent off 12 players and cautioned 30 others. Invited to address the SFA's Referees' Conference that year, McGinlay reckoned it was the most difficult League he had operated in. No sooner had he returned from the United States than he was off to Japan at the end of May to referee in the Japan Cup tournament. Due to this commitment he had to withdraw from refereeing the 2nd Replay of the Scottish Cup Final between Rangers and Hibernian, being replaced by Ian Foote. In 1982, he spent a short period in Abu Dhabi, refereeing in the Arabian Gulf Cup. During season 1986-87, he refereed in Dubai.

If having the chance of officiating around the world was a benefit of being a top-class referee, McGinlay was equally at home refereeing in minor football, which he did throughout his career. Summers were spent keeping his hand in by refereeing in the Forth & Endrick Welfare League. He just loved refereeing.

McGinlay had a fine record in the domestic cups in Scotland, with four Scottish Cup and three League Cup Finals and 14 Semi-Finals between the two competitions. He had the honour of refereeing the 100th Scottish Cup Final in 1985 between Celtic and Dundee United. His 14 Old Firm matches were over a 14 year period. Unusually perhaps, only one such match was in one of the Cups – a Scottish Cup 4th Round tie in 1992. He considered the most tense and nerve wracking match of his entire career was the League decider between Rangers and Aberdeen in April 1991, which Aberdeen lost whilst needing a draw to win the League.

Once he finished with refereeing, McGinlay was associated with Stenhousemuir in a commercial capacity for a number of years and was in much demand as an after dinner speaker.

Alistair MacKenzie
Born: 1930
Died: December 1997 aged 67
Admitted to SFA List: 1954-55

No. of seasons at Class 1: 16 (1960-61 to 1975-76)
No. of seasons as a FIFA Referee: 8 (1962-63 and 1969-70 to 1975-76)
3 A Internationals; 1 British International Championship match; 1 British Youth International Championship matches; 2 British Amateur International Championship matches; 1 League International; 1 U23 International;
UEFA: 2 European Championship matches; 14 Club Competition matches (2 ECCC, 5 ECWC (1 Q-F), 5 UC (2 Q-F), 2 ICFC)
1 Scottish Cup Final; 1 League Cup Final; 3 Old Firm matches

Alistair MacKenzie took the refereeing course along with his good friend Bobby Davidson. They attended the same school in Coatbridge and started their refereeing careers in the Airdrie & Coatbridge Amateur League. It took MacKenzie a little longer than Davidson to get on to the List, being admitted for season 1954-55, having been unsuccessful, along with 12 others, with a mid-term application the previous season.

Early promise was shown by his selection as a linesman for the 1955 League Cup Final. Once he got to Class 1 in 1960, his performances were such that he gained appointments to Amateur and Youth internationals in Northern Ireland and England during 1961-62 and earned FIFA status for season 1962-63. During that season he received an appointment in the Preliminary Round of the European Champion Clubs' Cup, Esjberg fB v Linfield, and handled an England U23 International against Belgium. MacKenzie served a single season on the FIFA List at this juncture but received another Amateur International in during 1963-64.

He regained FIFA status in 1969-70 and held his position for seven seasons, fully establishing himself in the top bracket of Scottish referees. The early 1970's proved to be the top period of his career.

His first A International was the friendly between Iceland and Denmark in 1970, a fixture he would repeat two years later. He handled Northern Ireland against England in the British International Championship in 1971, a match remembered for his penalising George Best for dangerous play against the

England goalkeeper Gordon Banks. With an audacious piece of skill, Best had flicked the ball away from Banks just after he had released it from his hands to kick it upfield. The goal Best scored was disallowed as a consequence. Selection as the referee for the friendly international, West Germany v Spain, in 1973, was a top appointment.

His 15 matches in the UEFA Club Competitions included several significant appointments. He refereed AFC Ajax v Olympique de Marseille in the European Champion Clubs' Cup in 1971. In 1973, he refereed AFC Ajax again, this time in the club's 1st Leg away tie in the unofficial Super Cup Final to Rangers (The match was not recognised by UEFA due to Rangers being banned at the time from competing in UEFA Competitions and was played as part of Rangers' centenary celebrations). MacKenzie was well regarded by UEFA as he appointed to three Quarter-Finals between 1973 and 1976, two in the UEFA Cup and the other in the European Cup Winners' Cup. The last of these matches was AC Milan v Club Brugge KV in the UEFA Cup in 1976. UEFA further recognised MacKenzie later that season when he was appointed to another Quarter-Final, this time in the European Championship – the 2nd Leg tie, USSR v Czechoslovakia.

MacKenzie refereed the Scottish Cup Final in 1972 and, later that year, the League Cup Final, with both matches featuring Celtic and Hibernian. He was in charge of the two clubs again in 1973 when he refereed the Final of the pre-season competition, the Drybrough Cup. On top of these Final appointments, MacKenzie refereed five Semi-Finals in the Scottish and League Cups in five seasons from 1969-70. One of these Semi-Finals, in the League Cup, was one of his Old Firm matches.

MacKenzie's last match was that European Championship Quarter-Final, as he chose to retire at the end of the season. Early in 1977, he was appointed as a Referee Supervisor for Edinburgh & District RA but he resigned due to business reasons after less than two years in the post. MacKenzie later became a Director of Falkirk and, from 1988-89 to 1992-93, was a member of the SFA Council. In his first season, he was a member of the Appeals Committee and thereafter he served on the Disciplinary & Referee Committee.

Steven McLean

Date of Birth: 1st April 1981
Admitted to SFA List: 2003-04
No. of seasons at Category 1: 18 (2007-08 to 2024-25)
No. of years as a FIFA Referee: 7 (2010 to 2016)
No. of years as a FIFA Video Match Official: 1 (2025)
1 A International
UEFA: 2 European Championship Qualifiers; 5 U21 Championship Qualifiers; 10 U19 Championship Qualifiers; U17 Championships (2011); 2 U17 Championship Qualifiers; 14 Club Competition matches (1 UCL, 13 UEL (1 PO, 3 G); 2 UEFA Regions Cup Qualifiers
1 Scottish Cup Final; 1 League Cup Final; 1 Youth Cup Final; 3 Old Firm matches

With his father Stuart having played for Kilmarnock and his younger brother Brian playing for a number of clubs over a long career, Steven McLean comes from a football family. Rather than playing, he determined that refereeing was to be his goal. He has enjoyed a solid career and is recognised as one of the most experienced referees in Scotland.

He was identified early in his career as a future talent and has more than justified that view. McLean's performances in his first three seasons at Category 1 marked him out as deserving of the opportunity to become a FIFA referee. Performances in his early UEFA appointments were rewarded by selection for the U17 Championships held in Serbia in 2011. He handled two group matches and the Semi-Final between Denmark and Germany.

His first European Championship match, San Marino v Sweden, came later that year and Latvia v Kazakhstan followed in 2015. McLean was regularly used in UEFA U19 and U21 Championship Qualifiers, and received an appointment to an U21 Play-off tie between Italy and Slovakia in 2014. His A International was the Wales v Northern Ireland match in 2016.

In the UEFA Club Competitions, McLean received 14 appointments in the Europa League. The majority were in the qualifying rounds but he received one Play-off match, RNK Split v Torino in 2014, and handled Group matches at Royal Standard de Liege, Qarabag FK and Club Brugge KV.

McLean received numerous appointments across a range of national team and club competitions as a Fourth Official and as an Additional Assistant Referee both during and after his time on the FIFA List. He returned to the FIFA List in 2025 as a VAR Official.

In the domestic Cups, McLean refereed the 2010 Youth Cup Final, the 2014 League Cup Final and the 2016 Scottish Cup Final, and has been appointed to six Semi-Finals in the two major Cups.

A physiotherapist who runs his own practice, McLean worked in the SFA's Referee Operations Department in the role of Recruitment and Education Officer on a job-sharing basis (with Craig Thomson) from 2011 to 2020.

Bobby Madden
Date of Birth: 25th October 1978
Admitted to SFA List: 2005-06
No. of seasons at Category 1: 14 (2008-09 to 2021-22)
No. of years as a FIFA Referee: 13 (2010 to 2022)
No. of years as a FIFA Video Match Official: 1 (2022)
3 A Internationals; World University Games
FIFA: 5 World Cup Qualifiers; U17 World Cup (2017);
UEFA: 6 European Championship Qualifiers; 3 Nations League matches; 2 U21 Championships (2017 and 2019); 3 U21 Championship Qualifiers; 4 U19 Championship Qualifiers; 2 U17 Championship Qualifiers; 56 Club Competition matches (16 UCL (6 G), 37 UEL (15 G, 6 R32, 2 R16), 3 UECL (2 G); 2 Regions Cup Qualifiers
1 Scottish Cup Final; 1 League Cup Final; 8 Old Firm matches

Bobby Madden was a Scottish Junior athletic internationalist and amateur football player before taking up refereeing, his athletics background giving him a strong foundation in his fitness levels for refereeing. Once at Category 3, he took just three seasons to reach Category 1, with his performances marking him out as a future prospect. The FIFA List was reached in 2010 and he proceeded to enjoy a fine career in international football.

In his first two years as a FIFA referee, he officiated at UEFA U17 and U19 qualifying tournaments in Portugal and Austria, a Regions Cup qualifying tournament in Hungary, a Qualifier in the Champions League and an U21 Qualifier in Albania. In 2011, he was selected for the World University Games in China, where he took charge of three matches.

After refereeing two Europa League Qualifiers at FK Vojvodina and IF Elfsborg at the start of season 2012-13, his first major appointment was received shortly afterwards – a World Cup Qualifier between Germany and the Faroe Islands. That autumn saw him referee three Group matches in the Europa League, as he started to establish himself on the European scene. During his career, he was regularly used in the Europa League and handled seven Play-Off ties, 19 Group matches, seven ties in the Round of 32 (featuring clubs such as Sevilla, Real Sociedad, SL Benfica and AS Roma) and two ties in the Round of 16 – Olympique Lyonnais v CSKA Moskva in 2018 and Young Boys v AFC Ajax in 2021. In the Champions League, he refereed six Group matches in the 2018-20 period, handling games involving SL Benfica, FC Bayern Munchen, FC Barcelona, Paris Saint-Germain and AFC Ajax.

Madden was selected for two UEFA U21 Championships – in 2017 in Hungary and 2019 in Italy. He officiated at two Group matches in each tournament. 2017 also saw him chosen for that year's FIFA U17 World Cup held in India, where he was in charge of Costa Rica v Guinea and Niger v Brazil in the Group Stages and appointed as the Fourth Official for the Round of 16 match, Paraguay v USA, and the Quarter-Final, Mali v Ghana.

Following his debut World Cup Qualifier in Germany, Madden handled four other Qualifiers involving Russia, Portugal, Denmark and Spain over the next decade. He accrued 10 appointments in total between the European Championship Qualifiers and the Nations League.

Madden was part of William Collum's team for the 2016 European Championships as an Additional Assistant Referee. In that role he had 28 appointments in the Champions League. Amongst his many Fourth Official appointments, he was part of Craig Thomson's team for a Europa League Semi-Final, SL Benfica v SC Braga, in 2011.

Madden's eight Old Firm matches reflects the place he held amongst Scottish referees of the time, and two Cup Finals topped a very solid career. Madden, who works in transport logistics, took up a job in England during 2022. A move to the English Football League's List of Referees was engineered and he was included in its National group of referees for season 2022-23, officiating at matches in Leagues One and Two in the north of England. The move did not quite work out as expected and he retired at the end of the season. For a year or two after, Madden appeared frequently on Scottish radio on football programmes offering his views on refereeing decisions and issues.

John Marshall
Born: 28th April 1859
Died: 23rd May 1938 aged 79
No. of seasons on List: 12 (1890-91 to 1903-04)
1 British International Championship match; 5 League Internationals
1 Scottish Cup Final

John Marshall can be regarded as the first great Scottish referee who emerged following the formalisation of the role in the Laws of the Game in 1891. As a player, he was capped four times for Scotland between 1885 and 1887. A speedy winger and a great dribbler, he played for a couple of clubs before joining Third Lanark in 1883 where he played for seven years, winning the Scottish Cup in 1889. He also played nine times for Glasgow in Inter-Association representative matches. Third Lanark held a benefit match for him against Rangers in 1891 after he had retired the previous year. On ending his playing career, he immediately took up refereeing and established himself very quickly.

By late 1896, he was described as being an "old stager with the whistle and in his day has refereed some of the most important games and is still likely to be in great demand". That indeed was the case as he refereed many significant matches during his career. He refereed four home Scottish League Internationals between 1893 and 1896 and Irish League v the Football League Internationals in 1896 and 1897. His British International Championship match was between Ireland and England in Dublin in 1900.

Marshall's Scottish Cup Final in 1894 was an Old Firm match, one of five that he controlled, and it is known that he refereed at least one Semi-Final tie - between Kilmarnock and Dundee in 1898. In 1895, he missed out on refereeing the Semi-Final between Renton and Dundee as Renton's bid to have him appointed as the referee was rebuffed.

A perhaps surprising omission from his record is the absence of appointments to the Finals of the Glasgow Cup and Glasgow Charity Cup. This may be down to his club connection with Third Lanark, as he was constantly referred to as J. Marshall (Third Lanark) in match reports. In a Glasgow Charity Cup Semi-Final between Celtic and Queen's Park in 1895, he had to intervene to stop fighting between players at an early stage of the match.

Marshall was on the committee of the Scottish Referees' Association in 1896, a forerunner of the Scottish Football Referees' Association. He worked as a spirit salesman.

Tommy Marshall
Admitted to SFA List: 1961-62
No. of seasons at Class 1: 6 (1967-68 to 1972-73)
No. of seasons as a FIFA Referee: 2 (1971-72 to1972-73)
1 A International; 1 British Amateur International Championship match; 1 U23 Representative match
1 UEFA Youth Tournament Qualifier

Tommy Marshall qualified as a referee in 1957 and had a slow but steady rise to Class 1. Prior to reaching FIFA status, he refereed two Northern Ireland home matches in the British Amateur International Championship against Wales and England in 1968 and 1969, respectively. Previously, Marshall had been a linesman in the 1964 British International

Championship match between Northern Ireland and England and in a home Scotland Youth Championship match against Wales in 1965.

His A International was received at the very start of his time as a FIFA referee, August 1971, when he was appointed to the friendly between Iceland and Japan. UEFA returned him to Iceland the following month to referee the Youth Tournament Qualifier against the Republic of Ireland. In January 1973, he officiated at the U23 Representative match between Scotland and the West German Olympic team. His one appointment as a linesman whilst a FIFA referee was to the World Cup Qualifier, Wales v England, in 1973.

Marshall decided to quit the SFA List in June 1973, making it known to a newspaper that he was disenchanted with the set up, and complaining that he had received very little in the way of international appointments in his two seasons on the FIFA List. A telecoms engineer, Marshall continued to referee in minor football.

Jimmy Martin
Date of Birth: 20th October 1899
Died: 12th March 1973 aged 73
No. of seasons on List: 18 (1930-31 to 1947-48)
No. of seasons as a FIFA Referee: 1 (1947-48)
3 A Internationals; 1 British International Championship match; 1 Wartime Representative match
2 Scottish Cup Finals; 5 Old Firm matches; 1 Junior international

Born in Glasgow, Martin's family moved to Fife when he was young and he played football for Cupar Hearts Juveniles and Rosslyn Juniors before turning his hand to refereeing. By the early 1930's he was refereeing Junior football in Fife and Stirlingshire and became prominent enough to be appointed to a Junior Cup Semi-Final between Tranent and Renfrew in 1933.

Once he started in senior football in 1933, he quickly made an impression with his performances, evidenced by being appointed to a friendly between Rangers and Manchester City in 1934. Two years later, in 1936, he was chosen to referee the

Scottish Cup Final between Rangers and Third Lanark, after having officiated at the Semi-Final involving Rangers. In season 1937-38, he refereed the Glasgow Cup and Glasgow Charity Cup Finals. The latter Final was between the Old Firm, one of five such games handled by Martin during his career. Also during that season he was the referee of the Junior international, Scotland v Wales.

His first A International followed in 1938-39 when he took charge of England's friendly against Norway, a match played at Newcastle. The Second World War interrupted his career with his only appointment of note being to the Representative match between an SFA XI and the Army XI (Scottish Command) in 1940.

Martin's second A International was an England v Netherlands match in November 1946. His performance must have pleased the Football Association as it requested him to officiate at its away international friendly against Belgium in 1947. His handling of the match came in for some criticism, with it being suggested that he had been too lenient towards Belgium, with his approach helping to keep the score down. An alternative point of view suggested that he had been supremely diplomatic and very tactful in his refereeing.

Martin, unusually even for the time, was happy to give a candid interview to an English newspaper. He accepted that he had had a 10 minute spell of leniency simply to save the game as a spectacle when England had already well won the match. He was quoted: "It would be a lie to say that I was not lenient during the last ten minutes' play. You know this continental habit of pushing. There was nothing violent in the pushing in this case and I do not see why I should have spoiled the spectacle by awarding several unnecessary penalty kicks. This so called leniency made no difference to the result. I believe in firm, honest refereeing but I also like to read a game with a sense of proportion and judgement. Those ten minutes must be viewed in relation to the whole of the game." England won the game 5-2.

Martin refereed England again the month after the Belgian match, this time in Wales in the British International Championship. This was his final season on the SFA List and he rounded off his career by being appointed to the Scottish Cup Final between Rangers and Morton. Martin was a hotelier and by this time had moved from Ladybank to take over the Angus Hotel in Blairgowrie. The business responsibilities had become too demanding to continue to referee. The hotel was the venue of a couple of Referee Supervisors' Executive Committee meetings in the late 1940's. His ownership of it probably explains why. Martin was the father of Norrie Martin, the Rangers goalkeeper of the 1960's.

George Mitchell
Date of Birth: 22nd February 1912
Died: 8th November 1996 aged 84
Admitted to SFA List: 1940-41
No. of seasons at Class 1: 20 (1942-43 to 1961-62)
No. of seasons as a FIFA Referee: 7 (1948-49 to 1954-55)
2 A internationals; 2 British International Championship matches; 1 Wartime Representative match
FIFA: World Cup (1950)
1 Summer Cup Final; 4 Old Firm matches

George Mitchell came from a football family. His father played for Falkirk and became a club director. He was a schoolboy internationalist, playing against England at Roker Park, Sunderland in 1926 and played juvenile football until work commitments in his then job as an insurance agent interfered. Mitchell took up refereeing at 25 and progressed to the List in 1940. Two seasons later, he was at Class 1 and gave sterling service for 20 seasons.
Prior to becoming Class 1, he had made sufficient impression to be appointed to referee the Wartime Representative match between an SFA XI and the Army (Scottish Command) in April 1942. In July that year he refereed the Summer Cup Final, Rangers v Hibernian.
The crowning glory of Mitchell's career was selection for the 1950 World Cup in Brazil – the first ever Scottish referee to be so chosen. The SFA had nominated him and Charlie Faultless to FIFA for consideration for selection. In the first round of Group matches, he refereed Sweden v Paraguay. During the

tournament, he received three appointments as a linesman with each of these matches featuring Brazil, the first being the match against Mexico in the Group Stages. Rather than there being knock-out rounds at the tournament, a further final Group was played and Mitchell was linesman for Brazil's matches against Spain and, crucially, the match against Uruguay. The way the results had gone, this match was held to be the "Final" to determine the winner of the World Cup and it has been regarded ever since as the 1950 World Cup Final. Mitchell thus became the first Scot to officiate at a World Cup Final.

Another distinction came Mitchell's way in 1951 when he became the last Scot to referee an England v Scotland match. The Football Association had favoured a neutral referee but the SFA pressed for Scottish officials and won the day, given that English referees had controlled the game at Hampden the previous year. It was a dream come true for Mitchell, as he had dreamed of playing at Hampden or Wembley as a boy.

Earlier that season he had refereed Northern Ireland's match against England in the British International Championship. 1951 was a big year for Mitchell as he handled two international friendlies – Wales v Switzerland and Netherlands v Finland. His last two seasons on the FIFA List were in the Deputy category.

In domestic football, although he officiated at five Semi-Finals in the Scottish and League Cups between 1949 and 1956, he missed out on being chosen for one of the Finals. His Old Firm matches were in 1950 and 1956 – two in each year. Mitchell was appointed to a number of prestigious club friendlies throughout his career, one of which was Falkirk v Newcastle United in 1953. This was the first live televised match (second half only) played under floodlights which was broadcast in the UK.

On retiring as a referee in 1962, Mitchell was appointed by the SFA as a Referee Supervisor and served in that capacity for 27 years, being attached to Stirlingshire RA for 22 years. He served on the Referee Supervisors' Executive Committee for 23 seasons, two of them as Vice-Chairman.

Mitchell was presented with the SFA's Honorary Long Service Award in November 1987 to mark 50 years of service to the

SFA as a referee and a Referee Supervisor. His had been a distinguished refereeing career and he had frequently been described as being "honest, fair and always a gentleman".

Les Mottram
Date of Birth: 5th March 1951
Admitted to SFA List: 1984-85
No. of seasons at Class 1: 9 (1988-89 to 1996-97)
No. of years as a FIFA Referee: 6 (1991-1996)
2 A Internationals; 1 B International
FIFA: World Cup (1994); 5 World Cup Qualifiers
UEFA: European Championships (1996); 2 European Championship Qualifiers; 2 U18 Championship Qualifiers; U16 Championships (1992); 1 U16 Championship Qualifier; 19 Club Competition matches (3 ECWC, 5 UC (1 Q-F), 10 UCL (7 G, 1 Q-F, 1 S-F), 1 SC)
1 Scottish Cup Final; 1 League Cup Final; 1 Challenge Cup Final; 5 Old Firm matches

Standing well over 6 feet, Les Mottram cut a commanding figure. He had an unswerving adherence to the Laws of the Game and gained a reputation as a disciplinarian. In what was a relatively brief time as a FIFA referee, and after a quiet first two years, he enjoyed a meteoric rise to the top of European and world refereeing, officiating at the 1994 World Cup and the 1996 European Championships.

Mottram played in Airdrie Academy's Scottish Shield winning team in 1967 and after leaving school signed for Airdrieonians in 1968, playing in the reserve team for two seasons. He then went on to play Junior football for a number of clubs in Lanarkshire and West Lothian for a decade before taking up refereeing in 1981 after becoming disenchanted with playing. Three years later, he made it on to the SFA List. During his second season at Class 3A he enjoyed his first international appointment when he ran the line to Bob Valentine in the all-Italian European Champion Clubs' tie between Verona Hellas and Juventus, a match played behind closed doors, and was selected as a linesman for the 1986 Scottish Cup Final.

Promotion to Class 2 followed, with progression to Class 1 in 1988 and the FIFA List in 1991.

His first match as a FIFA referee was the B International between Wales and England in February 1991. Later that year, he handled his first A International – Iceland v Denmark. A couple appointments in UEFA's youth competitions were fulfilled and he was then selected for the UEFA U16 Championships in 1992, played in Cyprus. He did so well that he was chosen to referee the Final, Germany v Spain. The tournament kick-started his ascent to the top. A World Cup Qualifier, Faroe Islands v Belgium followed quickly, and by December he was being appointed to a home Real Madrid CF match, against SBV Vitesse, in the UEFA Cup 3rd Round. A couple of months later, he refereed another World Cup Qualifier, Morocco v Tunisia, and was then appointed to a European Cup Winners' Cup Quarter-Final, Steaua Bucaresti v. Royal Antwerp.

Mottram handled three other World Cup Qualifiers during 1993, most notably a match between France and Bulgaria. France, just needing a draw to reach the Finals, lost the game in the last 10 seconds. Mottram described the match as extremely tense with the pressure in the build-up to it almost overpowering. Some 250 people in Bulgarian football consequently wrote a letter to the country's leading newspaper, praising Mottram's performance.

Selection for the World Cup in the United States was confirmed in March 1994 following a gathering of the candidates in Dallas. He was in charge of two Group matches – South Korea v Bolivia and Greece v Nigeria – and Fourth Official in another. In European football, Mottram was by now in the top group of referees. Over a four year period from 1992, he officiated seven Group Matches in the Champions League featuring clubs such as SV Werder Bremen, AFC Ajax, FC Barcelona and FC Porto. In 1995, he handled the Quarter-Final between IFK Goteborg and FC Bayern Munchen and the Semi-Final between AC Milan and Paris Saint-Germain. Another Quarter-Final followed in 1996, this time in the UEFA Cup – SK Slavia Praha v AS Roma. His crowning appointment at club level was the 2nd Leg of the 1996 Super Cup Final, AFC Ajax v Real Zaragoza, a match which saw him award three penalties to AFC Ajax and send off three Real Zaragoza players.

1996 was his final year as a FIFA referee and it was marked by being picked for the European Championships in England. He refereed Italy v Russia in the Group Stages and was considered to be in the running for the Final, although that was dependent on the progress of England in the tournament. As England reached the Semi-Finals, he was selected to referee the other Semi-Final between France and the Czech Republic.

That match was his last as a FIFA Referee. In March 1996, he had accepted an offer from Japan to referee in its J-league and to coach referees for three months in the autumn, managing to secure time away from his job as Head of a Technical Department at a school. He had been contemplating retiring from refereeing after the European Championships but grasped the opportunity to go to Japan. During his time there, he was offered a two-year contract commencing in March 1997 and, on his return to Scotland, intimated his intention to resign from the SFA List at the start of March. He passed the Fitness Test he was required to do and refereed his last match in Scotland on 22nd February at Alloa Athletic.

In domestic football, Mottram refereed the 1991 Challenge Cup Final and in 1995 handled that year's Scottish and League Cup Finals, Celtic v Airdrieonians and Aberdeen v Dundee, respectively. In four years from 1993, he was appointed to four Semi-Finals in the two Cups, the last in 1996 being an Old Firm match in the Scottish Cup.

Mottram managed to survive an infamous incident in a Partick Thistle and Dundee United match in 1993. Dundee United scored a goal which was not awarded – the ball rebounded from a stanchion into the field of play when it was then handled by a defender with play being allowed to continue without any action taken by Mottram or any signal for a goal or an offence being given by the standside linesman. Mottram was severely censured and the linesman censured by the SFA. The case had a lasting impact on Scottish football – as a consequence, the SFA decided that its member clubs should adopt the style of support for goal nets as recommended by FIFA and UEFA.

Throughout his career, Mottram had a great appreciation of the need for top class fitness and was an assiduous trainer. Described as being unflappable, he had rock-solid confidence in his ability and certainly did not hold back from enforcing the Laws of the Game and issuing sanctions. Mottram's views emerged in a radio interview he gave just prior to going to Japan. He put the cat amongst the pigeons when he called players in Scotland cheats, expressing the view that, as a referee of a match, it was him against 22 players who are out to break the Laws of the Game, something which he could not understand. He was also critical of managers attacking refereeing decisions. Mottram did not have kind words either about the media, being of the view that referees were correct not to speak about decisions after matches as he did not trust matters to be reported correctly. He was also bitter about the manner in which the media criticised referees. Predictably, the interview caused a storm of protest and Mottram had to issue an apology to the Players' Union for calling players cheats.

Mottram's term in Japan went extremely well to the extent that his contract was renewed twice. He was the only full-time referee in Japan, training every day and lecturing and coaching referees. Living outside Tokyo in an apartment provided by the J-League, he and his family enjoyed the Japanese lifestyle. For three years running, he was voted the J-League Referee of the Year. It was his view that he got far more respect as a referee in Japan compared to Scotland, which he attributed to the respectful nature of the Japanese. During his time in Japan, he invited a stalwart of Lanarkshire RA, John Dearie, over for a holiday. He had much to be grateful to Dearie for. In 1982, Mottram was on the point of quitting as a referee after failing to be accepted on to the Central Junior League's List of Referees. Dearie managed to get him included on the East of Scotland Junior League List. Had that not happened, Mottram would have been lost to refereeing and his life would have been entirely different.

When his contract expired in Japan, Mottram returned to Scotland and went back to teaching.

Jack Mowat
Date of Birth: 1st April 1906
Died: 12th March 1995 aged 88
Admitted to List: 1933-34
No. of seasons at Class 1: 14 (1946-47 to 1959-60)
No. of seasons as a FIFA Referee: 12 (1948-49 to 1959-60)
5 A Internationals; 3 British International Championship matches; 1 Amateur International match; 6 League Internationals; 2 Wartime Representative matches; 4 Representative matches
FIFA: World Cup (1958); 2 World Cup Qualifiers
UEFA: 3 Club Competition matches (3 ECCC (1 S-F, 1 F)
7 Scottish Cup Finals; 6 League Cup Finals; 4 Glasgow Cup Finals; 1 Glasgow Charity Cup Final

Jack Mowat is the most significant figure in the history of Scottish refereeing. Over 60 years, his contribution as a referee and as a Referee Supervisor in Scotland was immense. He also had an influence in world football through his membership of the FIFA Referees' Committee for six years during the 1970's.

Mowat played football as a goalkeeper and was with Queen's Park Hampden XI for one season. He took up refereeing in 1930 and was admitted to the SFA's List in 1933. He was selected as a linesman for the 1938 Scottish Cup Final between St. Bernards and East Fife and in 1940, he was a linesman in the War Emergency Cup Final, Rangers v Dundee United.

The Second World War intervened in his career, as he was called up to the RAF in August 1940. He served in the Equipment Branch, and was stationed in England as a Pilot Officer. He was not involved in football until being posted to Northern Ireland in March 1943. Shortly after, he was contacted by the Irish League and asked to referee in their competitions. By now a Flight Lieutenant, he refereed in Northern Ireland for the next two seasons and quickly made a name for himself as a "fearless and capable referee". During his spell there, he refereed the derby match, Belfast Celtic and Linfield, seven times. At Easter 1944, he was appointed to referee the Irish League v League of Ireland match and, in September, he refereed an Irish FA XI against the Combined Services XI. The

Combined Services XI was essentially a "Great Britain Select" and was filled with the star players of the day – Stanley Matthews, Tommy Lawton, Joe Mercer and Matt Busby. In July 1945, he was promoted to Squadron Leader and transferred to London. He continued to referee whilst in England.

Demobbed in June 1946, he returned to Glasgow. The SFA had retained him on the List throughout the war and he was promoted to Class 1. With the SFA having introduced its refereeing structure in 1945, Mowat was told by the SFA that he had to resign from Glasgow RA, which he had joined and fulfilled the requirement of passing the Refresher Examination, and become a member of Lanarkshire RA as Rutherglen, where he was now living, was under Lanarkshire's jurisdiction. He was required to sit the Refresher Examination again but was given dispensation to train with Glasgow RA at Helenvale.

His first significant appointment at Class 1 was to the 1948 Scottish Cup Semi-Final between Rangers and Hibernian and he broke through with an appointment to the British International Championship match, England v Wales, in October 1948. He went on to referee this match in each of the following two seasons, in Cardiff in 1949 and Sunderland in 1950. In line with the agreement amongst the four British associations on the appointment of referees for the Championship, the SFA put forward the names of three referees for consideration for the 1951 Wales v England match, one of them being Mowat. The FA of Wales decided that it did not want Mowat to be the referee but was happy with either of the other two. (Doug Gerrard refereed the match).

Mowat did not referee any more matches in the British International Championship during his career. By 1953, he was becoming curious as to why he was not receiving any appointments and was advised by the SFA that other Associations considered that "he was too strict with the players and liable to cause an international incident". An "international incident" had actually arisen after he officiated at the World Cup Qualifier, Portugal v Spain, in April 1950, when he became the first Scot to handle such a match. The Spanish FA wrote to the SFA complaining about Mowat and the Referee Committee passed the letter, and one from Mowat, to FIFA for "full investigation and any action deemed necessary". FIFA eventually informed the SFA that the Spanish FA had completely withdrawn its complaint. This did not go down well with the Referee Committee which thought that the Spanish FA should be instructed to write an apology to Mowat for making "such unfounded and unwarranted allegations".

The Football Association did not hold the same view of Mowat as the FA of Wales. He was held in high regard for his firm handling of matches, his natural authority and the respect he commanded during matches. Mowat refereed four home England international friendlies between 1949 and 1951, which is a very good indicator of the reputation he had forged. England's opponents were the Republic of Ireland, Italy, France and Austria. Matches against continental opposition carried huge importance in that era and the selection of the referee was considered crucial.

Mowat's job with the thread manufacturing company J& P Coats prevented him being a candidate for the 1950 and 1954 World Cups as he was unable to get the required time away but his circumstances had changed for the better by 1958 and he was selected to go to the Finals in Sweden. He refereed the Group match, Sweden v Hungary, and was a linesman in two others. Prior to the Finals, he refereed the international friendly between Belgium and the Netherlands.

After being appointed to the Glasgow Charity Cup Final in 1949, Mowat reigned supreme in domestic football during the 1950's. His first Scottish Cup Final was in 1950, Rangers and East Fife. He was then appointed to the Scottish and League Cup Finals in each of the next three seasons. He also refereed three successive Glasgow Cup Finals from 1951-52. Additionally, at the start of season 1951-52 the Scottish League organised two cups, one for each Division, to celebrate the Festival of Britain. Mowat was appointed to each Final. From April 1950, he refereed 12 Finals in a three year period. In his contribution to Glasgow RA's 50th Anniversary programme, Mowat recorded it "was something of a relief" when Charlie Faultless was selected for the 1954 Scottish Cup Final. Any relief did not last long though as Mowat was selected for the 1954 League Cup Final. The Glasgow Cup Final was his in

1956, and he closed the decade with the League Cup Finals of 1956 and 1957 and three successive Scottish Cup Finals from 1957. Over a 10-year period from 1949, Mowat had been appointed to 20 Finals, five of which went to a replay. He had one season when he did not have a Final - 1953-54. That season he refereed Semi-Finals in the Scottish and League Cups.

Mowat had three appointments in the European Champion Clubs' Cup. He handled the 1st Round match in 1957 between BV Borussia Dortmund and CC Bucharest and was appointed to take charge of the 1st Leg of the Semi-Final, Real Madrid CF v Club Atletico de Madrid in 1959. In the latter match, he took the unusual step of wearing a hat-cum-visor. His career was crowned by being chosen to referee the 1960 Final between Real Madrid CF and Eintracht Frankfurt at Hampden Park, the match which is probably the most revered game ever to be played in Scotland. He played his part in a superb match, with his willingness to let the game flow contributing greatly to a quite unforgettable occasion. For many years afterwards, his refereeing colleagues poked fun at him for being the cheapest referee UEFA had ever appointed to the Final. He had waived his expenses given that he lived just a few miles from Hampden Park. The SFA's Finance Committee minute on the Financial Statement for the Final records that the match officials' expenses amounted to £9, three shillings and sixpence. His linesman Donald Kyle and Jimmy Fulton, were from Glasgow and Edinburgh.

That Final was his last match as he decided to retire at the age of 54. His retirement was announced at the Referees' Conference in June. John Smillie the Chairman of the Referee Supervisors paid him tribute by saying "No man in the last 20 years has raised the prestige of refereeing as high as Jack Mowat, not only in this country but abroad." The SFA immediately appointed him as a Referee Supervisor for Glasgow RA. To mark his refereeing career, a presentation was made to him at an SFA Council meeting by the President, Bob Kelly. Kelly expressed the SFA's pleasure that Mowat had accepted the appointment as a Supervisor "in which capacity he would undoubtedly make a valuable contribution to the game".

Never a truer word was spoken as Mowat became the dominant figure in Scottish refereeing for the next 30 years.

He was soon appointed as Vice-Chairman of the committee and in 1962 became the Chairman after the sudden death of Smillie. Mowat served in the role for 28 years. A very close bond developed between Mowat and SFA Secretary Willie Allan and with his successor Ernie Walker, with his expertise and knowledge on the Laws of the Game being much relied upon in regard to the SFA's membership of the International FA Board, the body responsible for the Laws of the Game. He undoubtedly great carried influence in the SFA's conducting of business in refereeing matters. He provided much guidance and wise counsel and, through his Chairmanship, led the refereeing movement with much dedication. Many a referee benefited greatly from his advice and wise words, and he had a talent for identifying good referees at an early stage of their career. His addresses at the annual Referees' Conference regularly attracted press coverage.

A strong minded individual, it was Mowat's belief that changes to the Laws of the Game were the result of the weaknesses of referees in applying the existing Laws. He thought deeply about the Laws and he was an advocate of increasing the size of the goals, taking the view that humans had become taller since the start of football. There was a light-hearted side to him too, and when he spoke of increasing the size of the goals, he always said that he hoped he would get the world-wide contract to implement any change to the Law! For over 20 years, the Sunday People newspaper put his expertise on the Laws of the Game to good use by getting him to answer readers' questions on the Laws.

Mowat found his services to be in demand outside Scotland. In 1961, he spent two weekends in Northern Ireland at the invitation of the Irish FA. He addressed referees on the Laws and the control of matches. He also watched a match with the referees and gave on-the-spot comments on the refereeing of the game.

During season 1973-74, FIFA bestowed its Special Award and Diploma to him in recognition of his outstanding services to refereeing. He was presented with the Award by the SFA

President, Hugh Nelson, at a SFA Council meeting in April 1974. Mowat had an influence on refereeing world-wide from 1974 to 1981 when he served on FIFA's Referees' Committee. In this role, he attended the 1976 and 1980 Olympics and the 1978 World Cup. Through his efforts, he ensured that Scottish referees were selected for these tournaments. For the World Cup, he was given the responsibility of preparing the guidelines for the referees, bringing every existing refereeing instruction up to date, including tackling from the side, from behind, obstruction on the goalkeeper. On his return to Scotland and before the new season, he addressed a gathering of managers and coaches on the self-same instructions and their application in Scotland.

At the grand old age of 84, Mowat retired as the Referee Supervisors' Chairman in October 1990 having presided over 250 meetings in 28 years. His had been a remarkable career in refereeing. Essentially a modest man, he had a rather formal exterior but he was very friendly and helpful to many. A twinkle was never far from his eye.

As a lasting tribute to his remarkable contribution of 60 years to the refereeing movement, the SFA commissioned a trophy in his name to be presented to the referee who finished top of the Class 1 Referee assessment table each season. From 1994 the Trophy has been awarded to the referee of the Scottish Cup Final. Receiving the Jack Mowat Trophy is held in the highest regard by the recipients, given the esteem in which he is still held.

Alan Muir
Date of Birth: 10th May 1975
Admitted to SFA List: 1999-00
No. of seasons at Category 1: 20 (2004-05 to 2023-24)
No. of seasons at Specialist VAR: 1 (2024-25)
No. of years as a FIFA Referee: 3 (2009 to 2011)
1 B International
UEFA: 2 U21 Championship Qualifiers; 6 U19 Championship Qualifiers; 3 Club Competition matches (1 UCL, 2 UC); Regions Cup Qualifying Tournament
1 Challenge Cup Final

Alan Muir's early performances at Category 1 merited the opportunity of becoming a FIFA referee in 2009. He had been identified as a future talent when he was selected to officiate at a UEFA Regions Qualifying Group played in Luxembourg in 2000 and he gained further international experience in 2005 when he accompanied the Scotland U16 team to an invitational tournament in Portugal where he refereed two matches.

His debut as a FIFA referee came early in his first year when he officiated at a match between the Netherlands B team and Italy U21. UEFA used Muir regularly in its U19 Championship, officiating at qualifying tournaments in Portugal, Serbia and Sweden. His two UEFA U21 Championship appointments were Serbia v Slovakia and Switzerland v Turkey.

In the UEFA Club Competitions, Muir received his appointments to the early qualification rounds of the Champions League and the Europa League.

Muir received many appointments as a Fourth Official throughout his Category 1 career, with seven in the World Cup and European Championship Qualifiers during his time on the FIFA List. During the era of Additional Assistant Referees, Muir was heavily used in this role, receiving 25 appointments in the Champions League and the Europa League.

Muir was an Additional Assistant Referee in the 2014 Scottish Cup Final, St. Johnstone v Dundee United and fulfilled the role in several Semi-Final Ties. He was Fourth Official in the 2020 Final between Celtic and Heart of Midlothian. In 2019, he refereed the Challenge Cup Final, Connah Quay's Nomads v Ross County.

For season 2024-25, Muir was designated a Video Match official by the SFA. This led to his receiving seven appointments in this role in the UEFA Club Competitions in the first half of the season.

Tommy Muirhead
Date of Birth: 4th August 1938
Admitted to SFA List: 1967-68
No. of seasons at Class 1: 15 (1973-74 to 1987-88)
No. of seasons as a FIFA Referee: 2 (1979-80 and 1984-85)

UEFA: U16 Championships (1985); 1 Youth Tournament Qualifier

Tommy Muirhead was a stalwart of the Scottish refereeing scene over his 15 seasons at Class 1, his consistent performances bringing him two separate stints as a FIFA referee. His first season on the FIFA List was marked with just one refereeing appointment, to the UEFA Youth Tournament Qualifier, Wales v Northern Ireland. It was as a linesman when he received his major appointments that season, being selected as part of Brian McGinlay's team for the European Championships in Italy in 1980, where the Group match, West Germany v Greece was handled. In the build up to the Finals, Muirhead officiated with McGinlay on the friendly international between England and Argentina and a World Cup Qualifier, Finland v Bulgaria.

When he returned to the FIFA List in 1984-85, Muirhead was selected as a referee for the UEFA U16 Championships played in Hungary. He worked with McGinlay as a linesman again on the World Cup Qualifier, Cyprus and Hungary, that season. Over the course over his career, Muirhead received 10 appointments as a linesman in international football.

In domestic football, Muirhead was appointed to Semi-Finals of the League Cup in 1978 and 1980. A popular referee, Muirhead was presented with a ball autographed by the players of Dundee United and Heart of Midlothian after his last match in May 1988. During his career he had a business card with the following text, which is very appropriate for all referees: "When I am right, no one remembers. When I am wrong, no one forgets". He had come across the saying by accident and adopted it.

Bill Mullan
Date of Birth: 30th March 1928
Date of Death: 13th November 2018 aged 90
Admitted to SFA List: 1956-57
No. of seasons at Class 1: 18 (1960-61 to 1977-78)
No. of seasons as a FIFA Referee: 10 (1962-63 to 1963-64 and 1965-66 to 1972-73)

3 A Internationals; 2 British International Championship matches; 1 U23 International; 2 League Internationals
FIFA: 2 World Cup Qualifiers; Intercontinental Cup Final 2nd Leg (1971); Olympics (1972); 1 Olympic Qualifier
UEFA: European Championships (1972); 1 European Championship Qualifier; 13 Club Competition matches (4 ECCC, 3 ECWC, 1 UC, 1 ICFC)
1 League Cup Final; 4 Old Firm matches

Bill Mullan was a leading referee of the 1960's and 1970's. He was a FIFA referee for 10 out of 11 seasons from 1962-63, with 1964-65 being the season he missed out. In his own words, he had "drifted" into refereeing aged 21 as he was being kicked too much playing football. The result was an outstanding career and a lifelong commitment and contribution to the refereeing movement.

A PE teacher renowned for his great fitness, Mullan's first appointment as a FIFA referee, and his only one in his initial two-season spell on the FIFA List, was an Inter-Cities Fairs Cup tie in 1962 between Glentoran and Real Zaragoza. Once he returned to the FIFA List, his international career took off and it blossomed in the late 1960's and came into full bloom in the early 1970's. European club ties at KR Reykjavik and Sporting Clube de Portugal were fulfilled in the autumn of 1965 and the season was closed with two international friendlies – Republic of Ireland v West Germany and Iceland v Denmark. An Olympic Qualifier between France and Austria in May 1968 was followed in September by being appointed to referee Manchester United's European Champion Clubs' Cup tie in Waterford. A few weeks later he refereed the U23 International between Wales and England. His first British International Championship match was at the end of the season – Northern Ireland v England.

Appointments received to ties in the early rounds of the 1969-70 European Champion Clubs' Cup – Ferencvárosi TC v CSKA Sofia and Spartak Trvana v Galatasaray SK – reflected his growing standing in Europe. His third A International was in October 1970 when he was appointed to referee Netherlands v Yugoslavia.

A European Championship Qualifier between West Germany and Poland in October 1971 presaged his greatest international cup appointment. In late December he was chosen to referee the 2nd Leg of the Intercontinental Cup Final between Nacional and Panathinaikos, played in Uruguay. Mullan was one of three European referees selected for the match with none of them knowing who was to be the referee until half an hour before the kick-off. Normal preparations for a match were thrown totally out of the window but in a newspaper interview afterwards, Mullan considered it an excellent system as he considered that there was no pressure on him.

1972 was undoubtedly the best year of Mullan's career as he was selected for the European Championships and the Olympics. The European Championships were at that time a short tournament starting from the Semi-Finals, and Mullan handled the Semi-Final between the host country Belgium and West Germany. At the Olympics in Munich, he refereed Hungary v Brazil and West Germany v East Germany, the latter match being the first ever between the two countries at any level. He had two line appointments in the tournament. The autumn of 1972 was jam-packed with appointments: a UEFA Cup tie, a World Cup Qualifier, Norway v Belgium, a European Cup tie at Panathinaikos and another World Cup Qualifier, Wales v England. He had handled the two countries in the British International Championship at the end of the previous season. Mullan was at the peak of his career but, very unfortunately, early in 1973, he was badly injured in a car crash on the way home from a match. He suffered damage to his left eye and his days as a FIFA referee sadly came to an end at the close of the season.

Mullan regained fitness and returned to refereeing during the following season, wearing a contact lens on his damaged eye. He retired at the end of season 1977-78 at 50, the first season of the retiral age having been introduced. Mullan refereed the famous League Cup Final in 1971 when Partick Thistle shocked the football world by beating Celtic 4-1 and he handled four Semi-Finals in the Scottish Cup. His Old Firm matches were all during his early 1970's golden period. He was still well regarded after his return from his car crash, being appointed to a

League Cup Semi-Final in 1974 and selected to referee the Scottish League's international against the Football League in 1976.

The SFA appointed Mullan as a Referee Supervisor for Edinburgh & District RA in late 1978 and he served in the role for 21 seasons. For 15 seasons, he was a member of the Referee Supervisors' Executive Committee. He served his final season associated with the SFA as a Match Assessor in 1990-00. He had had a long involvement in the refereeing movement, acting as Secretary to Fife RA from 1957-58 to 1962-63 and then as Edinburgh & District RA's Secretary from 1963-64 until his appointment as a Referee Supervisor. Mullan was also a UEFA Referee Observer for a number of years.

David Munro
Date of Birth: 5th August 1990
Admitted to SFA List: 2009-10
No. of seasons at Category 1: 9 (2015-16 to 2023-24)
No. of years as a FIFA Referee: 5 (2020 to 2024)
1 C International
UEFA: 6 U21 Championship Qualifiers; 2 U19 Championship Qualifiers; 4 U17 Championship Qualifiers; 11 Club competition matches (2 UCL, 1 UEL, 4 UECL, 2 UYL)

David Munro was committed to being a referee from a young age and he made rapid progress in the early stages of his career, marking himself out as a future prospect, and reached Category 1 status at the age of 24. Selected for the UEFA CORE Course in 2017 to aid his development, he progressed to the FIFA List in 2020, having handled an England C International against Wales in 2019.
By the end of his first year as a FIFA referee, he had a Europa League Qualifier and two UEFA U21 Championship Qualifiers under his belt. A further four U21 Qualifiers were received over the next few seasons featuring countries such as Spain and Sweden, with his top tie being a Norway v Croatia match in 2022. AZ Alkmaar v FK Crvena Zvedva was the pick of the two appointments he received in the UEFA Youth League in 2022. He had a total of seven matches in the qualification

rounds of the Champions League, the Europa League and Europa Conference League.

As a Fourth Official, Munro had 11 appointments in international competitions, including three in the Europa League group stages.

In domestic football, Munro refereed the League Cup Semi-Final between Livingston and St. Mirren in season 2020-21 and was Fourth Official in the 2018 Challenge Cup Final and 2023 League Cup Final.

Due to a promotion in his job with a plant hire company, Munro decided to quit refereeing just before the start of season 2024-25, coming to the view that his new position would not allow him to devote sufficient time to refereeing.

Calum Murray
Date of Birth: 7th July 1967
Admitted to SFA List: 1998-99
No. of seasons at Category 1: 15 (2000-01 to 2014-15)
No. of years as a FIFA Referee: 5 (2005 to 2009)
3 U21 Internationals; 1 Women's A International
FIFA: 1 World Cup Qualifier
UEFA: 2 U21 Championship Qualifiers; 3 U19 Championship Qualifiers; 4 U17 Championship Qualifiers; 5 Club Competition matches (3 UC, 1 UEL, 1 UIC)
1 Scottish Cup Final; 1 Challenge Cup Final; 1 Youth Cup Final; 6 Old Firm matches

Remove the "u" from Murray's first name and you would have the perfect description of his refereeing style: "calm". It was a trait which served him well throughout his career. Five years at Class 1 brought him to the FIFA List for 2005. In the year before, he gained international experience by officiating at the Nordic U17 Cup in Finland and refereed the Final between Iceland and Denmark.

It was a busy first year as a FIFA referee, as he was appointed to UEFA U17 Championship Qualification tournaments in Austria and Poland, a UEFA U21 Championship match between Iceland and Malta, a UEFA Cup qualification tie, an

U21 friendly between the Republic of Ireland and Northern Ireland and a Scotland's Women's friendly against Iceland.

Things took a drastic turn for the worse unfortunately in the autumn of 2006 when Murray sustained an Achilles tendon injury which put him out of action for a year. The SFA kept faith with him and retained him on the FIFA List during this period in the knowledge that he would return. His injury absence, however, effectively held back his career as a FIFA referee. In his final two years in the role, further UEFA appointments in under-age competitions were received together with a UEFA Europa League qualifier. In 2008, he refereed Iceland v Denmark in an U21 friendly. His career was topped by being appointed to referee the World Cup Qualifier, Sweden v Malta in June 2009.

As a Fourth Official, Murray received appointments to two A Internationals, Wales v Paraguay, and South Korea v Ghana, and to a World Cup Qualifier, Moldova v Switzerland, and to a number of UEFA Club Competition matches, including a Round of 32 tie in the UEFA Cup, Galatasaray SK v Girondins de Bordeaux, in 2009. As an Additional Assistant Referee, he received five appointments to matches in the Champions League Group stages.

Murray recovered well after his year's injury absence and established himself in the top group of Scottish referees by the end of the 2000's. His six Old Firm matches came in the three years from 2009. A Scottish Cup 5th Round tie in 2010-11 went to a replay where his calmness was fully put to the test as he had to strive to maintain order, sending three Rangers players off, and deal with a confrontation between the two managers. He handled successive Old Firm matches at the end of the following season, the second as a late replacement for the originally appointed referee, Craig Thomson.

Murray refereed the 2008 Challenge Cup Final and the 2011 Scottish Cup Final. He was Fourth Official for the 2009 and 2012 League Cup Finals.

Murray chose to retire from refereeing at the end of season 2014-15. The SFA immediately capitalised on his experience by appointing him a Referee Observer and to membership of the Referee Committee. He acts as a Referee Observer for UEFA.

Robert Murray

No. of seasons on List: 18 (1899-00 to 1915-16)
2 British International Championship matches; 1 League International
2 Scottish Cup Finals; 1 Glasgow Cup Final; 2 Glasgow Charity Cup Finals; 9 Old Firm Matches; 3 Junior Internationals; 2 Junior Cup Finals

Murray was a top referee throughout his career. He quickly established himself and in his third season on the List was appointed to the Finals of the Scottish Cup, the Glasgow Charity Cup and the Junior Cup. His appointment to nine Old Firm games, played over a nine year period, further demonstrate his capabilities. Two of these matches were in the Finals of the Glasgow Charity Cup and the Glasgow Cup in 1911 and 1912, respectively.

His internationals came between 1905 and 1907. His League International was the Football League's match against the Irish League in 1905 and, in the following two years, he refereed England against Wales twice in the British Home International Championship. Murray was obviously well regarded in England, as the Football Association put forward his name, and David Philp's, to the Irish FA to be the referee of their 1908 International. The Irish were not agreeable however, with Tom Robertson being appointed.

Despite his standing in the game, Murray did not escape the odd bit of bother. In 1907, he was fined a guinea for arriving late for a Greenock Morton v Partick Thistle match, which eventually kicked-off 45 minutes late. In 1911, the SFA Referee Committee was moved to inform him that when he had no doubt about a point of play he must not consult the neutral linesmen. (Other referees, it may be supposed, were expected to act likewise). Whilst officiating in a Cowdenbeath 5-a-side tournament in 1904, he was so severely assaulted by a player who he had sent off that he was off work for more than a month. The case ended up in court but a verdict of not proven was reached, as witnesses, including Murray, could not identify the assailant – one of a pair of identical twins who were both playing in the match. When the case came before the SFA Referee Committee the twin brothers were banned for life.

Issues concerning the quality of Scottish referees were a running theme amongst clubs in the 1900's. Murray was a man of some principle in this matter as he refused a Glasgow FA appointment to referee the Glasgow Cup Semi-Final between Celtic and Queen's Park in 1906 as in the previous round Queen's Park and Rangers had agreed to use an English referee for their tie. His refusal resulted in another English referee being appointed in his place.

Murray was a committee member of the Scottish Football Referees' Association and refereed occasionally in the Irish League in the mid-1900's. Rather surprisingly perhaps, he was Secretary of Stenhousemuir in 1903.

Euan Norris
Date of Birth: 29th October 1977
Admitted to SFA List: 2000-01
No. of seasons at Class 1: 10 (2005-06 to 2014-15)
No. of years as a FIFA Referee: 5 (2009 to 2013)
UEFA: 1 European Championship Qualifier; 3 U21 Championship Qualifiers; U17 Championships (2010); 4 U17 Championship Qualifiers; 4 Club Competition matches (4 UEL (3 PO))
1 Challenge Cup Final; 1 Youth Cup Final

After playing schools' football and spending a season in Junior football with Carluke Rovers, Euan Norris started refereeing when he was 20. He followed in the footsteps of his father Les, with there only being a two season gap between Les retiring from the SFA List and Euan being admitted in 2000-01. He was promoted to Category 1 five seasons later with his performances gaining him a spot on the FIFA List in 2009.

By the end of his first year as a FIFA referee, he had officiated at two UEFA U17 Championship Qualification tournaments in France and FYR Macedonia and two UEFA U21 Championship Qualifiers in Iceland and Bulgaria. His performances in these matches were recognised by UEFA by appointing him to the

U17 Championships in Liechtenstein in 2010, where he took charge of the Semi-Final between Spain and Turkey.

Season 2010-11 started with two Europa League appointments – a qualification match and then a Play-Off tie between CS Maritimo and BATE Borisov – and another U21 Championship Qualifier, Sweden v Israel. In the summer of 2011, he received an appointment to a European Championship Qualifier, Kazakhstan v Azerbaijan. Further Europa League Play-Off appointments were received in each of the next two seasons.

As Fourth Official to William Collum, appointments were fulfilled in European Championship and World Cup Qualifiers in Bulgaria and Slovakia. Norris' time on the FIFA List coincided with the era of Additional Assistant Referees and it was in this capacity that he received 16 appointments, generally as part of William Collum's team, in Group matches in the Champions League and Europa League and to knock-out ties in the latter competition. Norris was chosen to be part of Craig Thomson's team for the European Championships in 2012 where he officiated at two Group matches.

Norris refereed the 2011 Challenge Cup Final between Queen of the South and Ross County and was appointed to League Cup Semi-Finals in 2012 and 2013. Injuries unfortunately began to impact on him and he was inactive throughout his last season on the List. Reaching the view that being able to return was not going to be possible, he resigned in March 2015. The SFA appointed him a Referee Observer a few months later and he has served on the Referee Committee since 2021.

John Paterson
Date of Birth: 24th February 1929
Died: 24th August 2021 aged 92
Admitted to SFA List: 1956-57
No. of seasons at Class 1: 16 (1961-62 to 1977-78)
No. of seasons as a FIFA Referee: 12 (1966-67 to 1977-78)
1 A International; 2 British International Championship matches; 1 British Youth International Championship match
FIFA: 1 World Cup Qualifier; Olympics (1976)

UEFA: 2 European Championship Qualifiers; 20 Club Competition matches (2 ECCC, 5 ECWC (1 Q-F, 1-S-F), 10 UC (1 Q-F, 1 S-F), 3 ICFC)
1 Scottish Cup Final; 2 League Cup Finals; 8 Old Firm matches

John Paterson had a very strong career as a referee, making his mark in European football as one of the top referees during the 1970's. He started refereeing in 1953 after playing as a goalkeeper in Junior football with Camelon and Bonnybridge. In his last season at Class 3A, he was selected as a linesman for the 1958 Scottish Cup Final. Earlier that season, he was a linesman to Jack Mowat in a European Champion Clubs' Cup tie at BV Borussia Dortmund. He made headlines at the very start of his time as a Class 1 referee when he sent off Pat Crerand and Mike Jackson of Celtic, and a Falkirk player, in a pre-season 5-a-side tournament.
His future potential was identified by an appointment to referee the British Youth International Championship match between Wales and England in 1963 and a Youth International, Norway and Sweden in 1964. The latter match was played the day before a full international between the countries and at which he was a linesman to Bobby Davidson. Davidson ran the line to Paterson in the Youth match.
FIFA status was gained in 1966-67 and he made a great start with appointments in the Inter-Cities Fairs Cup at Juventus and SL Benfica. His A International was a Netherlands v Belgium match in 1968. Over the next few seasons, he refereed the Republic of Ireland v Denmark in a World Cup Qualifier and Norway v France and Finland v Poland in European Championship Qualifiers. He was selected as a linesman to Bill Mullan in the European Championship Semi-Final, Belgium v West Germany, in 1972, and to Ian Foote in a 1977 World Cup Qualifier, South Korea v Iran. Paterson's two matches in the British International Championship were both England v Wales matches, in 1973 and 1975.
Paterson forged a name for himself in European club competitions. Between 1972 and 1975, he was appointed to Quarter-Finals in the European Cup Winners' Cup and the UEFA Cup and to Semi-Finals in each of the two competitions

– AC Milan v AC Sparta Praha in the UEFA Cup and VfB Stuttgart v Feyenoord in the Cup Winners' Cup. Between 1971 and 1977, he received 10 appointments in the UEFA Cup which, for the era, was quite an achievement.

Paterson's greatest success was selection for the 1976 Olympics in Montreal. He refereed Brazil v East Germany in the Group Stage and Brazil again in a Semi-Final against Poland. Although he had been provided with a blazer and trousers for the Olympics, in a sign of a pre-commercial age, he had to supply his own refereeing kit. With the Games being held in late July, Paterson prepared himself over the summer by refereeing Boys Brigade matches, training in the gym and by doing road running.

Paterson refereed the 1974 Scottish Cup Final, Celtic v Dundee United, and the League Cup Finals of 1969 and 1976 in which Celtic faced St. Johnstone and Aberdeen, respectively. In addition, he handled seven Semi-Finals in the two Cups, four of these being in the 1960's as he was starting to emerge as a force. His eight Old Firm matches from 1970 to 1977 reflect his standing within the game. One of these matches was the Final of the pre-season tournament, the Drybrough Cup, in 1974.

Paterson, a general manager with a packaging firm, chose to resign from the SFA List in January 1978. His final international appointment had been a UEFA Cup tie at FC Barcelona a couple of months previously, which was a pretty decent place to bow out. His had been a fine career. He had served refereeing well, having also been a long-serving Secretary to Lanarkshire RA from 1962 to 1978.

Jimmy Philip
Born: 7th May 1862
Died: 12th October 1930 aged 68
Olympics (1912 (1 Q-F))

A complete outlier in the context of Scottish international referees, the tale of Jimmy Philip is a very extraordinary one. Whilst being a football manager and an SFA Council member, he somehow managed to referee a Quarter-Final at the 1912 Olympic Games in Stockholm.

In the 1890's he had been a leading referee in Aberdeen and was in charge of the first game ever played at Pittodrie Stadium between the original Aberdeen club and Dumbarton in 1899. Rather than following a path in refereeing, however, Philip became the first manager of Aberdeen in 1903 when that original club merged with Victoria United and Orion. He held the position until he retired in 1924, at which point he became a club director. Philip served on the SFA Council from 1909 to 1927, representing the Division of Aberdeenshire, Invernessshire, Moray and Banffshire.

The SFA appointed Philip to be its representative at the annual FIFA Congress in Stockholm in 1912. The Organising Committee for the Olympic football competition had not invited any referees. The Official Report on the Games cutely records that the committee, beyond relying on Swedish referees, "could also reckon on the assistance of a number of well-known men from abroad who, before the Games began, informed the Football Committee of their intention to be present at these competitions and, at the same time, expressed their willingness to assist the Football Committee as referees". Thus, the door opened for Philip (and an Englishman, George Wagstaffe-Simmons), to turn their hand to refereeing. Phillip's match was Netherlands v Austria, played on 30th June, the same day as the FIFA Congress. Phillips had last refereed the year previously, when he took charge of some matches when Aberdeen went on a tour to what is now the Czech Republic, keen, apparently, to show the locals how it should be done. No doubt that chutzpah played a part in his fancying his chances at refereeing at the Olympics.

Philip's connection with refereeing was not done with his Olympic match. In 1918, Philip played an important role in encouraging Peter Craigmyle to become a referee. He served on the SFA Referee Committee from 1919-20 to 1926-27, and was its Chairman for his last three seasons. Through his membership of the committee, he was chosen to be Scotland's linesman in the home Victory International against Ireland in March 1919 and in the return match the following month.

Hugh Phillips
Date of Birth: 4th April 1921
Died: 18th February 1996 aged 74
Admitted to the SFA List: 1949-50
No. of seasons at Class 1: 16 (1952-53 to 1966-67)
No of seasons as a FIFA Referee: 15 (1952-53 to 1965-66)
8 British International Championship matches; 1 British Amateur International Championship match; 2 Amateur Internationals; 1 British International Youth Championship; 6 League Internationals; 1 U23 Representative match
FIFA: World Cup (1966); 5 World Cup Qualifiers
UEFA: 7 Club Competition matches (3 ECCC (1 Q-F), 2 ECWC, 2 ICFC)
3 Scottish Cup Finals; 4 League Cup Finals; 10 Old Firm matches; 1 Junior International; 1 Junior Cup Final

Hugh Phillips ranks as one of the best referees produced by Scotland. 15 consecutive seasons as a FIFA and selection for a World Cup is obvious evidence of a very successful career.
Phillips started refereeing during the Second World War whilst serving in India with the Royal Artillery. He was asked to referee some service games in an emergency and developed the refereeing bug. On his return to Scotland in 1946, he joined Lanarkshire RA. Three years later, he was in charge of a Scotland Junior international against Northern Ireland and refereed the Junior Cup Final between Auchinleck Talbot and Petershill after, rather amazingly, officiating at both Semi-Finals.
He had obviously created a very favourable impression as he was admitted the following season to the SFA's List at Class 2, rather than at the normal entry level at Class 3A. He needed just one season to reach Class 1 and two seasons to become a FIFA referee. His first international appointment was to an Amateur friendly between Scotland and Ireland at Ibrox Park in April 1952. The first of his six League Internationals was in October 1952 when the officiated at the Scottish League's match against the League of Ireland. The Scotland v England Youth International was in his charge at the end of the season. The next couple of seasons saw him handle a friendly Amateur

International between England and France and his first British International Championship match, Northern Ireland v Wales in April 1955.

Phillips served season 1955-56 in the Deputy category on the FIFA List and returned to full status the season after. His career then really started to take off. Two more British International Championship matches were handled in the autumn of 1956 and he finished the season by refereeing three World Cup Qualifiers in May 1957 – Northern Ireland v Portugal and then, quite remarkably, home and away matches between England and the Republic of Ireland. In October 1961, Phillips was appointed to the Qualifier between Hungary and the Netherlands. Phillips started to receive appointments in the European club competitions and was entrusted to take charge of some important ties in Denmark, the Netherlands, Belgium and West Germany. His major appointments were Tottenham Hotspur v Manchester United in the European Cup Winners' Cup in 1963 and Real Madrid CF v SL Benfica in the European Champion Clubs' Cup Quarter-Final in 1965. He received much praise in the press for his handling of the former match, particularly in his command of the game from the start. Real Madrid CF was reportedly pleased before the match with his appointment as referee as Phillips had impressed the club when he had refereed a friendly against Hibernian earlier that season. His final international club match was FC Barcelona v Hannover 96 in the Inter-Cities Fairs Cup in 1966.

The pinnacle of Phillips' career was reached when he was selected for the 1966 World Cup in England. In the Group stage, he refereed West Germany v Switzerland, and was a linesman in the Spain v Switzerland match. He was chosen as a linesman for the Quarter-Final, West Germany v Uruguay. It seemed hard for Phillips to avoid West Germany that year as, prior to the Finals, he had refereed its friendly in Northern Ireland.

Phillips resigned from the SFA List in September 1966. He had made his mind up to retire after the World Cup, which he regarded as the peak of his career, but when he returned home from it the opening set of Scottish League appointments had been issued and he felt obliged to fulfil the games which had been allocated to him. His last match was Rangers against Partick Thistle. Coincidentally, his first League match as a referee had been at Ibrox in 1950 for a game against Aberdeen.

Phillips, an accountant who worked in the civil service, had had a top class career. He had established himself very quickly amongst the top Scottish referees, being appointed to the Coronation Cup Final in 1953 and his first League Cup Final in 1955. He was at the peak of his career in the 1960's, being selected for the Scottish Cup Finals of 1961, 1964 and 1965 and three consecutive League Cup Finals from 1963, two of these being Old Firm matches. In 13 years from 1953, he was in charge of 10 Semi-Finals in the two Cups and the same number of Old Firm matches. Of small build and with a facial birth mark, Phillips developed an excellent reputation for his firm control of games and unobtrusive authority and was held in high esteem by players. In 1967, he turned down a lucrative offer to referee in the "rebel" American Soccer League, either for a month or the full April to September season.

He was the treasurer of Lanarkshire RA for much of the 1950's through to his retirement. Once he retired, he devoted himself to bowls, becoming Treasurer of the Scottish Indoor Bowling Association in 1977 and President of the World Indoor Bowls Council in 1995. He died from a stroke the day after he returned home from attending the World Indoor Bowls Championship at Preston.

David Philp
Date of Birth: 5th May 1875
Died: July 1931 aged 56
No. of seasons on List: 4 (1906-07 to 1909-10)
3 British International Championship matches; 1 Amateur International; 1 League International
1 Scottish Cup Final; 1 Glasgow Cup Final; 3 Old Firm matches

David Philp had a very brief but very eventful career as a referee, with a little bit of mystery and intrigue involved. He took up refereeing after playing as a left winger for Dunfermline Athletic and Cowdenbeath, and quickly made his mark with selection as the referee for the 1907 Scottish Cup

Final, Celtic v Heart of Midlothian. He had also refereed Celtic's Semi-Final against Hibernian, a tie that went to a Second Replay. His Glasgow Cup Final appointment was an Old Firm match at Hampden Park in October 1907, another tie which went to a Second Replay and thus accounted for his three Old Firm matches. His first international, England v Ireland (Amateur) was in December 1907, and was followed a few months later in March 1908 when he refereed his first British International Championship match, Wales against England in Wrexham. He officiated at the match between these two associations in England the following year. During this golden period for him, he also refereed occasionally in the Irish League.

After handling a Kilmarnock v Rangers match in March 1908, Philp reported to the SFA that, on the way to the railway station, he had been assaulted by a mob who threw stones and mud at him, drawing blood, and that he had only been saved from his antagonists through being taken on to the passing-by Rangers transport . The Referee Committee interviewed Philp in regard to his refereeing of the match and, after hearing his explanation, agreed to direct his attention to the instructions on rough play. It would seem that the committee felt that Philp was the author of his own post-match misfortune. The committee did agree to a claim from Philp of £1 five shillings and sixpence for attending the meeting and lost time through injuries sustained in the attack and instructed Kilmarnock to settle it. The club was also fined £50 in regard to Philp being attacked.

In November 1909, Philp's career took a very dramatic turn when he was deleted from the List of Referees by the Referee Committee. In keeping with the style of the time, no reason for the deletion is recorded in the meeting's minutes. Philp received a letter advising of his deletion effective from 15th November and that after that date he would be ineligible to referee in Scotland. The Scottish Football Referees' Association took his case up with the Referee Committee but got no joy, other than being told in general terms that referees were deleted as a result of being "officially inspected on the field". His removal from the List also excited some press comment, alluding to the reason being unknown, even to Philp himself.

Philp's name came to the fore later in the season at the Referee Committee's March meeting in surprising circumstances – he had been appointed to referee Wales v England in the British International Championship. The Referee Committee was compelled to draw the attention of the FA of Wales and the Football Association to the fact that Philp had been "struck off the List and suspended in November 1909". Philp was replaced as the referee by John B. Stark. This led to Philp writing to the Referee Committee, asking why his deletion from the List had been notified to the FA of Wales and the Football Association and requesting that his case be reconsidered. The request was refused. His story did not end there though. Rather incredibly, Philp accepted an invitation from the Football Association to referee England's international match against Ireland in February 1911. On his return from the game, Philp told the press that the English and Irish were "entirely satisfied with his decisions". The Referee Committee again wrote to the Football Association but it conveniently responded that it had "overlooked" Philp's deletion. The whole scenario is extremely curious and begs the question as to how Philp had been invited to referee the international whilst suspended as a referee in Scotland. It would certainly seem that the Football Association held him to be a good referee – it had put him forward along with Robert Murray to the Irish FA for the international in Ireland in March 1909 but the Irish FA proceeded to appoint Tom Robertson. There is no evidence to suggest the Philp had been refereeing outside Scotland after his deletion. Philp wrote to the SFA in 1913 requesting that his case be again reconsidered. The Referee Committee ruled this "out of order" and there was no further action on his part.

Philp had been prominent in the formation of a Fife Referees' Association in October 1909 and was elected its Vice President. He was a tailor until the outbreak of the First World War when he entered Admiralty service. At the time of his death, he was employed as a storeman in the Rosyth Dockyard.

Morag Pirie
Date of Birth: 27th June 1975
Admitted to SFA List: 2001-02
No. of seasons at Category 3: 11 (2003-04 to 2014-15)
No. of years as a FIFA Referee: 9 (2009 to 2017)
No of years as a FIFA Assistant Referee: 4 (2003 to 2007)
22 Women's A Internationals; 1 Women's U23 match; World University Games (2009)
FIFA: 7 Women's World Cup Qualifiers; Women's U17 Championships (2012); Olympic Youth Tournament (2014). As an Assistant Referee: 4 Women's World Cup Qualifiers
UEFA: 5 Women's Championship Qualifiers; Women's U19 Championships (2011); 10 Women's U19 Championship Qualifiers; Women's U17 Championships (2010); 2 Women's U17 Championship Qualifiers; 14 Women's Champions League matches (6 QG, 4 R32, 3 R16, 1 Q-F) As an Assistant Referee: 2 Club Competition matches (2 UCL); Women's U19 Championships (2006); 6 U19 Championship Qualifiers
4 Women's Scottish Cup Finals; 3 SWPL Cup Finals

Morag Pirie had a superlative career filled with accomplishments and packed with "firsts" as she blazed a trail for other Scottish women referees to follow. Her involvement in football started as a player with Aberdeen Accies but the refereeing bug caught hold after she was given the chance to referee in a girls' tournament. She qualified as a referee in 1996 and five years later became the first woman to be admitted to the SFA's List, enabling her to referee in Junior football. Two seasons later, she was promoted to Class 3, able to be an assistant referee in the Scottish League and to referee in the Highland League. Pirie quickly became accepted as a referee in the Highland League and regular line appointments in League football opened the door for her to be considered as an assistant referee for the FIFA List. The SFA wished to capitalise on her breakthrough from its own perspective of wishing to develop women referees and of promoting Pirie herself, given her obvious capabilities, and successfully nominated her as an assistant referee for the FIFA List in 2004 as a staging post for her eventually becoming a FIFA referee. Pirie proceeded to enjoy great success in both roles over the next 13 years.

She was an assistant referee for four years, the high point being in 2006 when she was selected for the UEFA Women's U19 Championships in Switzerland where she officiated at five matches including a Semi-Final and the Final itself, between Germany and France. Pirie also acted as an assistant referee in Champions League Qualifiers in Cyprus and Finland in 2005 and 2007, respectively. In domestic football, Pirie became the first female to be appointed to a national Cup Final when she ran the line in the 2007 Challenge Cup Final between Dunfermline Athletic and St. Johnstone.

Over a number of seasons, Pirie, an accountant, gained a wealth of experience as an assistant referee and as a Fourth Official in women's international football and that, combined with refereeing appointments she received for home Scotland Women's matches, provided a solid foundation for her to make the step to become a FIFA referee in 2009, after the serving of the obligatory year's gap between being nominated as an assistant and a referee.

Her first major appointment as a referee was to the World University Games held in Belgrade in 2009, where she handled a Quarter-Final between China and Brazil in the Women's Competition. The first of her seven Women's World Cup Qualifiers, Hungary v Romania, came along in October 2009. Over the next five years, she took charge of Qualifiers in Croatia, Switzerland, Hungary (again), Romania, Israel and Albania.

Given that UEFA's Women's U17 Championships in 2010 was a four team tournament in Switzerland (held close to UEFA's headquarters), Pirie's selection as one of the two referees for the competition was something of an achievement. She handled the Semi-Final, Netherlands v Spain, and the Third Place match between the Netherlands and Germany. The following year, 2011, saw Pirie selected as one of six referees for the eight team UEFA Women's U19 Championships, held in Italy. After refereeing two group matches, she was appointed to the Semi-Final, Germany v Switzerland.

Five Women's Championship Qualifiers were fulfilled between 2011 and 2016, with matches in Finland, Bosnia & Herzegovina, Sweden, Switzerland and Croatia.

Pirie received 14 appointments in the Women's Champions League, with eight matches in the knock-out rounds - four in the Round of 32, three in the Round of 16 and one Quarter-Final, VfL Wolfsburg v FC Barcelona in 2014.

Pirie's performances in Europe naturally drew her to the attention of FIFA. In the spring of 2012, she was selected by FIFA to attend a workshop for women referees held in Portugal and to officiate at the Algarve Cup for international women's teams which followed its conclusion. FIFA picked 13 referees and 26 assistant referees, with Pirie being one of five UEFA referees. The event was part of FIFA's programme to develop female refereeing with the objective of preparing the officials for future competitions. This led to Pirie's selection as one of 12 referees for the Women's U17 World Cup in Azerbaijan later that year. She was in charge of two Group matches, refereed the Quarter-Final between South Korea and Canada and was selected as the Fourth Official for the $3^{rd}/4^{th}$ Place match, Ghana v Germany.

Pirie reached the elite category of UEFA's women referees and was unfortunate to miss out on selection for the European Championships and the Women's World Cup when she was at the peak of her career. Her last major tournament was the Olympic Youth Tournament in China in 2014 where she was appointed to a Semi-Final, Venezuela v Mexico, in the Women's Competition. Her standing was such in Europe that she was much in demand to referee international friendlies. She refereed matches in the Republic of Ireland, Germany, Sweden and twice in England. Two matches were played in her "backyard" of Aberdeen in 2012 when the Cameroon Olympic team came to the city for a training camp prior to the London Olympics and played matches against Scotland and Northern Ireland. Quite remarkably, she refereed international matches on consecutive days in April 2017 – Sweden v Canada and England v Italy. Pirie was also appointed to 13 home Scotland Women's internationals.

The England v Italy match turned out to be Pirie's last as a FIFA referee as she chose to resign from the List in August. Small and slight of build, she had found it becoming increasingly hard over the previous three years to meet the requirements of the fitness test to maintain her place at Category 3 on the SFA List and to do the same for the FIFA test. She retired from refereeing at the end of season 2017-18 after spending it at Category 4.

Hers had been a wonderful career, laden with many fantastic appointments. She undoubtedly led the way for Scottish women referees in domestic and international football over her career.

Eddie Pringle
Date of Birth: 31st October 1933
Died: 2004 aged 70
Admitted to SFA List: 1961-62
No. of seasons at Class 1: 17 (1966-67 to 1982-83)
No. of seasons as a FIFA Referee: 1 (1980-81)
UEFA: U18 Championships (1981)
1 League Cup Final; 3 Old Firm matches

Eddie Pringle's career was fairly typical of a few other referees of the 1970's who served briefly on the FIFA List. His very steady performances over his lengthy stint at Class 1 firmly established him amongst the top group of referees in Scotland by his mid-40's and earned him numerous appointments to matches involving the major clubs. He served just one season on the FIFA List, with his only international appointment as a referee being selection for the 1981 UEFA U18 Championships held in West Germany.

He received six international appointments as a linesman during his career, the first of which was to Scotland's home British Youth International Championship match against Wales in 1963 in his second season on the SFA List. During his season on the FIFA List, he ran the line to Bob Valentine in a World Cup Qualifier, Cyprus v Belgium. Pringle was also appointed to a UEFA Cup Quarter-Final, Valencia CF v RSC Anderlecht, with Brian McGinlay in 1983.

Being appointed to three Old Firm matches between 1979 and 1980 was a mark of his capabilities as a referee and the excellent standard he set at that point in his career. His domestic performances were rewarded with selection for the 1981 League Cup Final between Rangers and Dundee United in his penultimate season on the SFA List.

Jimmy Provan
Born: 1905
Died: 10th February 1992 aged 86
No. of seasons on List: 3 (1937-38 to 1939-40 and 1947-48)
1 Old Firm match; 2 Junior Internationals; 2 Junior Cup Finals

Whilst he did not referee a senior international match, Jimmy Provan merits inclusion as an "international referee" on the basis of his being one of the Scottish referees who accepted contracts to referee in Argentina in 1948. During his time there, he refereed 31 matches in the country's Primera Division.
After playing football and running a Church team in his home town of Chapelhall, he took up refereeing in the 1930's. Admitted to the Scottish League's List in 1937-38, he was refereeing in the top division within two years. He quickly established himself and was respected for his vigorous enforcing of the Laws and deciding of any disputed points in matches. He was rewarded with the appointment to an Old Firm match – a Glasgow Charity Cup Semi-Final in May 1940. He certainly enforced the Laws in that game as he sent two players off and cautioned three others.
A paper maker to trade, the Second World War interrupted his career as he joined the Army. He was still able to officiate from time to time during the War, as he refereed a Junior Cup Semi-Final in 1943. He was demobbed in 1946.
Officiating in Junior football certainly seems to have been Provan's forte – he refereed Scotland's Internationals against Ireland in 1939 and 1947. He refereed another Semi-Final in the Junior Cup in 1947. He continued to referee in Junior football after he came off the SFA List at the end of season 1947-48 (when he was Class 2) and after he returned from Argentina. The Scottish Junior FA appointed him to the Junior Cup Finals

of 1951 and 1952 and to a Semi-Final in 1955, after which he retired from refereeing.

In 1957, he became the Chief Scout for Airdrieonians, a position he held until 1981. Over that period, he was responsible for bringing many well-known players to the club. Eight of the Airdrieonians team which reached the 1972 Texaco Cup Final had been brought to the club by him.

In an interview with a local newspaper on his retiral as Chief Scout, Provan looked back fondly on his time as a referee: "I tried to make myself a personality when refereeing. I liked to look smart on the field and took a pride in my kit. I felt that if you looked well and dressed well, efficiency would follow. I enjoyed every minute of my refereeing career. I loved football and money was always a secondary consideration".

Charlie Richmond
Date of Birth: 13th May 1968
Admitted to SFA List: 1996-97
No. of seasons at Category 1: 12 (2000-01 to 2011-12)
No. of years as a FIFA Referee: 7 (2003 to 2009)
5 A Internationals; 2 U21 Internationals
UEFA: 2 U21 Championship Qualifiers; 9 U19 Championship Qualifiers; 2 U17 Championship Qualifiers; 10 Club Competition matches (3 UC, 2 UCL, 1 UEL, 4 UIC)
1 Challenge Cup Final; 1 Youth Cup Final

Charlie Richmond revealed himself to be a referee of some promise early in his career and reached Category 1 within four seasons of being admitted to the List. His progress continued with elevation to the FIFA List in 2003. He enjoyed a seven year spell as a FIFA referee and during that time he officiated at five international friendlies. His first was in his debut year on the FIFA List when he was appointed to Finland v Canada in October 2003. Two years later, he handled Wales v Hungary and Northern Ireland against Germany. Richmond returned to Northern Ireland in 2007 to referee a friendly against Wales and later that year handled Malta against Armenia.

His introduction to international football as a FIFA referee had been an U21 friendly between Northern Ireland and Finland in

February 2003. In the UEFA U21 Championship Qualifiers he received appointments in Bosnia & Herzegovina and Slovenia in 2005 and 2009 for matches against Belgium and Ukraine, respectively.

In the UEFA Club Competitions, Richmond was predominantly used in the early qualifying rounds, particularly in the Intertoto Cup, refereeing ties at RC Lens, Grasshopper Club Zurich and Club Atletico de Madrid. His major appointments were in the 2nd Qualifying Round in the Champions League when he refereed FC Basel 1893 v IFK Goteborg in 2008, and Getafe CF v FC Twente in the 1st Round of the UEFA Cup in 2007.

Richmond refereed a match in the Tunisian League, Club Sportif Sfaxien against Esperance Sportive de Tunis, in January 2009, following a request by the Tunisian FA to the SFA provide a referee.

In domestic competitions, Richmond was appointed to the 2009 Challenge Cup Final, Dundee v Inverness Caledonian Thistle, and three Semi-Finals in the Scottish Cup and League Cup. Once his time on the FIFA List was over, Richmond's star began to wane in domestic football and he was used less regularly in the Scottish Premier League. He resigned from the List in April 2012 and, for a number of years thereafter, was a regular contributor to football programmes on the radio.

Don Robertson
Date of Birth: 14th February 1987
Admitted to SFA List: 2006-07
No. of seasons at Category 1: 13 (2012-13 to 2024-25)
No. of years as a FIFA Referee: 9 (2017 to 2025)
UEFA: 2 European Championship Qualifiers; 1 Nations League match; 5 U21 Championship Qualifiers; 5 U19 Championship Qualifiers; U17 Championships (2019); 6 U17 Championship Qualifiers; 24 Club Competition matches (4 UCL, 4 UEL (1 G), 11 UECL (1 PO, 3 G, 1 LP), 5 UYL (1 R16)
2 League Cup Finals; 1 Junior Cup Final

A youth goalkeeper for Queen's Park, Partick Thistle and St. Mirren, Robertson's talent as a referee was identified very early once he took up the whistle aged 17. He quickly progressed to the SFA List and handled the Junior Cup Final in 2012 prior to reaching Category 1.

His steady climb up the domestic rankings saw him being admitted to the FIFA List for 2017. His first taste of international competition had come in 2013 when, through his participation on UEFA's CORE Course, he was selected by UEFA to referee a match between Italy and Ukraine in the International Challenge Trophy, a competition for U23 players not yet capped at full international level.

He served his UEFA apprenticeship in various U17 and U19 Championship Qualifying tournaments in his first couple of years, achieving selection for the 2019 U17 Championships in the Republic of Ireland. He refereed three Group matches and the Semi-Final between the Netherlands and Spain and was the Fourth Official for the Hungary v Spain Quarter-Final.

In the UEFA Youth League, Robertson has had some notable appointments, among them PSV Eindhoven v FC Barcelona, Real Madrid CF v FC Shakhtar Donetsk and a Round of 16 match between FC Bayern Munchen and GNK Dinamo Zagreb. He has had three Group matches and one League Phase match in the Europa Conference League and one Europa League Group match.

Robertson has been regularly appointed to UEFA U21 Championship Qualifiers, refereeing France in three of his six matches. Turkey v Andorra in the European Championship Qualifiers in 2019 was his first full international. He was appointed to Iceland v Slovakia in the European Championship Qualifiers in 2023. In the Nations League, he has officiated Luxembourg v Cyprus and Austria v Kazakhstan.

During his career, Robertson has fulfilled numerous appointments as a Fourth Official, Additional Assistant Referee and as a VAR.

Robertson, an accountant, was appointed to the 2021 and 2023 League Cup Finals. He was thrust into action in the first of his three Old Firm matches when, as Fourth Official, he had to replace William Collum as the referee of the 2023 Scottish Cup Semi-Final between the clubs after Collum picked up an injury during his warm-up. Robertson's calm, unflustered manner helped him greatly in taking control of the match at such short notice.

Paul Robertson
Date of Birth: 17th July 1985
Admitted to SFA List: 2007-08
No. of seasons at Class 1: 5 (2011-12 to 2015-16)
No. of years as a FIFA Referee: 1 (2014)

Paul Robertson can unquestionably be regarded as a lost talent to refereeing as injury brought his career to a premature end just as it was about to blossom. His abilities were evident at the outset of his career when he was admitted to the SFA List aged 22. He served a four season apprenticeship in the lower categories before being promoted to Category 1. Despite a youthful appearance, he had an innate ability to control matches in a calm and firm manner, gaining the respect of the participants. These qualities led to him being regarded as a decided prospect for the future. Nominating him for inclusion in the FIFA List for 2014 was seen by the Referee Committee as the necessary step in his career development after two seasons at Category 1. This happened despite Robertson sustaining an Achilles injury at the start of season 2013-14. Robertson and the Referee Committee were confident that a full recovery would be achieved. Sadly, this confidence ultimately proved to be misplaced as the surgery Robertson underwent was not successful. The door was kept open for him to make a return in the hope that fitness would be regained but this, unfortunately, did not prove possible. The inevitable had to be faced and Robertson, regrettably, resigned from the List in January 2016.

Tom Robertson
Date of Birth: 9th December 1863
Died: 25th January 1924 aged 61
No. of seasons on List: 24 (1894-95 to 1918-19)
1 A International; 24 British International Championship Matches; 2 Amateur Internationals; 13 League Internationals; 7 Inter-Association matches

5 Scottish Cup Finals; 2 Glasgow Cup Finals; 6 Glasgow Charity Cup Finals; 27 Old Firm matches; 8 Junior Internationals; 8 Junior Cup Finals; 8 Irish Cup Finals

Tom Robertson has a justifiable claim to be regarded as one of Scottish football's most important figures due to his accomplishments as a player and as a referee.
His playing career began at Possil Bluebell as a boy in 1878 and he joined Northern in 1881-82 before moving to Cowlairs where he played for four seasons. An engineer, he moved to England to take up a job offer and played for Aston Villa and other local Midlands clubs during season 1886-87. A half-back, he developed a fine reputation at Aston Villa. He returned to Scotland after a year and rejoined Cowlairs, with whom he won the Glasgow Exhibition Cup in 1888. He then joined Queen's Park and enjoyed a distinguished spell over the next six seasons. The Scottish Cup was won in 1890. He was capped four times for Scotland and captained the team in three of these matches, including his debut against Ireland in 1889. Robertson also played nine times for Glasgow in Inter-Association matches against Sheffield, London and Edinburgh. His last club was St. Bernard's of Edinburgh whom he joined in January 1895 and with whom he won the Scottish Cup that season for the second time.
Robertson remained an amateur player throughout his career, resisting the temptation to turn professional a few times. Being an amateur, he was able to move freely. From time to time he returned to the Midlands in England and on one occasion played a league match for Nottingham Forest in 1892.
He stopped playing in November 1895 and immediately took up refereeing, encouraged to do so by John McDowall, the SFA Secretary. He proceed to make a great reputation for himself as a referee, based on a comprehensive knowledge of the rules, intelligent observation of play and prompt decisions. His reputation was forged throughout the British Isles as he refereed in all of the constituent countries, with his services being in constant demand for many important games.
His ability as a referee was recognised quickly, being appointed to his first British International Championship match, Wales v

England, in March 1896. He was described in 1897 as a "first class knight of the whistle" and was praised for bringing his past playing knowledge to refereeing. Major appointments began to flow steadily in his direction.

He became popular with the Football Association and, in the days when appointments were agreed between the competing associations, it is remarkable to note that Robertson refereed England in 21 Internationals – 10 at home and 11 away. He did two Scotland v England Internationals – one home match for each association. Five Ireland v England matches and five Wales v England matches were in his charge. He refereed the Scottish League v the Football League three times and nine other League Internationals outwith Scotland, five of them being the Irish League against the Football League. At senior level, he refereed a remarkable 40 internationals, comprising the British International Championship, an A International and League and Amateur internationals.

If there was such a thing as a professional referee in the early 1900's, Tom Robertson was it. He became a "whistle for hire" as it were. He was included in various Referee Lists outwith Scotland – the Football League, the Southern League, the Irish League and the Lancashire FA. There was a period when he was officiating more outwith Scotland than in the country. He was undoubtedly regarded as one of the top referees in England, if not the best. In an article in the Birmingham Daily Mail in 1903, William MacGregor, a Scot who was a founding member of the Football League, insightfully commented that "Robertson is now one of the finest referees in the country. One of the few men who have the real referee instinct, and that is all important. It is not so much a knowledge of the game. All referees are supposed to have that, but there is a thing as the refereeing instinct, and I do not wish to be offensive when I say that few referees have it. Mr. Robertson, however, does posses it." Robertson was appointed to many of the major League matches in England during this decade – fixtures such as Manchester City v Wolverhampton Wanderers, Arsenal v Liverpool, Newcastle United v Preston North End and Manchester United v Middlesborough.

When he was added to the Southern League's List of Referees in 1904, one attendee at the meeting said "it would cost clubs no more to bring Robertson down to London from Glasgow than it would to bring certain Lancashire officials down". Clubs were evidently happy to pay his travelling expenses.

Indeed, having refereed a match at Tottenham Hotspur, it was reported that "it seems a long way to bring a referee, but he is such an excellent official that no club would begrudge the expense. He is strict, impartial and very much down on rough play, qualities lacking in many officials of the present day." Expense certainly was no object in 1908 when Robertson was obliged to attend a Football Association disciplinary hearing in regard to his sending-off a West Ham United player in a Southern League match against Millwall.

In a report on the Arsenal v Liverpool match, the following tribute was paid: "The refereeing of Robertson was about as perfect an exhibition given on the Manor Ground. Indeed, though I remember most of the men of the whistle whose names have been made famous, I do not remember to have derived so much satisfaction in all my experience. Always up with play, ever watchful, never at fault with his decisions, and absolutely without that fastidiousness which mars some of our big-wig refs, I can well understand how this gentleman gets engagements so far south. I shall forever regard Mr Tom Robertson as my ideal referee until I see better."

Further tribute came from an unnamed English League official in 1906: "The majority of League Managers in my country will bear me out that Tom Robertson is the best referee in Britain and every one of us would have him on the same afternoon if that were possible. He just knows the game and he gives his decisions fairly. He never turns a player away with a sore heart. If the player tells Tom he could not help tripping an opponent or fouling the ball, Tom, like the canny man he is, will just remark that it is all right; better luck next time. That is how Tom Robertson won his name as a referee. A player requires to be humoured, and so long as a referee is friendly with the players, the better the game is contested."

Robertson refereed ties in the FA Cup but, if such a thing can be said, the significant omission in his appointments is that of the

FA Cup Final. However, it is hard to imagine the Football Association appointing a non-English referee for that match.
Robertson's commitment to refereeing was exemplified in December 1913 when he refereed two Southern League matches in Wales on consecutive days. On Christmas Day he officiated at Cardiff City v Merthyr and the following day he refereed the return fixture at Merthyr. Rather amazingly, he travelled back up to Scotland to referee Morton v Falkirk on 27th December.
Tom Robertson refereed regularly throughout the 1900's in Ireland, handling eight Irish Cup Finals between 1901 and 1911. It would have been nine but for the postponement due to snow of the 1908 Final and being unavailable for the rescheduled match. He also refereed five Finals in other cup competitions. One such Final was a County Antrim Shield Final between Distillery and Linfield in 1900. The rivalry between the clubs and their supporters was such that it was thought advisable to secure the services of Robertson as the referee, an indication he had quickly established his reputation in Ireland. The regard in which he was held was reflected in the Irish FA inviting him to referee a trial match between home players and an Anglo-Irish team in 1910. (In Scotland, Robertson did ten trial matches between Home Scots and Anglo-Scots.)
Robertson has a remarkable tally of 27 Old Firm matches, which is unlikely ever to be surpassed. Seven of these matches were in Cup Finals – one Scottish Cup, two Glasgow Cup and four Glasgow Charity Cup.
He played a key role in the formation of the Scottish Football Referees' Association in 1903, and served as a committee member in its initial existence.
Robertson was in great demand in Scotland throughout his career and was appointed to numerous local association cup finals throughout Scotland. He officiated at various levels of the game and handled Schools' Internationals as well being a prominent referee in Junior football, reflected by his appointments to Junior internationals and Junior Cup Finals. He often refereed every night of the week in the Juniors at the end of each season in the spring and early summer. Given his playing connection with Queen's Park, he regularly refereed the

club's annual friendly against Corinthians. His popularity prompted him to postpone his retirement from time to time until his eyesight began to bother him and he found the pace of the game too fast for him.

Robertson submitted a letter of resignation the Scottish League in May 1919 and was warmly thanked for his services to the game. His resignation was well reported throughout Scotland, with his contribution as a referee being fully recognised. His refereeing days were not exactly over though. He came out of retirement in October 1923 to referee his one A International, Sweden v Denmark, thus becoming the first Scot to referee such a match involving two non-British teams. To get there, he travelled by ferry from Newcastle to Gothenburg and then on to Stockholm. Press reports referred to his having refereed many internationals, being a sprightly 54 year old (even though he was 60 at the time), and among the best referees to have officiated at the stadium.

Just a few months afterwards, Robertson died suddenly due to heart failure at his home in Bishopbriggs on 25th January 1924. His death was widely reported in newspapers throughout Britain. He was considered to be "a household name" with one report stating that he had "stood for all that was best in football. He was one of the few big figures in football, well known in Scotland, England and Ireland. He was a personality. Somewhat an autocrat on the field when refereeing, he held the esteem of the players. His thorough knowledge, not only of the rules of the game, but of the spirit in which it should be made, was undisputed, and his decisions seldom questioned."

Robertson was well remembered by those in the game who had come across him in his career. In 1923, the Preston North End Manager, James Lawrence, looked back on referees of the past and said of Robertson: "He was acknowledged to be a strong type of referee. He'd been a player in his time and was considered to be a "tousy yin" – he knew all the tricks of the trade. To a player who might protest his innocence, Robertson would reply "If I hadn't done it often myself, I might believe you."

In 1929, Steve Bloomer, the famous England international held to the greatest player of his era at the turn of the 20th century, commented that he considered Tom Robertson "as being the most perfect of all referees".

John Rowbotham
Date of Birth: 5th December 1955
Admitted to SFA List: 1991-92
No. of seasons at Class 1: 12 (1993-94 to 2004-05)
No. of years as a FIFA Referee: 6 (1995-2000)
1 A International
FIFA: 4 World Cup Qualifiers
UEFA: 3 U21 Qualifiers; 2 U18 Championship Qualifiers; 15 Club Competition matches (1 ECWC, 11 UC, 1 UCL, 2 UIC)
1 Scottish Cup Final; 3 Challenge Cup Finals; 2 Old Firm matches; 1 Junior Cup Final

John Rowbotham was the beneficiary of an SFA decision to introduce the principle of "accelerated promotion" for referees in the early 1990's. He started refereeing in 1987 after he stopped playing amateur football and quickly demonstrated a natural aptitude and skill. Admitted to the SFA List in 1991 at 35, he took just two seasons to be promoted to Class 1, with his appointment to the 1993 Junior Cup Final being an indicator of his swift rise. A further two seasons were taken to reach the FIFA List.

During his six years as a FIFA Referee, Rowbotham did very well to receive appointments to four World Cup Qualifiers - in Cyprus, Russia, Switzerland and Liechtenstein. He made his mark in the UEFA Club Competitions too, being particularly used in the early rounds of the UEFA Cup handling ties such as RC Lens v SS Lazio, Udinese Calcio v Widzew Lodz, PAOK Thessaloniki v Club Atletico de Madrid and FC Basel 1893 v Feyenoord.

Rowbotham, a sales representative for a Kirkcaldy confectionary firm, was regularly used as a Fourth Official and had appointments to a Quarter-Final in the Champions League in 1995 and Semi-Finals in the UEFA Cup in 1995 and 1998.

His A International was Northern Ireland v Belgium in 1997.

Tall, lean and instantly recognisable due to being bald as a result of alopecia, Rowbotham enjoyed a fine career, fully justifying his rapid promotion through the SFA List with his 12 seasons service at Class 1 and becoming a FIFA referee. Following his first Old Firm match in September 1995, he did well to recover from a bad performance in a Rangers and Aberdeen League match a couple of months later which generated much media focus on him at the time. Having refereed three Challenge Cup Finals between 1995 and 2002, Rowbotham's final season on the SFA List was crowned by being appointed to the 2005 Scottish Cup Final between Dundee United and Celtic.

Rowbotham was appointed as a Referee Observer and as the Association Manager for Stirlingshire RA for season 2005-06 but resigned from both positions in February 2006 due to personal reasons.

Tom Small
Born: 1891
Died: October 1969 aged 78
No. of seasons on List: 17(1919-20 to 1935-36)
1 British International Championship Match; 2 League Internationals
1 Glasgow Cup Final; 10 Old Firm matches; 2 Junior Internationals; 3 Junior Cup Finals

Tom Small was a popular, well-regarded referee of some personality. He lived up to his surname as he was small in stature, standing just over five feet tall. In advance of his British International Championship match between Ireland and England in October 1929, an English newspaper described him as a "Harry Lauder in shorts", but not in a disparaging way, as he was "flowing with personality". Another report indicated that occasionally he would stop play and go over to spectators to lecture them. The newspaper also conveyed that he was reckoned to be Scotland's No. 2 referee after Peter Craigmyle. The press described him as "that super regulator of football traffic", as having an "eager and short-stepping" running style and that "his gesticulations made sure that his decisions were understood by players and spectators alike".

He started refereeing in the late 1910's and quickly progressed to the SFA's List. A Dundonian, he refereed three Cup Finals, senior and Junior, in Angus in successive Saturdays in May 1922. He made his mark in Junior football, refereeing the 1923 Junior Cup Final, the appointment resulting from making a good impression in one of the Semi-Finals. He went on to referee the 1928 and 1931 Junior Cup Finals. The Scottish League included him in its List from 1924-25. At the end of that season, he handled his first Junior International, Scotland v Ireland. His first League International came along in October 1926 when he was appointed to the Scottish League's match against the Irish League.

By the time of his second league International, the Scottish League v the Football League in 1928, it was held that he was rapidly coming to the fore, being the unanimous choice of the two Leagues. In official circles he was thought to be the likeliest successor to the mantle long worn by Tom Dougray. In the phraseology of that time, it was regularly considered that Small had given the "utmost satisfaction" in his handling of games.

Small was regularly in the mix when it came to the appointment of referees for the Scottish Cup Semi-Finals and Finals, but missed out in the voting process and only managed to secure selection for one Semi-Final, in 1928. He was chosen on five occasions to be the Reserve Referee for the Semi-Finals and twice for the Final. The one disappointment in his career was not being appointed to the Cup Final. He had small compensation to some degree by being a linesman in the 1931 Final.

His talents were reflected in his taking charge of 10 Old Firm matches over seven seasons from 1924-25. He was something of an expert in gaining replays in cup-ties between the two clubs – a Glasgow Cup Semi-Final in 1925 went to three matches and the 1929 Final was over two matches.

Small decided to retire from the List at the end of season 1935-36 when he was 45. Rather magnanimously of him, he took the view that younger referees should be given the chance. He did not stop refereeing altogether though as he continued to referee charity games in Dundee as he had done throughout his career.

He had been prominent in the activities of the Angus Referees' Association and the training of referees in particular and was awarded life membership of the association in 1937 for his "good and lengthy service".

Small kept involved in football, attending matches at all levels of the game. By 1945, he was scouting for Heart of Midlothian. When the SFA set up its refereeing system that year, he was the ideal man to be appointed as the Referee Supervisor for the new Angus & Perthshire RA. He took on the role with some relish but unfortunately had to resign in January 1946. Employed as a school janitor, he was unable to take the necessary time off work to attend meetings in Glasgow on a regular basis.

Two tales portray the personality of Small. In 1954, watching the World Cup on television, Small was much impressed by the Italian referee, Vincenzo Orlandini, and wrote to congratulate him on his performance. Orlandini replied expressing his thanks, much flattered by the interest taken in him. Two years later, in 1956, Small won the "Letter of the Week" in the Sunday Post's football section. He had been compelled to write to stick up for referees given recent comment in the newspaper: "I think the referees of today are just as good as they were in my time, but we had a little more freedom. I would like to see the Referee Committee do away with the black book and allow the referee to air his views to the press if any sensational incident occurred on or off the field. In my opinion, if this were carried out, we would have fewer incidents and a better understanding."

Tom Small spent the last five years of his life in Motherwell, where he had moved to live with his daughter after he was widowed.

George Smith
Date of Birth: 14th October 1943
Died: 13th May 2019 aged 75
Admitted to SFA List: 1966-67
No of seasons at Class 1: 21 (1971-72 to 1991-92)
No of seasons/years as a FIFA Referee: 15 (1974-75, 1978-79 to 1991)

4 A Internationals; 1 British International Championship match; 2 British Amateur Championship matches; 1 British Youth International Championship match; World University Games (1987)

FIFA: World Cup (1990); 2 World Cup Qualifiers; 2 Olympic Qualifiers

UEFA: 4 U21 Championship Qualifiers; U18 Youth Tournament (1979); 1 U18 Championship Qualifier; UEFA U16 Championships (1986); 19 Club Competition matches (3 ECCC (1 Q-F), 7 ECWC (1 Q-F), 9 UC (1 Q-F)

3 Scottish Cup Finals; 2 League Cup Finals; 7 Old Firm matches

George Smith ranks as one of the best referees produced by Scotland. He enjoyed a lengthy career at Class 1 and his 15 years as a FIFA referee is testament to the high standards of performance he reached and maintained.

A player in the same school team as the future Hibernian player Pat Stanton, Smith took up refereeing at 16 years of age. After a referee failed to turn up for a match at the boys' club Smith helped out at, he was asked to fill in as a replacement. That led to him taking the refereeing course during season 1959-60. After five seasons in the minor grades and one season in Junior football, he progressed to the SFA List at the age of 23. An early taste of international football came his way in 1968 when he was a linesman to Bobby Davidson in a British International Championship match, Wales v Northern Ireland. 1968 also saw him being appointed as a linesman to the Scottish Cup Final between Dunfermline Athletic and Heart of Midlothian.

Promotion to Class 1 was achieved in 1971-72. During that season, he was appointed to the British Youth International Championship match, Wales v England. Two British Amateur International Championship matches followed in the next two seasons. His excellent performances in his first three seasons at Class 1 seasons brought him to the FIFA List for 1974-75, although it was just for that season. Whilst he did not receive any refereeing appointments during the season, he was selected as a linesman to Bobby Davidson for the 1975 European Cup Winners' Cup Final, Dynamo Kyiv v Ferencvarosi TS.

Smith returned to the FIFA List for 1978-79 and he served continuously through to 1991. The end of that first season was marked by selection for the UEFA Youth Tournament in Austria. Over the next few seasons, experience was built up in the UEFA Club Competitions, handling ties involving clubs such as Juventus, 1.FC Koln, VfB Stuttgart and FK Crvena Zvedva. Smith took charge of the Wales and Northern Ireland match in the British International Championship in 1982, an Olympic Qualifier between Italy and the Netherlands in 1984 and the England v Republic of Ireland international in 1985.

Selection for the UEFA U16 Championships in Greece in 1986 heralded the start of his peak years as a FIFA referee. Between 1987 and 1990, he was appointed to 2nd Leg ties in Quarter-Finals in each of the UEFA Club Competitions – Malmo FF v AFC Ajax in the 1987 European Cup Winners' Cup, AC Milan v Werder Bremen in the 1989 European Champions Clubs' Cup and AJ Auxerre v AC Fiorentina in the 1990 UEFA Cup. He refereed at the 1987 World University Games in Albania and was chosen for the 1989 FIFA U16 World Cup held in Scotland. A calf injury sustained in the pre-competition Fitness Test caused his withdrawal from the Finals but this disappointment was more than made up the following year when he was selected for the World Cup in Italy. There, he refereed the group match between Austria and Czechoslovakia and ran the line in the Italy v Czechoslovakia match.

The first of Smith's seven Old Firm matches was the Scottish Cup Final in 1980, a match marred by a full scale riot between both sets of supporters on the pitch after the match ended. Quite blameless for what had taken place, Jack Mowat remarked afterwards that Smith had given the best performance of any participant in the Final. By the late 1980's Smith was at the absolute peak of his career and was appointed to two Scottish Cup Finals and two League Cup Finals between 1988 and 1990. Smith contemplated retiring after the 1990 World Cup but continued for another two seasons, ending his career one season before the retiral age of 50. A civil servant in the Scottish Office, Smith was often characterised as having a "schoolmaster" approach to his handling of players. He was certainly a very firm referee and resolute in his disciplinary approach. Having the strength of character to take tough decisions, he could handle the toughest situations. A Rangers and Aberdeen match in 1985 was a violent and indisciplined match which saw Smith send off two Rangers players and caution seven others. A police escort was required when leaving the stadium after the match. In a UEFA Cup match between Valencia CF and FC Porto in 1989, and at a venue known to be a cauldron, Smith sent off four Valencia CF players.

The SFA appointed Smith as a Referee Supervisor for Edinburgh & District RA immediately on his retirement, wishing to capitalise on his vast experience. At the same time, he was also appointed to the Referee Supervisors' Executive Committee. He served in that role for a decade and, once that committee was transformed into the Referee Committee, for a further few seasons until the end of season 2006-07. He continued to act as a Referee Observer through to the autumn of 2018 when he retired due to health reasons, thus completing 58 years in the referee movement. Smith acted as a Referee Observer for UEFA for a number of years. He was an excellent Observer and a great judge of a referee. He took great delight in passing on the benefits his experience to younger referees he had assessed and watching them progress in their careers.

John B. Stark
Born: 19th April 1878
Died: 29th March 1941 aged 62
No. of seasons on List: 9(1904-05 to 1912-13)
5 British International Championship matches; 1 Amateur International; 2 League Internationals; 1 Inter-Association match
1 Scottish Cup Final; 4 Old Firm matches

Stark grew up in a football-loving family in Airdrie and, as a boy, cleaned the boots of the Airdrieonians players. He played schools' and juvenile football and was encouraged to take up refereeing by an Airdrieonians player. He quickly progressed through the grades and made the Scottish League's List for season 1904-05. It did not take him long to be appointed to First Division matches. During that first season, it was reported that in a Heart of Midlothian match against St. Mirren, he was inclined to talk to the players. The famous internationalist Bobby Walker told him at half-time that he was doing fine but advised him that he must stop talking to the players.

Stark suffered a setback in his career during season 1907-08. He was suspended by the SFA Referee Committee for a month following a disciplinary hearing on a Celtic home match against Airdrieonians when Celtic was fined £15 for missile throwing by spectators. As part of its investigation, the committee formed the opinion that Stark, "had not shown a proper conception of his duties in suppressing rough play" in the match. This affair did not deter Stark and he put it behind him and was rewarded by being selected to referee a Scottish Cup Semi-Final that season.

Stark's first international was in October 1908 when he refereed the Irish League against the Football League. Other major appointments flowed that season – the Amateur international between Ireland and England in November and the match between the two associations in the British International Championship in February. He ended the season by refereeing the England v Scotland game (a match where the Football Association preferred to give Stark the opportunity over Tom Robertson, whom the SFA had proposed) and the Scottish Cup Final between Celtic and Rangers. After the English international, Bradford FC, the host club, presented him with a solid silver whistle to mark his first international in the country.

The Scottish Cup Final was drawn as was the replay. The crowd unfortunately rioted at the end of the replay and invaded the pitch, destroying parts of the ground, all in the belief that extra-time should have been played, rather than the tie going to a second replay. The outcome was that the Cup was withheld at the request of both clubs. In the first match, Stark had confidently awarded a goal to Celtic taking the view that the ball had crossed the line with the Rangers goalkeeper clutching it. Despite the inevitable outcry, he was commended for his integrity for his decision.

Stark's last international was the British International Championship match between England and Wales in March 1911.

Stark officiated frequently in Ireland in the late 1910s' and was selected to referee the 1909 Mid-Ulster Cup Final between Glenavon and Portadown.

In 1913, Stark emigrated to Detroit in the United States. He established himself extremely quickly to the extent that he was selected by the Michigan Soccer Association to referee its State Cup Final in each of his first three seasons there. Considered to be the best referee in the Mid-West, he was held in great esteem elsewhere in the United States as clubs regularly sought his services for matches. Stark handled an Inter-City match between Detroit and Cleveland in 1914. He became closely involved with the Referees' Association in Michigan and worked hard to establish that body on a sound footing.

David Syme
Date of Birth: 15th June 1944
Died: 27th October 2020 aged 76
Admitted to SFA List: 1968-69
No. of seasons at Class 1: 21 (1973-74 to 1993-94)
No of seasons/years as a FIFA Referee: 14 (1977-78 to 1991)
2A Internationals; 1 British International Championship match; 1 British Youth International Championship match;
FIFA: 5 World Cup Qualifiers; U19 World Cup (1985 (F)); 7 Olympic Qualifiers
UEFA: 1 European Championship Qualifier; 2 U21 Championships (1986 ((1S-F) and 1990 (1 Q-F)); 5 U21 Championship Qualifiers; Youth Tournament (1978); 1 U18 Championship Qualifier; 1 U16 Championship Qualifier; 1 27 Club Competition matches (3 ECCC (1 S-F), 6 ECWC (1 Q-F), 18 UC (1 Q-F, 1 S-F)
2 Scottish Cup Finals; 2 League Cup Finals; 12 Old Firm matches

By any standard, David Syme had an outstanding career in domestic and international football. He can be regarded as one of the top referees produced by Scotland, serving the game extremely well over his 21 seasons at Class 1 and 14 continuous seasons on the FIFA List. Son of Willie Syme and no doubt influenced by him to follow in his footsteps, he started refereeing in 1963 when he was 19 after a series of ankle breaks brought his playing days in amateur football to an end. He was admitted to the SFA List five years later.

His talent was such that he was promoted to Class 1 after four seasons and so commenced his long run as a top-class referee. During his first season at Class 1, to give him an introduction to international football, he was appointed to the Wales v Northern Ireland match in the British Youth International Championship. Over the next few seasons he received several appointments as a linesman to major international matches at club and country level and graduated to the FIFA List for season 1977-78. He had obviously made a favourable impression in domestic football as he had been selected to referee the Scottish Cup Semi-Final between Heart of Midlothian and Rangers in 1977.

As was the case with a few other Scottish FIFA referees, Syme's first international was a match in Iceland, against Norway, in 1977. He ended his first season as a FIFA referee by being chosen for the UEFA Youth Tournament held in Poland.

Syme did not take long to make a mark in European club football. In his first few seasons, he was handling matches involving clubs such as VfL Borussia Monchengladbach and FC Barcelona and in 1982 was appointed to the 2nd Leg of the European Champion Clubs' Cup Semi-Final, FC Bayern Munchen v CSKA Sofia. He returned to FC Bayern Munchen in 1989 to referee its Semi-Final against SSC Napoli in the UEFA Cup. A UEFA Cup Quarter-Final appointment to Victoria Bucuresti and SG Dynamo Dresden had preceded the Bayern match. Another Quarter-Final, this time in the European Cup Winners' Cup between Dynamo Kyiv and FC Barcelona, was received in 1991. These appointments in the knock-out stages of the club competitions reflect the standing in which Syme was held throughout his career by UEFA. 18 appointments in the UEFA Cup is a fine achievement. He was also appointed to Quarter-Finals and Semi-Finals in the UEFA U21 Championships in 1986 and 1990.

Syme, a salesman for a watch company and then a holiday home company, developed a fine record at national level too, as five World Cup Qualifiers would testify. His tally of seven Olympic Qualifiers is remarkable. In March 1988, FIFA sent him to New Zealand to officiate in an Olympic Qualifying tournament where he refereed Chinese Tapei's matches against Australia and New Zealand. It is something of an oddity that he only refereed one European Championship Qualifier, Iceland v France, in 1990.

The late 1980's were the peak of his international career but his greatest accomplishment had been in 1985 when he was selected for the FIFA U19 World Cup, held in Russia. After refereeing the Group match, Paraguay v China, he was appointed to the Final between Brazil and Spain.

From the late 1970's to the end of his career, Syme firmly established himself as one of Scotland's top referees. Being appointed to 12 Old Firm matches is an indication of his capabilities. His first such match was the League Cup Final of 1978 and he took charge of the teams again in the 1986 Final in the same competition. His two Scottish Cup Finals were Aberdeen v Rangers in 1983 and Motherwell's memorable triumph over Dundee United in 1991.

Syme was never far from controversy at times in Scottish football, being locked in his dressing room at Tynecastle in 1989 after a Heart of Midlothian and Rangers match and being vilified by Airdrieonians for erroneously awarding a penalty against the club in a League Cup Semi-Final against Dunfermline Athletic in 1991 which the club held to have "cost" them the game. Big in stature, he was a strong, no-nonsense referee. His career ended on a sad note as a consequence of dropping his trousers as part of a bet at a charity dinner and he found himself heavily criticised by the SFA for "comprising his integrity as a referee by his undignified actions". Syme considered it to have just been a bit of fun and decided to resign from the List at the end of April 1994. He was in any case due to retire at the end of the season on age grounds.

Willie Syme
Born: 1917
Died: 11th July 1970 aged 53
Admitted to SFA List: 1951-52
No. of seasons at Class 1: 15 (1954-55 to 1968-69)
No. of seasons as a FIFA Referee: 6 (1963-64 to 1968-69)

5 A Internationals; 1 U23 International
FIFA: 1 World Cup Qualifier
UEFA: 1 European Championship Qualifier; 9 Club Competition matches (1 ECCC, 8 ICFC (1 S-F))
1 Scottish Cup Final; 3 Glasgow Cup Finals; 2 Glasgow Charity Cup Finals; 8 Old Firm matches

Willie Syme had a fine, solid refereeing career. Having played Junior football as a goalkeeper for Benburb, he began refereeing in 1949 once he returned to Glasgow after serving as an army sergeant as he wished to continue to be involved in football. Once he was admitted to the SFA List in season 1951-52, his talents soon became apparent as he was promoted to Class 1 midway through season 1952-53. By the end of the decade, he had refereed the Finals of the 1957 Glasgow Charity Cup and the 1958 Glasgow Cup. The first of his Old Firm matches was in 1960 and in 1963-64 and 1966-67 he handled two matches between the clubs in each season.

His performances brought him to FIFA status in 1963-64 and he proceeded to accomplish much in this latter period of his time as a referee. As a pre-cursor to becoming a FIFA referee, Syme was selected by the SFA to officiate in the Football Association's eight-team Centenary Amateur International Tournament in May 1963. He refereed England's match against West Germany in Middlesbrough, a match which featured the future West German goalkeeper Sepp Maier.

He was appointed to eight matches in the Inter-Cities Fairs Cup, handling matches involving clubs such as 1.FC Koln, Club Atletico de Madrid, Eintracht Frankfurt, SL Benfica and Bologna. Remarkably, in his first season as a FIFA referee, Syme was appointed to a Semi-Final in the competition – Real Zaragoza v RFC Liege. His other club match was a preliminary tie in the European Champion Clubs' Cup in 1964 – FK Lyn v Reipas Lahti.

Syme took charge of an U23 International between Northern Ireland and Wales in his first season on the FIFA List. His European Championship Qualifier was Norway v Portugal in 1967. He suffered the misfortune of having to abandon his only World Cup Qualifier, the Republic of Ireland and Denmark in

1968, early in the second half due to fog. (The match was replayed the following season when Syme was no longer a FIFA referee and was refereed by John Paterson).

The undoubted high point of Syme's international career was the month he spent in Brazil with Tom Wharton and Archie Webster prior to the 1966 World Cup. During that period, he refereed five Brazil internationals against Chile, Peru (twice), Poland and Czechoslovakia. As he only refereed five A internationals during his career, it is surely quite unique that he refereed Brazil in every single one!

Syme's performances in domestic football were rewarded by being appointed to the 1967 Scottish Cu Final between Celtic and Aberdeen. He chose to resign from the List at the end of season 1968-69, his last honour being the referee of the Rangers and Partick Thistle Glasgow Cup Final.

In July 1970, Syme, a works manager in a Glasgow joinery company, was the subject of a profile in a spin-off of the Scotsport football programme on Scottish Television. His jovial personality, which had made him a popular character in the game, came across in the interview. Tragically, a week later, Syme was killed in a road accident.

Stanley Tait
Born: 1937
No. of seasons as a FIFA Referee: 3 (1966-67, 1969-70 and 1974-75)

From Edinburgh, Tait emigrated to Canada in the late 1950's/early 1960's. By that time, he had already qualified as a referee and he continued to referee in Canada. He progress was such that he was appointed to the FIFA List for season 1966-67. Tait served on the FIFA List for two other single seasons, 1969-70 and 1974-75. A record of any international appointments has not been established.

Tait would have been influenced to take up refereeing by his father Bill, who was on the SFA's List from 1952 to 1965, serving at Class 3A and Class 3B before being a Referee Supervisor for Edinburgh and District RA from 1965 to 1977.

Craig Thomson
Date of Birth: 26th June 1972
Admitted to SFA List: 1997-98
Promoted to Category 1: 2000-01
No. of seasons at Category 1: 19 (2000-01 to 2018-19)
No. of years as a FIFA Referee: 15 (2003 to 2017)
9 A Internationals; 1 U21 International
FIFA: 9 World Cup Qualifiers; 2 U17 World Cups (2007and 2013(F))
UEFA: 2 European Championships (2008 (as Fourth Official) and 2012); 9 European Championship Qualifiers;U21 Championships (2007); 4 U21 Championship Qualifiers; 6 U19 Championship Qualifiers; 2 U17 Championship Qualifiers; 71 Club Competition matches (41 UCL (6 PO, 26 G, 2 R16, 2 Q-F), 10 UC (4 G, 2 R32, 2 R16), 17 UEL (3 PO, 3 G, 3 R32, 5 R16, 1 Q-F, 2 S-F), 3 UIC)
3 Scottish Cup Finals; 4 League Cup Finals; 1 Challenge Cup Final; 1 Youth Cup Final

Craig Thomson was Scotland's leading referee over the first two decades of the 21st century. His talent was identified early and his quick promotion to Category 1 after just three seasons on the SFA List was more than fully justified over his outstanding career in domestic and international football. From an early stage, he was deemed to be a future FIFA referee and he reached that status after two seasons at Category 1.

His early career was carefully nurtured by the SFA. International experience was gained at the 2002 Algarve Women's Cup, a tournament for national teams, and he was selected for the 2002 Youth Cup Final. The SFA also provided him with the opportunity to officiate at the 2005 Toulon U21Tournament where he refereed a Semi-Final between Portugal and Mexico. Thomson's career path with UEFA followed the intended route, serving his apprenticeship with appointments in the Under-Age Championships and to ties in the qualification rounds of the UEFA Club Competitions. In 2007, UEFA selected him as a referee for its U21 Championships in the Netherlands where he refereed two Group matches. His star was certainly on the rise that year as FIFA chose him as one of the referees for the U17 World Cup in South Korea. After handling three Group matches, he refereed the Round of 16 tie between Germany and the USA.

By 2008, Thomson had progressed into the Elite category of UEFA referees and his career took off. He was used as a Fourth Official in the European Championships that year in Austria/Switzerland and had three appointments in the Group matches. Four years later, he was chosen as a referee for the European Championships in Poland/Ukraine where he refereed the Group matches, Denmark v Portugal and Czech Republic v Poland and acted as the Fourth Official for the Spain v France Quarter-Final.

FIFA selected Thomson for the U17 World Cup once more in 2013, when it was held in the United Arab Emirates. After taking charge of one Group match, he was appointed to the Round of 16 tie between Morocco and the Ivory Coast. He then received the ultimate accolade by being chosen for the Final, Nigeria v Mexico. Despite this achievement, Thomson sadly missed out on selection for the 2014 World Cup in Brazil having been a candidate in the lead up to the tournament. That disappointment aside, Thomson's tally of nine Qualifiers in each of the World Cup and the European Championships is a fine record. He was entrusted to handle many important matches, with one such match, the European Championship Qualifier, Italy v Serbia in 2010, having to be abandoned after only six minutes due to crowd trouble by the Serbian supporters.

To have refereed nine A Internationals in the modern era is a significant achievement. Thomson was introduced to national team football in 2004 when he refereed Northern Ireland and Norway. Amongst his other friendly internationals, he refereed three home France matches against Slovakia, Spain and Russia and one away match against Belgium. South Africa and Uruguay were the Republic of Ireland's opponents in two other internationals he handled. He also refereed another Republic of Ireland international, against Northern Ireland, in the Carlsberg Cup tournament in 2011.

Gaining elite status in UEFA enabled Thomson to receive many appointments in the UEFA Club Competitions. In the

Champions League, he was in charge of 29 matches in the Group Stages involving many of the top European clubs. Further, he was appointed to four matches in the knock-out rounds: two matches in the Round of 16, both featuring FC Barcelona in 2012 and 2013 and two Quarter-Finals in 2011 (FC Barcelona v Shakhtar Donetsk) and in 2013 (BV Borussia Dortmund v Malaga CF). An equally fine record was achieved in the Europa League. Whilst sparingly used in the Group Stages due to his Champions League appointments, UEFA relied heavily on him in the knock-out rounds, appointing him to 11 matches. Three were in the Round of 32 (featuring ties such as Sevilla v FC Porto and Olympique Marseille v Athletic Club Bilbao), five in the Round of 16, one Quarter-Final, Valencia CF v Club Atletico de Madrid in 2010 and two Semi-Finals – SL Benfica v SC Braga in 2011 and Club Atletico de Madrid v Valencia (again) in 2012. Given that these latter two matches were played in the Iberian Peninsula, it was fitting that Thomson's final international club match was between Spanish and Portuguese clubs: FC Barcelona v Sporting Clube de Portugal in December 2017. The quality of the appointments Thomson received were such to confirm his status as one of the leading referees of his generation in Europe.

Thomson was, naturally, a dominating presence in domestic Scottish football throughout his career as his tally of three Scottish Cup and four League Cup Finals over a nine year period indicates. Additionally, he refereed 12 Semi-Finals between the two Cups over his career. Three of these Semi-Finals were Old Firm ties and one other in his total of 14 games between the two clubs was the League Cup Final of 2011.

Thomson, a lawyer by profession, was a tall commanding presence in matches and his calm, unflustered and resolute approach served him very well. His performance levels were such that he rarely became the subject of "controversy", a rare thing for a referee to achieve. For five years from 2011 to 2016, Thomson worked in the SFA's Referee Operations Department as a Recruitment and Education Officer on a job-sharing basis (with Steven McLean) until a job promotion with the company he worked for required that he step down. After retiring from refereeing in 2019, Thomson was appointed a few months later as a Referee Observer, a role which he fulfilled until the end of season 1923-24.

Eddie Thomson
Born: 1928
Died: 10th May 2010 aged 82
Admitted to SFA List: 1963-64
No. of seasons at Class 1: 13 (1965-66 to 1977-78)
No. of seasons as a FIFA Referee: 2 (1973-74 and 1975-76)
1 British Amateur International Championship match
UEFA: 1 Youth Tournament Qualifier
3 Old Firm matches; 1 Junior Cup Final

Eddie Thomson, an Edinburgh civil servant, had a career fairly typical of other referees in the 1960's and 1970's who graduated to the FIFA List in their 40's. His steady and consistent performances in domestic football brought him to FIFA status for two separate seasons, which gave him little chance to become established in European football. His only appointment as a FIFA referee was to a UEFA Youth Tournament Qualifier between Iceland and the Republic of Ireland in 1973. His match in the British International Amateur Championship, Northern Ireland v England, had been in 1967, the appointment being a reflection of his potential for the future. He was recognised as a referee of some talent early in his career, being appointed to referee the 1963 Junior Cup Final between Irvine Meadow and Glenafton Athletic in the season prior to admission to the SFA List. Once on the List, he took just two seasons to reach Class 1. In his one season at Class 3A, he was selected as a linesman with Tom Wharton for an Inter-Cities Fairs Cup Quarter-Final, Real Zaragoza v Juventus in 1964. He returned to Zaragoza a couple of months later with Willie Syme for the club's Semi-Final against RFC Liege. Thomson was the referee in charge of one of Scottish football's most famous matches, Berwick Rangers' stunning Scottish Cup victory over Rangers in 1967.
Thomson's second season as a FIFA referee, 1975-76, saw him being appointed as a linesman to another European Quarter-Final, this time in the European Champion Clubs' Cup for the

tie SL Benfica v FC Bayern Munchen, with the referee being John Gordon. Thomson had also run the line to Gordon in an Olympic Qualifier, Iceland v USSR, the previous season. Returning to FIFA status brought Thomson his first appointment to an Old Firm match. It speaks highly of his capabilities that he was appointed to referee the match again in each of the following two seasons when no longer a FIFA referee. Recognition of his services to the game was made by his being chosen for the League Cup Semi-Final between Rangers and Forfar Athletic in his last season on the List, 1977-78. He was one of the first referees to be captured by the introduction of the retiral age of 50 but he had no qualms with having to retire, being of the view that it would give younger men the chance of quicker promotion.

In 1989, as part of a revamp of the supervisory system, Thomson was appointed by the SFA as a Referee Supervisor for Edinburgh & District RA and he greatly appreciated the opportunity to give something back to refereeing. Another supervisory re-shuffle saw him being moved to Stirlingshire RA in 1991, where he served for nine seasons and was instrumental in developing the careers of the referees under his charge. He acted as a Match Assessor in season 1999-00 before retiring.

Jimmy Thomson
No. of seasons on List: 20 (1926-27 to 1947-48)
1 British International Championship match; 1 Amateur International; 1 League International; 1 Inter-Association match
1 Glasgow Cup Final; 2 Old Firm matches; 1 Irish Cup Final

Once he was admitted to the List, Jimmy Thomson took just a few seasons to establish himself at the top level as a referee. He enjoyed a golden spell in the two seasons from 1929-30, refereeing all his major appointments in this period. An Old Firm League match in October 1929 started the ball rolling. This was followed by an appointment to the Scottish Cup Semi-Final between Heart of Midlothian and Rangers in 1930 where he won the vote over four other referees nominated for the tie. He was then selected to be the Reserve Referee for the Final itself.

After taking charge of the Glasgow v Sheffield Inter-Association match in September 1930, he then had an exceptional run of appointments in October. His League International was the Scottish League v the Irish league on 8th October, the Glasgow Cup Final between Rangers and Celtic was on 11th October, and this sequence was concluded by refereeing England v Ireland in the British International Championship on 20th October.

Celtic submitted a complaint to the SFA about his handling of the Glasgow Cup Final and also issued it to the Press. The club was of the view that a Rangers player should have been sent off and that their players had allegedly been fouled to their injury repeatedly throughout the match without any action being taken, all of which were held to be disadvantageous to the club. A Celtic "goal" had also been disallowed. The Referee Committee "enjoined referees to entirely disregard the communication of Celtic FC to the Press". The Scottish Football Referees' Association consequently submitted a letter to the committee expressing their "very keen appreciation of the action taken" in the matter.

A further international came Thomson's way later in the season – the Amateur International between England and Wales in February 1931.

That was the last major appointment Thomson received. It is hard to escape the thought that the Glasgow Cup Final perhaps had an influence on his standing thereafter. Regardless, Thomson gave sterling service in the rest of his career. He also officiated regularly in Northern Ireland in the early to mid-1930's and was rewarded for his endeavours by being appointed to the 1932 Irish Cup Final between Linfield and Glentoran. His last two seasons on the List were as a Class 2 referee.

Joe Timmons
Date of Birth: 4th April 1952
Admitted to SFA List: 1977-78
No. of seasons at Class 1: 11 (1979-80 to 1983-84 and 1989-90 to 1994-95)
No. of years as a FIFA Referee: 3 (1992 to 1994)
1 A International

UEFA: 1 U21 Championship Qualifier; 3 U16 Championship Qualifiers; 2 Club Competition matches (1 ECWC, 1 UCL)
1 Challenge Cup Final; 1 Junior International; 1 Junior Cup Final

Joe Timmons' talent was indicated by his selection by the Scottish Junior FA to referee the 1977 Junior Cup Final at the age of 25 before he was on the SFA List. He was admitted the next season. Timmons was championed by Jack Mowat, then acting as the Referee Supervisor for Ayrshire RA, and was promoted mid-season to Class 2 and reached Class 1 for season 1979-80. In March 1978, he was selected as a linesman with Ian Foote on a European Cup Winners' Cup Quarter-Final, Real Betis Balompie v Dynamo Moskva and he took charge of his Junior International, Scotland v Wales, later that season.

A banker by profession, a job move took him to Newcastle-upon-Tyne in the autumn of 1983. He continued to referee and, starting from scratch, he quickly made his mark. He rose through the ranks of non-league football and he gained promotion to the Football League's Referee List for season 1987-88. By his second season, he was refereeing in the Second Division (now the English Championship).

His bank transferred him back to Scotland during 1989 and he was able to return to Class 1 for season 1989-90. His performances over the next couple of seasons took him to the FIFA List for 1992. The year augured well for him – a UEFA U16 Championship Qualifier between the Republic of Ireland and Wales in February kick-started his international refereeing career and this was followed by officiating at the Toulon U21 Tournament, where he refereed France v Mexico. An international friendly, Iceland v Israel, was handled in August and a tie in the Preliminary Round in the European Cup Winners' Cup in the Faroe Islands in September. Later that month however, he picked up a knee injury refereeing an amateur match when he was free from a Scottish League appointment. Injury to his knee struck again when he was officiating at the Challenge Cup Final in December and he had to be replaced by the Fourth Official midway through the first half.

In 1993, he handled a UEFA U21 Championship Qualifier in the Netherlands and a Champions League Qualifier at Spartak Moskva. Timmons fulfilled three Fourth Official appointments in the autumn of 1994 in European Championship Qualifiers. Knee injury problems continued to bedevil Timmons, unfortunately, and he chose to bow to the inevitable in November 1994 and resigned from the List.

Timmons had a career that promised so much when he started out and he could easily be forgiven for thinking "what if" on a few counts – what might have happened had he not been transferred by his employers to England, what might have happened had continued to work in England (refereeing in the First Division would surely have been in his grasp) and what might he have achieved had he not had to retire prematurely due to injury.

The SFA utilised Timmons as a Match Assessor from 1999 to 2002.

John Underhill
Date of Birth: 5th January 1961
Admitted to SFA List: 1991-92
No. of seasons at Class 1/Category 1: 14 (1994-95 to 2007-08)
No. of years as a FIFA Referee: 2 (2001 to 2002)
UEFA: 2 U21 Championship Qualifiers; 1 U19 Championship Qualifier; 1 U18 Championship Qualifier; 4 Club Competition matches (2 UC, 2 UIC)
1 Junior Cup Final

An Englishman, Underhill moved to Scotland in 1989 to take up a position as a lecturer in geophysics and geology at the University of Edinburgh. He had begun refereeing in 1980 in Bristol after playing for the University there and, after moving to Cardiff to continue his studies, graduated to refereeing in the Welsh League. A job move took him to the Netherlands where he continued to referee before another move to London led to him refereeing in the Southern League and the Football Conference.

Underhill started in Junior football when he moved to Scotland and was admitted to the SFA List within two seasons. His appointment to the Junior Cup Final between Glenafton Athletic and Largs Thistle in 1994, in his last season at Class 2, reflected the reputation he had developed in that grade of football. It is a Final remembered for four players (two from each side) being sent off for violent conduct.

Once at Class 1, Underhill's steady performances brought him into the top group of referees and he was rewarded with two years on the FIFA List. He enjoyed a variety of appointments from UEFA – an U18 Championship Qualifier, Denmark v Netherlands, an U19 Championship Qualifier, Belgium v Yugoslavia, and two U21 Championship Qualifiers – Slovenia v Russia and Estonia v Belgium. At club level, he refereed Intertoto Cup ties at Artmedia Petrzalka and 1.FC Kaiserslautern and UEFA Cup matches at Viking FK and Legia Warszawa.

During his spell as a FIFA referee, Underhill received 12 appointments as a Fourth Official, including three World Cup Qualifiers, one European Championship Qualifier and three Group matches in the Champions League.

Underhill was a popular figure amongst his fellow referees and was elected as the first President of the Scottish Senior Football Referees' Association when it was formed in 2005. He held the position for three years until he retired from refereeing.

Bob Valentine
Date of Birth: 10th May 1939
Admitted to SFA List: 1965-66
No. of seasons at Class 1: 18 (1971-72 to 1988-89)
No. of seasons/years as a FIFA Referee: 11 (1978-79 to 1986-87 and 1988)
2 A Internationals; 1 British International Championship match; 1 British Youth International Championship match
FIFA: World Cup (1982); 6 World Cup Qualifiers; U19 World Cup (1981); Olympics (1980); 1 Olympic Games Qualifier
UEFA: 2 European Championships (1984 and 1988); 2 European Championship Qualifiers; 33 Club Competition matches (11 ECCC (1 Q-F, 1 S-F), 5 ECWC (2 Q-F), 17 UC (3 Q-F, 2 S-F, 1 F)

3 Scottish Cup Finals; 4 League Cup Finals; 12 Old Firm matches

Bob Valentine ranks amongst the very best of Scottish referees. In his 11 years as a FIFA referee he established a record of achievements which will be hard to surpass. At national team level, he was selected for a World Cup, two European Championships, the Olympics and a FIFA U19 World Cup. At international club level, amongst a host of major appointments, he refereed a UEFA Cup Final and the UEFA Super Cup.

Valentine took up refereeing in 1961 and progressed to the SFA List for season 1965-66. He received an early introduction to international football during that first season when he was appointed as a linesman to a British Youth International Championship match, Scotland v Northern Ireland. Other international line appointments followed in the ensuing seasons, together with a Scottish Cup Semi-Final in 1967.

Promotion to Class 1 was gained for season 1971-72, during which he refereed England v. Northern Ireland in the British Youth International Championship. After taking a season or so to find his feet, Valentine's career began to take off during the mid-1970's, culminating in being appointed to the 1977 Scottish Cup Final between Celtic and Rangers, and reaching the FIFA List in 1978. His first A International was at the end of his debut season on the FIFA List –the Republic of Ireland against the world champions Argentina. After refereeing a couple of matches in the UEFA Club Competitions and an Olympic Qualifier, France v Belgium, during season 1979-80, Valentine received his first major appointment when he was selected as one of the 24 referees for the 1980 Olympics in Moscow. There, he ran the line in the opening match, USSR v Venezuela, and refereed the USSR's Group match against Cuba. Valentine had the honour of refereeing the Bronze Medal match, which rather incredibly, again featured the USSR, this time against Yugoslavia.

That the Olympics was Valentine's breakthrough is evidenced by the appointments he received the following season – ties at FC Bayern Munchen and Real Sociedad in the UEFA Club Competitions and two World Cup Qualifiers, one of which was

Malaysia v Thailand, a match played in Kuwait. His progress continued with selection for the third edition of the FIFA U19 World Cup, held in Australia, in 1981. After handling two Group matches, he was appointed to the Semi-Final between Romania and West Germany and was a linesman in the Final, West Germany v Qatar. His star was on the ascendancy and selection for the 1982 World Cup in Spain followed. In the first Group Stage, he was in charge of the infamous Austria v West Germany match, the two teams being happy to play out a 1-0 win for West Germany to ensure their advancement to the Second Group stage. Valentine was one of 12 referees retained for the latter stages, taking charge of Poland v USSR in the second Group Stage and being selected as a linesman for the Semi-Final, West Germany v France.

Valentine, a Dundonian who worked as a compositor for DC Thomson, was now firmly established in the top rank of UEFA's referees and he was selected for the 1984 European Championships in France. His selection gave him the distinction of becoming the first referee to officiate at the World Cup, the Olympics, the FIFA U19 World Cup and the European Championships. At the Finals, he officiated at the home nation's Group match against Belgium. Valentine repeated his selection for the European Championships four years later in West Germany, where he handled the host nation's Group match against Denmark.

The standing in which Valentine was regarded by the football authorities is encapsulated by what happened in April 1985. He had flown to Switzerland for a World Cup Qualifier against the USSR and, on his arrival, was advised by FIFA that he was being required to referee another Qualifier three days later, this time the United Arab Emirates against Saudi Arabia in Doha. The surprise appointment was certainly a bonus for his two linesmen, Kenny Hope and Norman Carnegy, who both had to hurriedly arrange further time away from work to assist Valentine.

Valentine was heavily used in the UEFA Club Competitions during the 1980's and he was called upon to handle many major appointments. In five years from 1983, he handled a remarkable total of six Quarter-Finals and three Semi-Finals in the three

Cups. In the European Cup Winners' Cup, he had a Quarter-Final, Dynamo Moskva v Larissa in 1985, and a Semi-Final, Club Atletico de Madrid v FK Crvena Zvedva, in 1986. In the UEFA Cup, he had three Quarter-Finals and two Semi-Finals, one of the latter being the 2nd Leg between Real Madrid CF and FC Internazionale Milano in 1985. The UEFA Cup, regularly regarded at the time as being the toughest European club competition to win, was Valentine's speciality in many ways and he was chosen to referee the 2nd Leg of the 1986 Final, 1.FC Koln v Real Madrid CF. He was also involved in the UEFA Cup Final the following year, when, in the days before the role of Fourth Official was formalised, he was used as the standby referee for Dundee United's home leg against IFK Goteburg.

He refereed Real Madrid CF again in the Semi-Final of the European Champion Clubs' Cup against FC Bayern Munchen in 1987. Valentine took charge of four Real Madrid CF matches in a three year period from 1985, the other being a home tie against Juventus in the 2nd Round of the European Champion Clubs' Cup in 1986.

Valentine's complemented his UEFA Cup Final appointment by being selected to handle the UEFA Super Cup Final 1st Leg between AFC Ajax and FC Porto in 1987-88, confirmation of the regard UEFA held for his abilities.

In domestic football, Valentine's tally of seven national Cup Finals (and eight Semi-Finals) over 12 years reflects his standing in the game. A particular highlight was being chosen to referee the two Dundee clubs in the 1980 League Cup Final. Three of his Finals were matches between the Old Firm. His first such match was the 1977 Scottish Cup Final and his last match before retiring was the 1989 Scottish Cup Final. Valentine also refereed the Old Firm in the 1979 Drybrough Cup Final, a pre-season competition.

Once he retired from refereeing, the SFA appointed Valentine as a Referee Supervisor for Angus & Perthshire RA. He served on the Referee Supervisors' Executive Committee from 1990 through to 2003 when it effectively became the Referee Committee. He was a member of that committee until 2009. From 2003 to 2005, Valentine was the last Chairman of the Referee Supervisors' Committee before the SFA changed its refereeing structure from Referee Supervisors to Association Managers and Referee Observers. He served as a Referee Observer until 2011.

Valentine was a UEFA Referee Observer for a number of years. Given his outstanding career as an international referee, it was no surprise when UEFA utilised his services as a Referee Mentor when it introduced its Talents programme in 2000. He fulfilled the role for five years, guiding the referees under his charge with the benefits of his vast experience.

Sgt-Major J. Vick
No. of seasons on List: 4 (1911-12 to 1913-14 and 1915-16)
1 League International
1 Glasgow Charity Cup Final (1913); 2 Old Firm matches

An instructor with the Army Gymnastic staff, and stationed at Maryhill Barracks, Vick had a relatively short career but in that time he developed a reputation as a highly capable referee.

His Old Firm matches were the New Year Derbies of 1913 and 1914. He was selected for the Scottish League's match against the Southern League in October 1913 and handled the 1914 Glasgow Charity Cup Final between Celtic and Third Lanark.

Vick refereed a benefit match held in 1913 for Jimmy Brownlie, Third Lanark's famous international goalkeeper, and was in charge of a Celtic v Everton friendly the following year. He was called up in August 1914 to serve in the First World War (as were eight other top referees of the time). Attached to the 2nd Yorkshire and Lancashire Regiment, Vick kept in touch "back home" by sending postcards to contacts he had in the Daily Record football staff. He was wounded in November 1914. During his time in Glasgow, he was also a prominent cricketer.

Andrew Waddell
Date of Birth: 26th September 1950
Admitted to SFA List: 1973-74
No. of seasons at Class 1: 20 (1978-79 to 1997-98)
No. of years as a FIFA Referee: 8 (1989 to 1996)
2 A Internationals; 1 B International
FIFA: 2 World Cup Qualifiers

UEFA: 1 European Championship Qualifier; 2 U21 Championship Qualifiers; 1 U18 Championship Qualifier; U16 Championships (1990); 1 Women's Championship Quarter-Final; 1 Women's Championship Qualifier; 11 Club Competition matches (2 ECCC (1 Q-F), 2 ECWC, 6 UC (1 Q-F), 1 UIC)
2 Old Firm matches; 1 Junior Cup Final

Andrew Waddell took up refereeing in 1965, initially in rugby before quickly moving to football, whilst a pupil at Hutcheson's School in Glasgow. Admitted to the SFA List in 1973, he was selected in his last season at Class 3A as a linesman to Alistair MacKenzie for a European Championship Quarter-Final between the USSR and Czechoslovakia in 1976. Whilst at Class 2, he refereed a Junior Cup Semi-Final in 1977 and the Final itself, between Bonnyrigg Rose and Stonehouse Violet, the following year.

Waddell, a medical scientist, made a good impression early in his Class 1 career, being chosen to referee a League Cup Semi-Final between Aberdeen and Morton in 1979-80 in his second season. Over the ensuing seasons, he slowly but surely established himself amongst the top Scottish referees. He came into the public eye in 1982 due to a famous photograph when he was confronted eyeball to eyeball by the Celtic manager, Billy McNeill, when officiating at a match against Aberdeen.

Waddell's performances brought him to the FIFA List for 1989. As a precursor to his elevation, he was selected as a linesman as part of Bob Valentine's team for the 1988 European Championships. He had a fairly quiet debut year, officiating at just a UEFA U18 Championship Qualifier in Denmark but that was followed by selection for the 1990 UEFA U16 Championships held in East Germany. The early 1990's proved to be his best years at international level. Appointments to matches at Brondby IF and Malmo FF in the UEFA Club Competitions were followed in 1990 by a Quarter-Final between the Netherlands and Denmark in the UEFA Women's European Championships. Despite his relative newness at that level, Waddell was appointed to a European Champion Clubs' Cup Quarter-Final, Real Madrid CF v Spartak Moskva in 1991.

Another Quarter-Final appointment was received in 1992, this time in the UEFA Cup – Torino v B1903 Kobenhavn. For only receiving 11 appointments in the UEFA Club Competitions, being selected to officiate at two Quarter-Finals was a remarkable achievement.

Waddell handled a European Championship Qualifier, Cyprus v USSR in 1991, with his two World Cup Qualifiers being the Baltic derby, Latvia v Lithuania, in 1992 and Luxembourg v Greece in 1993.

Waddell was the Fourth Official for the 1994 Scottish Cup Final between Dundee United and Rangers. He handled two Semi-Finals in the Scottish Cup, one of being an Old Firm match in 1992. That was his second such match, the first being a Quarter-Final in 1991 when he sent off three Rangers players. Graeme Souness, the Rangers manager, apologised for his players' behaviour afterwards. Waddell's decisions were entirely correct and encapsulated his trademark resolute approach to refereeing.

Injuries started to impact on Waddell in his latter years on the SFA List and he decided to retire two years early at 48. Waddell became involved with Preston Athletic some years later and acted as the Chairman of the Lowland League for a few years when the League was formed in 2013. He represented the League on the SFA Congress for a period and served on the SFA's Professional Game Board. In recent years Waddell has become Secretary of Edinburgh University.

Nick Walsh
Date of Birth: 23rd December 1990
Admitted to SFA List: 2009-10
No. of seasons at Class 1: 12 (2013-14 to 2024-25)
No. of years as a FIFA Referee: 8 (2018 to 2025)
3 A Internationals
FIFA: 1 World Cup Qualifier
UEFA: 2 European Championship Qualifiers; 1 Nations League match; U21 Championships (2025); 5 U21 Championship Qualifiers; 4 U17 Championship Qualifiers; 26 Club Competition matches (1 UCL (1LP), 11 UEL (1 PO, 3 G, 1 LP), 11 UECL (1 PO, 5 G, 2 LP), 3 UYL (1 R16)

2 Scottish Cup Finals; 1 League Cup Final; 1 Challenge Cup Final; 5 Old Firm matches; 1 Junior Cup Final

Nick Walsh marked himself out as a real talent as soon as he started refereeing and was admitted to the SFA List for 2009-10 aged 19. Appointed to the 2013 Junior Cup Final, he was promoted to Category 1 mid-way through season 2013-14. Two seasons later, he was refereeing in the Scottish Premiership and FIFA status was gained in 2018.

A UEFA U17 Championship qualifying tournament in Madeira in March started his international career and by the end of the year he had officiated at a Europa League Qualifier in Iceland and an U21 Championship Qualifier in Luxembourg.

The first of his three A Internationals was a friendly between Gibraltar and Estonia in March 2019. A year later, he was in charge of Wales against the USA and in 2022 he handled the Republic of Ireland and Belgium. His World Cup Qualifier was San Marino v Hungary in 2021 and in the European Championship Qualifiers he has refereed in Moldova and Andorra. He has handled matches in Finland and Lithuania in the Nations League.

Walsh, a PE Teacher, has been well used in the UEFA Club Competitions. After an initial period of receiving appointments in the Qualifying rounds, he has handled Play-Off ties in the Europa and Conference Leagues, five Group matches in the Conference League and three in the Europa League. Following the introduction of the new format for these competitions for season 2024-25, Walsh had two League Phase matches in the Conference League, one in the Europa League and one in the Champions League, a match between Stade Brestois and SK Sturm Graz. In the Youth League, he was appointed to a Round of 16 tie, Paris Saint-Germain v Sevilla in 2022.

The high point of his FIFA career to date was his selection as one of the 12 referees for the 2025 UEFA U21 Championships in Slovakia. He refereed two Group Matches – Portugal v Poland and Spain v Italy – and the Semi-Final between Germany and France.

Walsh's domestic performances have brought him the 2017 Challenge Cup Final, the 2021 and 2024 Scottish Cup Finals and the 2023 League Cup Final. His last two Finals have been matches between the Old Firm. He has controlled five such games to date and to do so before the age of 35 is testament to his qualities and his refereeing skills. Small in stature, he has exuded natural authority during matches throughout his career.

Hugh Watson
No. of seasons on List: 17(1925-26 to 1941-42)
4 British International Championship matches; 2 Amateur Internationals; 3 League Internationals; 2 Inter-Association matches
2 Scottish Cup Finals; 2 Glasgow Charity Cup Finals; 8 Old Firm matches;1 Junior Cup Final

Watson had thoughts of becoming a senior player when he started playing in goals for Sighthill UF in the Glasgow Churches League. After two seasons, he progressed into Junior football with Kilsyth Emmett. His time as a player was brought to an end after a number of injuries and in 1922 he decided to take up refereeing. Starting off in the Glasgow Churches League, by the following season, he was refereeing in Junior football. He continued to progress and was included in the Scottish League's List in 1925. He was operating in the First Division within a couple of seasons and quickly established himself, going on to become one of the top referees of the 1930's.

International honours soon came his way and, in the three seasons from 1930-31, he handled nine such matches. His first was the League International between the Irish League and the Football League in September 1930. In the next two months, he was appointed to the Amateur International, Ireland v England, and the British International Championship match, Wales v England. All told, he did five "Ireland v England" matches at various levels, either in Ireland or England. He refereed a home Scottish League International just once, in October 1932, against the Irish League.

Watson refereed in Ireland from 1929-30 through to the mid-1930's. He quickly developed a fine reputation there and in that first season he was appointed to the County Antrim Shield

Final. He was held in high regard and was even popular, a relatively rare thing for a referee to be. He was considered to be "one of the best Scotland has sent us since the days of Tom Robertson", which was a compliment indeed. He was considered to keep himself in condition and to be fit to follow play, something which was not always the case with other referees.

When Watson refereed in Ireland, it was predominantly in Northern Ireland but occasionally he officiated in the League of Ireland. After the end of a Dundalk v Shelbourne match in 1931 he was seen running off the pitch and was subsequently given an escort by Civic Guards. He might not have been so popular at that match!

Watson was known for his courteous and confident manner and his ability to control players and to be close to play. Tact was used in the British International Championship Match, Ireland v England, in 1933, when, after the English player Cliff Bastin was carried off injured, he seemed to be on the point of sending off the Irish player who had fouled him but appeared to change his mind once he realised that the Irish player was injured himself.

In addition to his two Scottish Cup Finals of 1935 and 1938, Watson also handled a Semi-Final in 1932.

In 1933-34, Watson had a remarkable run of five consecutive Old Firm matches. On top of doing the two League matches, the Semi-Final of the Glasgow Cup went to a replay and he finished with the Glasgow Charity Cup Final.

Watson did two matches in one Monday in September 1934. Firstly, he refereed Aberdeen v Kilmarnock in the League at 11:00am and then officiated at the Jack Harkness benefit match, Heart of Midlothian v Huddersfield Town, later that day.

He lectured to the Highland Referees' Association in Inverness in January 1935 on the "problems of refereeing", a talk which was open to the public. His popularity in Northern Ireland was reflected by being appointed to referee a Schoolboys' International against Wales in 1938. He decided to retire from refereeing at the end of season 1941-42, along with his good friend Mungo Hutton.

Lorraine Watson (nee Clark)
Date of Birth: 12th June 1985
Admitted to SFA List: 2005-06
No. of seasons at Category 1 Development: 5 (2017-18 to 2020-21)
No. of years as a FIFA Referee: 13 (2013 to 2025)
No. of years as a FIFA Assistant Referee: 2 (2010 to 2011)
10 A Internationals
FIFA: 6 Women's World Cup Qualifiers
UEFA: 7 Women's European Championship Qualifiers; Women's U19 Championships (2015); 20 Women's Champions League matches (6 QG, 4 G, 5 R32, 4 R16); As Fourth Official: 2 Women's European Championships (2017 and 2022); Women's U17 Championships (2013) Women's Champions League matches (2 R32; 2 S-F)
3 Scottish Women's Cup Finals; 4 SWPL League Cup Finals;2 SWFL Cup Finals

Lorraine Watson has had an exceptional career as a referee. In domestic football she progressed further than any other female as a referee, spending five seasons as a Category 1 Development referee. At this category, she refereed several matches in SPFL League 2. In her last season at Category 2, she refereed Linlithgow Rose v Auchinleck Talbot in the 1st Leg of a Junior Cup Semi-Final in 2017.
She built up a bank of experience as an assistant referee across a wide range of women's competitions in international football before spending two years from 2010 as a FIFA Assistant Referee. Her experience as an assistant was added to domestically when she was re-classified to Category 3 in January enabling her to run the line in the Scottish League. An appointment to a Rangers v Berwick Rangers Third Division match in January 2013 generated excellent publicity for her and for females in refereeing.
Once she became a FIFA referee in 2013, Watson quickly established herself in European football and in her first year she was selected as a Fourth Official for the UEFA Women's U17 Championships, held in Wales. Two years later, she was one of the referees for the UEFA Women's U19 Championships in

Israel. Qualifiers in the Women's European Championships and the Women's World Cup followed with some significant appoints such as Austria v Norway and Croatia v Denmark. Watson was twice selected as a Fourth Official for the Women's European Championships – in the Netherlands in 2017 and in England in 2022. In the first Finals, she was one of two referees selected for the role and she had seven appointments, including the Germany v Denmark Quarter-Final. Amongst her friendly international appointments was Germany v France in 2018, the year in which she was included in UEFA's Elite Category for women referees, and Australia v South Africa (a match played in England).

At club level, she has had 20 matches in the UEFA Women's Champions League. Beyond involvement in the qualification and group stages, she has received regular appointments to the knock-out rounds with four in the Round of 16. As a Fourth Official, she officiated with a team of Romanian officials at a Semi-Final between FC Barcelona and Paris Saint-Germain in 2017.

In recent seasons, becoming a mother twice has interrupted her career as has some injury spells. This resulted in her choosing to drop down to Category 4 in Scottish domestic football. She has a fine record in refereeing in the various Women's Cup Finals in Scotland.

Willie Webb

Date of Birth: 8th April 1904
Died: 21st August 1973 aged 69
No. of seasons on List: 24 (1927-28 to 1949-50)
No. of seasons as a FIFA Referee: 3 (1947-48 to 1949-50)
4 A internationals; 9 British International Championship matches; 1 Wartime Representative match; 3 League Internationals; 3 Amateur Internationals
1 Scottish Cup Final; 1 League Cup Final; 4 Glasgow Cup Finals; 1 Glasgow Charity Cup Final; 4 Old Firm matches; 3 Junior Internationals; 2 Junior Cup Finals

Willie Webb was one of the leading Scottish referees of the 1930's and 1940's. Refereeing in the Scottish League from

1930, a significant early appointment was the 1931 Glasgow Cup Final between Queen's Park and Rangers. His first international was the Amateur match between Scotland and England in 1934. The first of his nine British International Championship matches followed in 1935, England against Ireland. Over the next two years he refereed the England and Ireland fixture three more times (once in England and twice in Ireland). In this period he also refereed two England and Wales matches. After the Second World War he did a further two Ireland and England matches and one other England v Wales match.

Remarkably, Webb refereed England in 12 internationals. He was in charge of the international played between Scotland and England to mark the Silver Jubilee of King George V in 1935, a friendly in the Republic of Ireland in 1946 and a home match against Sweden in 1947. Webb also refereed a Republic of Ireland international against Germany in 1936. The quality of these appointments demonstrate the standing in which Webb was held within football during his career. That regard was also shared by the Scottish Junior FA as it engaged him to referee three internationals between 1934 and 1936 and two Junior Cup Finals in 1935 and 1939. His first Old Firm match came in 1935, in the Glasgow Cup Final. Webb was much in demand in the mid-1930's.

After refereeing three Semi-Finals in the preceding seasons, Webb was appointed to the 1939 Scottish Cup Final, Clyde v Motherwell. Like other referees of his time, the Second World War interrupted his career. He handled just one Representative match during the War – the SFA XI v FA XI in 1940. In domestic football, he was appointed to the Wartime Emergency Cup Final, Dundee United v Rangers, in 1940 and the Southern League Cup Final between Rangers and Motherwell in 1945. The Southern League Cup Final of 1946 between Rangers and Aberdeen was also in his charge.

Webb was still very much to the fore after the Second World War, refereeing five internationals and two League internationals between 1946 and 1948. In May 1948, he was invited by the Portuguese FA to referee Arsenal's tour matches against SL Benfica and Oporto. The 1949 League Cup Final,

East Fife v Dunfermline Athletic was his last major domestic appointment.

After working as a train engine driver, Webb became a school attendance officer/inspector for Glasgow Education Authority. Given his standing within Scottish refereeing, he was an obvious choice to become a Referee Supervisor for Glasgow, Lanarkshire, Dunbartonshire and Renfrewshire RA when the SFA introduced its refereeing structure in 1945. As a few others did, he combined the role with refereeing and gave many talks on the Laws of the Game at boys' clubs throughout the West of Scotland. During 1948, Webb made a few appearances on a BBC radio sports programme, discussing the Laws and aspects of the game with a supporter. The cut and thrust of the discussions were well received.

In the autumn of 1948, speculation emerged that Webb might become a Referee Inspector for the Scottish League, as the creation of such a position was under consideration by the League. This eventually materialised in November 1949 when Webb was one of four Inspectors appointed by the League, the others being two former players and a former referee, John Scott. This appointment by necessity led to Webb's resignation as a referee and a Referee Supervisor. Just prior to accepting the League's position, Webb had been nominated by the SFA to FIFA as a potential candidate for the 1950 World Cup.

Webb's had been a fine career, being considered to have been one of Britain's best referees, and renowned for his fitness and ability to keep up with play. He was known for not being able to be intimidated no matter how hostile the atmosphere was and for retaining a sense of humour when refereeing.

Archie Webster
Date of Birth: 8th February 1927
Died: 14th July 2008 aged 81
Admitted to SFA List: 1957-58
No. of seasons at Class 1: 13 (1962-63 to 1974-75)
No. of seasons as a FIFA Referee: 3 (1964-65 to 1965-66 and 1973-74)

2 A internationals; 1 British International Championship match; 1 British Amateur International Championship match; 4 U23 Internationals
FIFA: 1 World Cup Qualifier
1 Summer Cup Final; 1 Old Firm match

After taking five seasons to reach Class 1, Archie Webster quickly made a favourable impression with his performances as he became a FIFA referee after his second season at Class 1. An U23 friendly international between Wales and England in October 1964 was his first match as a FIFA referee. He closed the season by refereeing a Scottish Cup Semi-Final, Motherwell v Celtic and handling both legs of the Scottish League's Summer Cup Final between Motherwell and Dundee United.
The following season 1965-66, was his best. After refereeing a Rangers friendly against SL Benfica in late September, he was in charge of the Wales v England match in the British International Championship the week after. Later in October, he handled Denmark v USSR in a World Cup Qualifier. His star was so in the ascendancy at this stage that he was nominated by the SFA, along with Hugh Phillips, as a potential candidate for the 1966 World Cup in England. Although he missed out on selection to Phillips, the highlight of his international career came at the end of the season as he travelled to Brazil with Tom Wharton and Willie Syme in May and June to referee some of Brazil's preparatory matches for the World Cup. Webster took charge of matches Brazil played against Poland and Czechoslovakia.
Webster's two season stint as a FIFA referee came to an end at that point as he had been overtaken in the domestic rankings by another referee. Webster returned to the FIFA List for 1973-74 but he did not receive any appointments as a referee during that season, nor, rather unusually, as a linesman. However, in the period between his two spells as a FIFA referee, he did receive a number of international refereeing appointments. He was appointed to England v Wales U23 matches in 1969 and 1972 and a British Amateur International Championship match, Wales v Northern Ireland, in 1971.

Webster also refereed an U23 friendly between Norway and France in September 1971, the day before he ran the line to John Paterson in a European Championship Qualifier between the two countries.

These appointments which Webster received suggest that he must have been almost continuously on the fringes of returning to the FIFA List. He was certainly a reliable referee over his career, as is evidenced by his appointment to an Old Firm match in 1969 and another Scottish Cup Semi-Final, Hibernian v Rangers, in 1972.

A shopkeeper in Stirlingshire, Webster was persuaded by the SFA to take up the position of Referee Supervisor for Fife RA in May 1975, which cut short his Class 1 career. In that role, he gave sterling service to the SFA for 24 years. He was a member of the Referee Supervisors' Executive Committee for 19 seasons and was the Vice-Chairman for seven of these. He acted as a Match Assessor for season 1999-00 before retiring. Webster also acted as a Referee Observer for UEFA for a period.

Tom Wharton
Date of Birth: 3rd November 1927
Died: 9th May 2005 aged 77
Admitted to SFA List: 1948-49
No. of seasons at Class 1: 17 (1951-52, 1956-57 to 1970-71)
No. of seasons as a FIFA Referee: 13 (1958-59 to 1970-71)
8 A Internationals; 3 British International Championship matches; 1 British Youth International Championship match; 1 B International; 1U23 International; 4 League Internationals
FIFA: 2 World Cup Qualifiers
UEFA: 2 European Championship Qualifiers; 25 Club Competition matches (6 ECCC (2 Q-F), 5 ECWC (2 Q-F, 1 F), 14 ICFC)
4 Scottish Cup Finals; 4 League Cup Finals; 4 Glasgow Cup Finals; 2 Glasgow Charity Cup Finals; 23 Old Firm matches

Tom Wharton, an imposing and commanding figure, is a giant of refereeing in all senses of the word. He is undoubtedly one of the most significant figures produced by Scottish refereeing and, through his decade-long membership of the FIFA Referees' Committee, he also had a great influence on refereeing world-wide. Instantly recognisable, he became popularly known by his nick-name of "Tiny" – the complete opposite of his standing six foot four inches tall and weighing 15 stone.

Raised in the East End of Glasgow, Wharton played as a defender for Calton Parish in the Glasgow Churches League and was a member of the Scottish Churches Youth Cup-winning team of 1945-46. He was introduced to refereeing at the start of the following season when he was asked to referee his team's game when the appointed official did not turn up. After the match the opposing team's secretary suggested to Wharton, without wishing to cause any offence, that he would make a better referee than a player. Then aged 18, Wharton went to the referee training classes in January 1947 and passed the examination with a mark of 86. At a time when there was an acute shortage of referees, Wharton could have refereed almost every night of the week in the spring. Experience was gained and it was soon suggested that to him that he should consider moving from amateur to Junior football. The advice was taken and Wharton quickly made his mark, being selected to referee an international between Scotland and the Republic of Ireland in 1948 after just 12 Junior matches.

Identified as a talent, he was admitted to the SFA's List midway through season 1948-49. Wharton's first appointment in senior football was as a linesman to Peter Craigmyle and, two games later, he ran the line to Jack Mowat. His progress was rapid, being promoted to Class 1 for season 1951-52, aged 24. However, after just one season, he returned to Class 2 where he gained more experience over the next three seasons. Promotion back to Class 1 was achieved for season 1955-56 and Wharton never looked backed, serving the game with distinction for the next 16 seasons. During season 1955-56, he was chosen to referee Scotland's British Youth International Championship match against England. FIFA status was reached after two seasons. His first season as a FIFA referee was ended by officiating the British International Championship match, Northern Ireland v Wales.

Wharton's first international friendly, Iceland v West Germany, in August 1960 was followed a couple of months later by a World Cup Qualifier, Sweden v Belgium. Season 1961-62 was his first in the UEFA Club Competitions and, remarkably, after just two matches, he refereed a Quarter-Final, 1.FC Nurnberg v SL Benfica, in the European Champion Clubs' Cup, and then a Final, Club Atletico de Madrid v AC Fiorentina in the European Cup Winners' Cup, a match played at Hampden Park.

Over the next decade, Wharton would be appointed to an impressive four Quarter-Finals and three Semi-Finals in these competitions. The Quarter-Finals, in the European Champion Clubs' Cup and the European Cup Winners' Cup, featured clubs such as Real Madrid CF, FC Bayern Munchen, Juventus and Olympic Lyonnais. His Semi-Final appointments were all in the Inter-Cities Fairs Cup – Valencia CF v AS Roma in 1963, RSC Anderlecht v FC Internazionale Milano in 1970 and the all-English clash between Leeds United and Liverpool in 1971.

A significant chapter of Wharton's career came prior to the 1966 World Cup when he travelled to Brazil with Willie Syme and Archie Webster to referee some of Brazil's many preparatory matches. He refereed two matches against Wales and one against Chile. Wharton fulfilled his ambition of refereeing at Wembley when he took charge of England's British International Championship match against Wales in November 1966. In the Qualifiers for the 1968 European Championships he controlled Netherlands v West Germany and Italy v Switzerland. He was in charge of Switzerland again in its match against Romania in a World Cup Qualifier in 1969.

Wharton's standing in the game during the 1960's was reflected in his being chosen to referee a couple of prestigious club friendlies in England – Manchester United v SL Benfica in 1962 and Chelsea v Real Madrid CF in 1965. In 1969, he flew to Toronto to take charge of a challenge match between AC Milan and AC Sparta Praha for the Canadian National Exhibition Cup of Champions.

In domestic football, Wharton's rise through the ranks was rewarded by being selected for the first of eight national Cup Finals when he was appointed to the 1960 League Cup Final between Rangers and Kilmarnock. His first Scottish Cup Final,

Rangers v St. Mirren, followed in 1962. Wharton was closely associated with Old Firm matches during his career, officiating 23 games over 12 seasons, a remarkably tally. He refereed three Scottish Cup Finals (1963, 1966 and 1971), two League Cup Finals (1966 and 1970) and the Glasgow Cup Final (1970) between the clubs. Each of the Scottish Cup Finals was drawn. Amongst colleagues in the refereeing world, Wharton often made play, jokingly, of being able to secure a replay. (That had failed him though in his Cup Winners' Cup Final. The drawn match was played again early the following season in West Germany and refereed by Kurt Tschenscher).

The 1971 Scottish Cup Final was his last match in Scottish football as he chose to retire, aged 44, after handling a friendly international between Sweden and West Germany in June. It was a wise choice to go out at the top. He was no doubt aware of the physical demands of continuing and the effort that needed. Given his size, he was never renowned for getting about the pitch but he put great store in his positioning to indentify foul play and being in command of the game. He was also well known for using his sense of humour to control players. In professional life, Wharton had trained as a draughtsman in the steel industry and after completing his apprenticeship, started his own business as a structural engineer. By the time of his retiral, his business commitments were increasing and he required time to devote to them.

He was not lost to refereeing and football though. The second half of his refereeing career began when the SFA appointed him as a Referee Supervisor for Glasgow RA immediately after he retired. He became Vice-Chairman of the Referee Supervisors' Committee in 1975 and succeeded Jack Mowat as the Chairman in 1990. He served in that role until the end of season 2002-03. At a time when the SFA's committee structures were starting to change, he was appointed as a co-opted member of the Referee Committee from 2001 to 2003. In his time as a Referee Supervisor, he contributed a great deal to Scottish refereeing, with many a referee benefitting from his words of wisdom. He was very much in the mould of a "wily politician" and at times during his Vice-Chairmanship it often seemed that it was him against the rest of committee as he fought to look after his

Glasgow referees. That said, he was a dogged defender of the interests of refereeing and he made the most of his stature to get his point of view across a range of football business.

These qualities were put to good use when Wharton was appointed to the FIFA Referees' Committee in 1980 in place of Jack Mowat. In that role, he was very influential in ensuring that Scottish referees were appointed to FIFA competitions during a decade of service on the committee. In 1986, he was charged with supervising the referees' course at the World Cup in Mexico. His tenure on the committee ended after the 1990 World Cup, following the appointment of David Will, a former SFA President, as Chairman of the committee. FIFA recognised Wharton twice – firstly, in 1976 when it bestowed its Special Award and Diploma on him in recognition of his services to refereeing, (the award was presented to him at an SFA Council meeting in May 1976) and secondly in 1994 when he was awarded the Order of Merit in Gold Award, the first and only referee ever to be a recipient. In its media release announcing the award, FIFA referred to him as "always having made a stylish impression, partly because of his striking stature that must have deterred many a player from muttering a meek protest" and of having "had that rare quality of showing the players firmly but politely who was in charge on the field, without inhibiting their play."

Wharton's business background played a part in another role which he fulfilled for many years from 1980 – as a member of the United Kingdom's Football Grounds Improvement Trust and then of its successor body, the Football Trust, of which he was Vice-Chairman from 1990 to 2000. The Trusts disbursed funds received from football pools companies to British clubs for ground improvements. Wharton played an invaluable role in directing over £100 million to many Scottish clubs for stadium improvements over his period as a member of the Trust. The Scottish Junior FA presented for a number of years the Tom Wharton Award to the referee of the Junior Cup Final, as a means of recognising Wharton's role with the Trust and for the part he played in the provision of funding for its member clubs.

Wharton stepped down as Chairman of the Referee Supervisors at the end of the 2003 Referees' Conference, commanding respect as he always did for his chairing of proceedings. Glasgow RA held a Gala Dinner later in the year in his honour and to mark his contribution to refereeing and to football. Wharton is the only referee who has been inducted into Scottish Football's Hall of Fame.

Alex Williamson
No. of seasons on List: 13(1925-26 to 1938-39)
2 League Internationals; 1 Inter-Association match

Prior to getting on to the Scottish League's List, Williamson had a fall-out with the Scottish Football Referees' Association, resigning from its membership and strongly protesting about being fined £5 by it for allegedly touting for an appointment in the Dunbartonshire Cup. He soon returned to the fold and quickly made his mark by handling his two League internationals, both between the Football League and the Irish League in 1927 and 1928. He also refereed the Glasgow v Sheffield Inter-Association match in 1928.
In later life, he was the Scottish Secretary of the British Empire Cancer Campaign.

Hugh Williamson
Date of Birth: 28th December 1945
Admitted to SFA List: 1976-77
No. of seasons at Class 1: 14 (1981-82 to 1994-95)
No. of years as a FIFA Referee: 1 (1992)
UEFA: 1 Club Competition match (1 ECWC)
1 Challenge Cup Final; 1 Junior International

Hugh Williamson, who took up refereeing in 1970 after playing amateur football, was the last Scot to be admitted to the FIFA List when in his 40's. He served just one year on the List due to FIFA's decision to lower the retiral age of international referees from 46 to 45. As he turned 47 at the end of 1992, it was a brief time on the List. Nonetheless, Williamson had realised his ambition to become a FIFA referee, and although he received just one appointment as a referee in that year - a UEFA Cup tie in Finland between Turun Palloseura and Trabzonspor - he was selected as a Fourth Official for three matches. Two were with Brian McGinlay - in the European Cup Winners' Semi-Final between AS Monaco and Feyenoord, and the 2nd Leg of the UEFA U21 Championship Final between Sweden and Italy. The third match was a World Cup Qualifier between Lithuania and Latvia, refereed by Andrew Waddell. He was also a linesman to Jim McCluskey in an international friendly between England and Brazil.

During his career, Williamson, a training instructor with an assurance company, had received a good number of international line appointments, his most memorable being the UEFA Cup Semi-Final 2nd Leg, Real Madrid CF v FC Internazionale Milano, in 1986, a match refereed by Bob Valentine. Williamson had operated with Valentine previously, his early promise at Class 1 leading to his being chosen to be part of Valentine's team at the 1984 European Championships. As part of the preparations for the Finals, Valentine and his team officiated at a UEFA Cup Quarter-Final between HNK Hadjuk Split and AC Sparta Praha.

During the 1980's, Williamson was regularly appointed by the SFA to referee Youth international friendlies and as a linesman for various home matches in the UEFA U16 and U18 Championship Qualifiers. In 1990, he refereed a match played between the Shetland Islands and the Faroe Islands, a game arranged to assist the Faroese following their recent admission into UEFA membership. The deployment of Williamson on such games indicates his capabilities and his one year as a FIFA referee was due reward for his application and commitment. That was reflected in his appointment to the 1994 Challenge Cup Final between Dundee and Airdrieonians in his final season on the List.

Williamson was appointed by the SFA as a Match Assessor in February 1999 and he served in that role through to the end of the following season.

Willie Young
Date of Birth: 21st December 1955
Admitted to SFA List: 1985-86
No. of seasons at Class 1: 15 (1990-91 to 2004-05)

No. of years as a FIFA Referee: 6 (1994 to 1999)
No. of years as a FIFA Linesman: 2 (1992 to 1993)
6 A Internationals; 2 U21 Internationals
FIFA: 1 World Cup Qualifier
UEFA: 1 European Championship Qualifier; 3 U21 Championship Qualifiers; 3 U18 Championship Qualifiers; 15 Club Competition Appointments (2 ECWC, 8 UC, 1 UCL, 4 UIC); 1 Women's Championship Qualifier; 1 Women's Championship Semi-Final 2nd Leg
1 Scottish Cup Final; 1 League Cup Final; 1 Challenge Cup Final; 4 Old Firm matches; 1 Junior International; 1 Junior Cup Final

Willie Young, a player with Craigmark Burntonians in the Ayrshire Juniors in the mid-1970's, freely admits that his whole approach to refereeing was changed as a result of receiving his first international appointment as a linesman with David Syme, on the UEFA Cup match, FC Nantes Atlantique v Torino in 1986. Up to that point, Young regarded refereeing to be a hobby and a way of continuing to have an involvement in football after he finished playing. The whole experience of being on the match opened his eyes to the opportunity that refereeing could offer. Then at Class 3A, he wanted a piece of the action as a referee and determined to reach Class 1 and then to get on to the FIFA List. His ambitions were achieved. He became a Class 1 referee in 1990, after refereeing that year's Junior Cup Final, and achieved FIFA status in 1992 as a linesman. After two years in that role, he became a FIFA referee in 1994.
In his two years as a FIFA linesman, he had various appointments in World Cup Qualifiers and UEFA Club Competition matches which helped him gain experience for becoming a FIFA referee. A notable appointment was running the line to Jim McCluskey in an England v Brazil friendly in 1992.
Young's first taste of international football as a referee came at the 1994 Toulon U21 Tournament, where he refereed France and the USA. Season 1994-94 brought his first A International, a friendly between Sweden and Lithuania, and saw him handle a UEFA Women's Championship Qualifier, Germany v

Switzerland, and a 2nd leg of a Semi-Final in the competition between Sweden and Norway. After early appointments in the UEFA Youth Championships, appointments to ties in the UEFA Club Competitions were regularly received, most predominantly in the UEFA Cup. He was in charge of ties such as FC Dinamo Minsk v Lillestrom SK, AS Roma v FC Zurich and Udinese Calcio v Polonia Warszawa.

Amongst his A Internationals, Young refereed three Northern Ireland friendlies against opponents of the quality of Germany, France and Yugoslavia. A trip to Hong Kong in 1998 for the Carlsberg Cup tournament saw him referee a match between Egypt and Bulgaria. Georgia v Greece was refereed in the European Championship Qualifiers in 1999 and he was in charge of Norway v Armenia in a World Cup Qualifier in 2000.

Young had 14 Fourth Official appointments during his career, the highlight being his appointment to the 1999 UEFA Cup Final, AC Parma v Olympique Marseille, in Moscow, as part of Hugh Dallas' team.

A lawyer, Young was a dominant personality in domestic football throughout his career. He displayed great strength in controlling matches, stood no nonsense but also used his sense of humour as a tool to exert control and diffuse situations. Young refereed nine Semi-Final ties and the Final of each of the three national Cup Finals, a total which speaks highly of his capabilities, particularly as one of the Semi-Finals was an Old Firm match. These appointments were due reward for a highly successful time as a referee. He was hampered by fitness issues in the latter stages of his career but the 2005 League Cup Final between Livingston and Hibernian capped his time on the List before retirement.

An accomplished after-dinner speaker, Young took time out from refereeing for a couple of years before being appointed by the SFA as a Referee Observer in 2007. He became a member of the Referee Committee in 2009 and was appointed its Chairman in 2019. Young also acts as a Referee Observer for UEFA. It is safe to say that the goal he set himself in 1986 was more than achieved, and then some.

Ernie Youngson
Born: 1923
Died: 2002 aged 79
Admitted to SFA List: 1953-54
No. of seasons at Class 1: 2 (1955-56 and 1956-57)
No. of seasons as a FIFA Referee: 1 (1956-57)
1 Junior Cup Final

Ernie Youngson, an Aberdonian, had a very brief career as a referee on the SFA List. He gained admittance after refereeing a Junior Cup Semi-Final and the Final itself, between Vale of Leven and Annbank United, in 1953. Class 1 was reached two seasons later followed by FIFA status the season after, albeit in the Deputy category. The hand of Peter Craigmyle, also an Aberdonian and the Chairman of the SFA Referee Supervisors' Committee during the 1950's, can be perhaps detected behind Youngson's meteoric rise. There is no known record of Youngson having received an international appointment at any time during his career.

In domestic football, Youngson came to notice on a few occasions. In December 1955, he allegedly stopped a Hibernian v Celtic match four minutes early. The following year he caused a stir by consulting the captains of Dundee and Airdrieonians as to whether they felt if the light was good enough to continue the match. The SFA was apparently none too happy about his action, as it weakened the view that the referee is the sole judge of everything relating to the game. On a happier note, a newspaper report on an East Fife v Celtic match in March 1957 complimented him on his good decisions which had been indicated by "quite magnificent gestures". It is not known why Youngson's career ended after season 1956-57.

A janitor at an Aberdeen Primary School where he took the football team, Youngson had a pivotal role in identifying and nurturing the talent of the future Aberdeen player Neale Cooper.

Linesmen/Assistant Referees

1891 was an important year in the development of the Laws of the Game due to the formalisation of the roles of referee and linesmen. The role of the linesman, however, remained subservient to that of referees for many years. For major matches such as internationals and Cup Finals, the linesmen continued to be appointed from those holding positions with associations and leagues. Presidents and other Office Bearers regularly filled the role. As clubs provided their own linesman for their matches, it was no doubt a natural thing to carry things through in the same manner for such games. This approach carried through to the late 1920's. For international matches, the Scots' linesman was selected from the members of the SFA's Selection Committee. Similarly, members of the Scottish League's Management Committee acted as linesmen in League Internationals. Referee Committee members officiated at Scottish Cup Semi-Finals and Finals. Slowly but surely, change occurred. The early 1930's saw referees being utilised as linesmen on a more regular basis, with the top referees of the day tending to be appointed.

The appointment of linesmen evolved in the post-war period, with direction being given by FIFA that linesmen for internationals should be drawn from officials who regularly acted in the role. That enabled selections to be made from Classes 3A and 3B. Over time, that altered to Class 3A only, and by the 1980's the SFA adopted an approach where each Class 3A official stood the chance of receiving one international appointment during the time spent at that category. By this time, Class 1 referees were appointed as the senior linesman, for the purposes of taking over from the referee in the event of injury or illness. FIFA referees acted as the senior linesman in World Cup Qualifiers from the 1970's. In several instances, such appointments as a linesman were the only international appointments that a FIFA referee might receive. The only time these referees acted as a linesman was on an international appointment, which was not actually doing much favour for the game in which he was officiating, nor for the official himself.

It took football a long time to reach the point where referees who regularly operated as linesmen were deemed necessary and appropriate for international football, given that the roles of referee and linesman are quite distinct. The turning point was the 1990 World Cup, where much concern was expressed on the standard of officiating. This led to FIFA introducing linesmen into the International List for 1992 and the sense in doing so has been of huge benefit to the game. It is worth noting comment made by Peter Craigmyle in a talk in Northern Ireland in 1952 when he said he "did not believe many were capable of being a great referee and a great linesman. It was as great an achievement to be a great linesman as to be a great referee."

The door was opened to referees to forge a career as an international linesman, or assistant referee, as the role was renamed in 1996. In the first few years, several Class 1 referees served in the role, given that at the time they were regularly operating as linesmen in domestic football. Several linesmen were drawn from Class 2 on the same basis. Once the SFA created the category of Specialist Assistant Referee in 1998, a proper pathway was created for referees to follow. Not every referee will make it to Category 1 but going down the route of becoming a Specialist Assistant Referee provides a chance of progressing to the FIFA List.

Many of the Scottish FIFA linesmen/assistant referees have enjoyed excellent careers and have received a sizeable amount of significant appointments in their own right. One thing that the creation of the role of an international assistant referee has undoubtedly achieved is that recognition can be received on merit on an individual basis and in that respect the approach taken by FIFA and UEFA in recent years to directly select assistant referees for major competitions has been of huge benefit to the individuals concerned.

By way of illustration, Martin Cryans was selected by FIFA for the 2004 Olympics in Athens and, after officiating at two group matches, was appointed to a Quarter-Final, a Semi-Final and then the Gold Medal Final match, an outstanding achievement. Other male assistant referees have often been selected for the Finals of UEFA competitions at Under Age level. Kylie Cockburn had an exceptional record at international level, being selected for two FIFA Women's U17 World Cups in Jordan (2016) and Uruguay (2018) (where she officiated at the 3rd/4th Place Match) and the 2019 Women's World Cup in France where she was officiated at a Round of 16 tie.

In recent years, the number of appointments fulfilled by assistants can be huge, particularly if a long career is enjoyed. That is only possible by maintaining a very high standard of performance in both domestic and international football. Assistant referees regularly receive criticism for perceived failings but their worth is fully appreciated by their refereeing colleagues.

FIFA Linesmen-Assistant Referees

Molly Alexander
Date of Birth: 29th May 1978
No. of seasons on SFA List: 5 (2017-18 to 2021-22)
No. of seasons as Category 4 Referee: 5 (2017-18 to 2021-22)
No. of years as a FIFA Assistant Referee: 4 (2017-2020)
4 Women's A Internationals;
UEFA: 1 Women's European Championship Qualifier; 4 Women's Champions League matches (2 R32, 2 R16); 3 Women's U19 Championship Qualifiers
1 Scottish Women's Cup Final

Graeme Alison
Date of Birth: 24th April 1959
No. of seasons on SFA List: 19 (1986-87 to 2004-05)
No. of seasons at Class 1: 5 (1994-95 to 1998-99)
No. of seasons as Specialist Assistant Referee: 5 (1999-00 to 2004-05)
No. of years as a FIFA Linesman/Assistant Referee: 5 (1993 to 1998)
2 A Internationals
FIFA: 2 World Cup Qualifiers
UEFA: 6 European Championship Qualifiers; 2 U21 Championship Qualifiers; 1 U18 Championship Qualifier; 11

Club Competition matches (2 UCL, 3 UC, 5 ECWC (1Q-F), 1 UIC)
1 Scottish Cup Final; 1 League Cup Final; 1 Challenge Cup Final; 5 Old Firm matches

Vikki Allan
Date of Birth: 15th October 1992
No. of seasons on SFA List: 4 (2021-22 to 2024-25)
No. of seasons as Category 3 Development Referee: 4 (2021-22 to 2024-25)
No. of years as a FIFA Assistant Referee: 9 (2017 to 2025)
2 Women's A Internationals
FIFA: 7 Women's World Cup Qualifiers
UEFA: 6 Women's European Championship Qualifiers; 1 Women's Nations League match; Women's U17 Championships (2022); 3 Women's U17 Championship Qualifiers; 14 Women's Champions League matches (4 QG, 4 G, 2 R32, 1 R16)

Francis Andrews
Date of Birth: 24th August 1966
No. of seasons on SFA List: 19 (1995-96 to 2013-14)
No. of seasons as Specialist Assistant Referee: 13 (2001-02 to 2013-14)
No. of years as a FIFA Assistant Referee: 8 (2004 to 2011)
2 A Internationals; 1 U21 International
UEFA: 6 European Championship Qualifiers; 4 U21 Championship Qualifiers; 32 Club Competition matches (16 UCL (8 G and 1 Q-F), 10 UC (2 R32), 4 UEL (1 S-F), 2 UIC)
1 Scottish Cup Final; 1 League Cup Final; 1 Challenge Cup Final; 8 Old Firm matches

James Bee
Date of Birth: 12th September 1967
No. of seasons on SFA List: 20 (1995-96 to 2014-15)
No. of seasons as Specialist Assistant Referee: 12 (2002-3 to 2013-14)
No. of years as a FIFA Assistant Referee: 8 (2004 to 2008 and 2010 to 2012)

5 A Internationals
UEFA: 5 European Championship Qualifiers; 5 U21 Championship Qualifiers; 3 U17 Championship Qualifiers; 22 Club Competition matches (3 UCL, 9 UC, 7 UEL, 3 UIC (1 F))
1 Scottish Cup Final; 1 League Cup Final; 1 Challenge Cup Final; 8 Old Firm matches

Kevin Bisset
Date of Birth: 28th March 1958
No. of seasons on SFA List: 12 (1989-90 to 2000-01)
No. of seasons as Class 1 Referee: 6 (1995-96 to 2000-01)
No. of years as a FIFA Linesman/Assistant Referee: 3 (1995 to 1997)
2 A Internationals
UEFA: 2 U21 Championship Qualifiers; 1 U18 Championship Qualifier; 5 Club Competition matches (4 ECWC, 1 UC); 1 Women's European Championship Semi-Final
1 Challenge Cup Final

Jim Carlin
Date of Birth: 7th July 1955
No. of seasons on SFA List: 10 (1985-86 to 1994-95)
No. of seasons at Class 2: 5 (1990-91 to 1994-95)
No. of years as a FIFA Linesman: 1 (1992)
FIFA: 2 World Cup Qualifiers
UEFA: 1 U18 Championship Qualifier; 1 U16 Championship Qualifier; 1 Club Competition match (UC Q-F)
1 Scottish Cup Final; 1 League Cup Final; 1 Old Firm match

Sean Carr
Date of Birth: 8th November 1983
No. of seasons on SFA List: 19 (2008-09 to 2024-25)
No. of seasons as Specialist Assistant Referee: 11 (2014-15 to 2024-25)
No. of years as a FIFA Assistant Referee: 7 (2016 to 2023)
6 A Internationals
FIFA: 3 World Cup Qualifiers
UEFA: 5 European Championship Qualifiers; 1 Nations League match; 12 U21 Championship Qualifiers; 3 U19 Championship

Qualifiers; 16 Club Competition matches (5 UCL, 17 UEL (10 G), 3 UECL, 4 UYL (2 R16))
1 League Cup Final; 1 Challenge Cup Final; 1 Old Firm match

Iain Cathcart
Date of Birth: 7th December 1950
No. of seasons on SFA List: 18 (1977-78 to 1994-95)
Promoted to Class 1: 1982-83
No. of seasons as Class 1: 7 (1982-83 to 1988-89)
No. of seasons as Class 3B/Class 3: 6 (1989-90 to 1994-95)
No. of years as a FIFA Linesman: 3 (1993 to 1995)
3 A Internationals; 1 British International Championship match
FIFA: 1 World Cup Qualifier
UEFA: 2 European Championship Qualifiers; 3 U16 Championship Qualifiers; 11 Club Competition matches (1 ECCC (Q-F), 4 ECWC (1Q-F), 1 UCL (S-F), 5 UC (1F))
1 Scottish Cup Final; 1 League Cup Final; 1 Youth Cup Final; 2 Old Firm matches

Graham Chambers
Date of Birth: 14th April 1971
No. of seasons on SFA List: 24 (1999-00 to 2022-23)
No. of years as Specialist Assistant Referee: 15 (2008-09 to 2022-23)
No. of years as a FIFA Assistant Referee: 8 (2009 to 2016)
6 A Internationals; 1 Women's A International
FIFA: 5 World Cup Qualifiers; U20 World Cup (2011)
UEFA: 6 European Championship Qualifiers; 5 U21 Championship Qualifiers; 3 U19 Championship Qualifiers; 35 Club Competition matches (10 UCL (4 G, 1 R16, 2 Q-F), 24 UEL (11 G, 1 R32) and 1 SC (F)); 1 Women's Champions League match
1 Scottish Cup Final; 1 League Cup Final; 5 Old Firm matches

Frank Connor
Date of Birth: 30th December 1981
No. of seasons on SFA List: 19 (2006-07 to 2024-25)
No. of years as Specialist Assistant Referee: 13 (2012-13 to 2024-25)

No. of years as a FIFA Assistant Referee: 11 (2015 to 2025)
6 A Internationals; 1 U21 International
FIFA: 9 World Cup Qualifiers
UEFA: European Championships (2016); 9 European Championship Qualifiers; 7 Nations League matches; U21 Championships (2019); 1 U21 Championship Qualifier; 68 Club Competition matches (22 UCL (11 G, 2 R16, 2 Q-F), 34 UEL (19 G, 3 R32, 4 R16, 2 Q-F), 9 UECL (2 G, 2 LP and 1 R16), 3 UYL (1 R16))
2 Scottish Cup Finals; 2 League Cup Finals; 11 Old Firm matches

Willie Conquer
Date of Birth: 27th March 1970
No. of seasons on SFA List: 14 (2004-05 to 2017-18)
No. of seasons as Specialist Assistant Referee: 12 (2006-07 to 2017-18)
No. of years as a FIFA Assistant Referee: 8 (2009 to 2015)
2 A Internationals; 1 Women's A International
FIFA: 4 World Cup Qualifiers
UEFA: 3 European Championship Qualifiers; 3 U21 Championship Qualifiers; 33 Club Competition matches (16 UCL (10 G, 2 R16), 3 UC, 13 UEL (7 G))
1 Scottish Cup Final; 1 Challenge Cup Final; 4 Old Firm matches

Martin Cryans
Date of Birth: 4th February 1969
No. of seasons on SFA List: 23 (1991-92 to 2013-14)
No. of years as Specialist Assistant Referee: 13 (2001-02 to 2013-14)
No. of years as a FIFA Assistant Referee: 12 (2003 to 2014)
5 A Internationals; 1 Women's A International
FIFA: 8 World Cup Qualifiers; Olympics (2004 (1F)); U20 World Cup (2011); U17 World Cup (2003)
UEFA: 2 European Championship Qualifiers; 5 U21 Championship Qualifiers; 6 U19 Championship Qualifiers; 49 Club Competition matches (24 UCL (18 G and 2 R16), 14 UC (2 R32, 2 R16), 8 UEL (2 R32, 3 Q-F), 1 UIC (1 S-F))

1 Scottish Cup Final; 2 League Cup Finals;9 Old Firm matches

Alan Cunningham
Date of Birth: 22nd February 1966
No. of seasons on SFA List: 16 (1995-96 to 2010-11)
No. of seasons as Specialist Assistant Referee: 12 (1999-00 to 2010-11)
No. of years as a FIFA Assistant Referee: 11 (2001 to 2011)
11 A Internationals; 5 U21 Internationals
FIFA: 3 World Cup Qualifiers
UEFA: 4 European Championship Qualifiers; Meridian Cup (2001); 2 U21 Championship Qualifiers; 1 U19 Championship Qualifier; 16 Club Competition matches (2 UCL, 13 UC (1 R32), 1 UIC (1 R16)
1 League Cup Final; 1 Challenge Cup Final; 11 Old Firm matches

Andy Davis
Date of Birth: 11th April 1961
No. of seasons on SFA List: 14 (1992-93 to 2005-06)
No. of seasons as Specialist Assistant Referee: 7 (1999-00 to 2005-06)
No. of years as a FIFA Assistant Referee: 6 (2000 to 2005)
5 A Internationals; 1 U21 International
FIFA: 2 World Cup Qualifiers
UEFA: 3 European Championship Qualifiers; 2 U21 Championship Qualifiers; 19 Club Competition matches (16 UC, 3 UIC)
1 Scottish Cup Final; 1 League Cup Final; 6 Old Firm matches

David Doig
Date of Birth: 14th February 1959
No. of seasons on SFA List: 11 (1993-94 to 2003-04)
No. of seasons as Specialist Assistant Referee: 6 (1998-99 to 2003-04)
No. of years as a FIFA Assistant Referee: 5 (1999 to 2003)
4 A Internationals; 1 U21 International
FIFA: 1 World Cup Qualifier

UEFA: 3 European Championship Qualifiers; 3 U21 Championship Qualifiers; 3 U18 Championship Qualifiers; 22 Club Competition matches (12 UCL (7G), 7 UC, 2 UIC, 1 SC (F)
1 Scottish Cup Final; 1 League Cup Final; 8 Old Firm matches

Martin Doran
Date of Birth: 19th July 1959
Died: 2nd March 2023 aged 63
No. of seasons on SFA List: 15 (1989-90 to 2003-04)
No. of seasons as Specialist Assistant Referee: 6 (1998-99 to 2003-04)
No. of years as a FIFA Assistant Referee: 3 (2000 to 2003)
2 A Internationals
FIFA: 1 World Cup Qualifier
UEFA: 1 U19 Championship Qualifier; 1 U18 Championship Qualifier; 8 Club Competition matches (4 UC, 1 UCL, 3 UIC)

George Drummond
Date of Birth: 6th January 1967
No. of seasons on SFA List: 16 (1998-99 to 2013-14)
No. of years as Specialist Assistant Referee: 11 (2003-04 to 2013-14)
No. of years as a FIFA Assistant Referee: 7 (2006 to 2012)
3 A Internationals; 1 B International
FIFA: 3 World Cup Qualifiers
UEFA: 4 European Championship Qualifiers; 3 U21 Championship Qualifiers; 3 U19 Championship Qualifier; 16 Club Competition matches (4 UCL, 3 UC, 8 UEL (1 R32, 1 R16, 1 Q-F), 1 UIC)
2 Scottish Cup Finals; 2 League Cup Finals; 1 Challenge Cup Final; 5 Old Firm matches

Jim Dunne
Date of Birth: 5th December 1959
No. of seasons on SFA List: 18 (1986-87 to 2003-04)
No. of seasons as Specialist Assistant Referee: 1998-99 to 2003-04)
No. of years as a FIFA Assistant Referee: 5 (1998 to 2002)

1 A International
UEFA: 4 European Championship Qualifiers; 1 U21 Championship Qualifiers; 13 Club Competitions matches (8 UCL (5 G, 1 S-F), 4 UC, 1 UIC)
1 Scottish Cup Final; 2 League Cup Finals; 1 Youth Cup Final; 8 Old Firm matches

John Fleming
Date of Birth: 20th September 1957
Died: 22nd October 2019
No. of seasons on SFA List: 16 (1988-89 to 2003-04)
No. of seasons as Class 1/Category 1 Referee: 6 (1994-95 to 2003-04)
No. of years as a FIFA Linesman/Assistant Referee: 4 (1995 to 1998)
2 A Internationals
FIFA: 1 World Cup Qualifier
UEFA: European Championships (1996); 1 European Championship Qualifier; 18 Club Competition matches (1 ECCC, 3 ECWC (1 Q-F), 7 UCL (5 G, 1 Q-F), 6 UC (1 Q-F, 1 S-F), 1 SC (F)
1 Scottish Cup Final; 1 League Cup Final; 3 Old Firm matches

Bob Gunn
Date of Birth: 28th September 1955
No. of seasons on SFA List: 10 (1990-91 to 1999-00)
No. of seasons as Specialist Assistant Referee: 2 (1998-99 to 1999-00)
No. of years as a FIFA Assistant Referee: 5 (1995 to 1999)
FIFA: 2 World Cup Qualifiers
UEFA: 3 European Championship Qualifiers; 1 U18 Championship Qualifier; 17 Club Competition matches (1 ECWC (Q-F), 9 UCL (5 G), 6 UC, 1 UIC)
1 Scottish Cup Final; 1 Youth Cup Final; 2 Old Firm matches

Gavin Harris
Date of Birth: 5th June 1986
No. of seasons on SFA List: 11 (2007-08 to 2017-18)

No. of seasons as Specialist Assistant Referee: 6 (2012-13 to 2017-18)
No. of years as a FIFA Assistant Referee: 2 (2013 to 2014)
UEFA: 1 U21 Championship Play-off match; 9 U19 Championship Qualifiers; 3 U17 Championship Qualifiers; 4 Club Competition matches (2 UCL, 2 UEL (1 Q-F))
1 Youth Cup Final

Jim Herald
Date of Birth: 30th July 1950
No. of seasons on SFA List: 18 (1982-83 to 1999-00)
No. of seasons as Class 1 Referee: 12 (1988-89 to 1999-00)
No. of years as a FIFA Linesman: 4 (1992 to 1995)
3 A Internationals
FIFA: 2 World Cup Qualifiers; 1 Olympic Qualifier
UEFA: 1 European Championship Qualifier; 1 U21 Championship Qualifier; 1 U18 Championship Qualifier; 12 Club Competition matches (3 ECCC, 2 ECWC (1 Q-F), 5 UC (1 Q-F), 2 UCL)

Hayley Irvine
Date of Birth: 14th January 1989
No. of years as a FIFA Assistant Referee: 2 (2015 to 2016)
3 Women's A Internationals
FIFA: 4 Women's World Cup Qualifiers
UEFA: 1 Women's Championship Qualifier; 6 Women's U17 Championship Qualifiers; 8 Women's Champions League matches (3 Q-F, 3 R32, 1 Q-F)

Wilson Irvine
Date of Birth: 1st August 1959
No. of seasons on SFA List: 17 (1987-88 to 2003-04)
No. of seasons as a Specialist Assistant Referee: 6 (1998-99 to 2003-04)
No. of years as a FIFA Assistant Referee: 6 (1998-2003)
2 A Internationals; 1 U21 International
FIFA: 5 World Cup Qualifiers
UEFA: 3 European Championship Qualifiers; 2 U21 Championship Qualifiers; 33 Club Competition matches (1

ECWC, 11 UC (1 S-F), 17 UCL (12 G, 1 Q-F), 3 UIC (1 F), 1 SC (F)
1 Scottish Cup Final; 1 League Cup Final; 1 Challenge Cup Final; 7 Old Firm matches

Joe Kelly
Date of Birth: 14th June 1954
No. of seasons on SFA List: 14 (1985-86 to 1998-99)
No. of seasons as Class 1 Referee: 4 (1991-92 to 1994-95)
No. of seasons as Specialist Assistant Referee: 1 (1998-99)
No. of years as a FIFA Linesman/Assistant Referee: 5 (1994 to 1998)
Class 3: 1995-96 to 1997-98
3 U21 Internationals
UEFA: 1 European Championship Qualifier; 3 U21 Championship Qualifiers; 1 U18 Championship Qualifier; 10 Club Competition matches (3 ECWC (1 Q-F), 5 UC, 1 UCL, 1 UIC); 2 Women's Championship Qualifiers
1 League Cup Final; 1 Challenge Cup Final; 3 Old Firm matches

Stuart Logan
Date of Birth: 14th May 1961
No. of seasons on SFA List: 22 (1985-86 to 2006-07)
No. of seasons as Specialist Assistant Referee: 5 (1998-99 to 2002-03)
No. of years as a FIFA Assistant Referee: 5 (1999 to 2003)
1 A International
FIFA: 1 World Cup Qualifier
UEFA: 1 European Championship Qualifier; 1 U21 Championship Qualifier; U16 Championships (1999) 11 Club Competition matches (1 ECWC, 4 UC, 4 UCL (3G, 2 UIC (1F))
1 Scottish Cup Final; 1 League Cup Final; 5 Old Firm matches

Jim Lyon
Date of Birth: 6th July 1969
No. of seasons on SFA List: 19 (1993-94 to 2011-12)
No. of seasons as Specialist Assistant Referee: 11 (1999-00 to 2009-10)

No. of years as a FIFA Assistant Referee: 5 (2003 to 2007)
3 A Internationals
UEFA: 3 U21 Championship Qualifiers; U19 Championships (2003); 3 U19 Championship Qualifiers; 20 Club Competition matches (13 UC, 2 UCL, 5 UIC (1F))
1 Scottish Cup Final; 4 Old Firm matches

Stuart Macaulay
Date of Birth: 31st December 1966
No. of seasons on SFA List: 23 (1992-93 to 2014-15)
No. of seasons as Specialist Assistant Referee: 15 (1999-00 to 2013-14)
No. of years as a FIFA Assistant Referee: 6 (2003 to 2008)
5 A Internationals; 3 U21 Internationals
FIFA: 1 World Cup Qualifier
UEFA: 1 European Championship Qualifier; 4 U21 Championship Qualifiers; 3 U19 Championship Qualifiers; 3 U17 Championship Qualifiers; 14 Club Competition matches (8 UC (1 R32), 2 UCL, 4 UIC (1 F)
1 League Cup Final; 2 Challenge Cup Finals; 5 Old Firm matches

Gordon McBride
Date of Birth: 25th January 1960
No. of seasons on SFA List: 16 (1989-90 to 2004-05)
No. of seasons as Specialist Assistant Referee: 7 (1998-99 to 2004-05)
No. of years as a FIFA Assistant Referee: 6 (1997 to 2002)
5 A International Appointments; 1 U21 International; 1 Women's A International
UEFA: 1 European Championship Qualifier; 2 U21 International Qualifiers, 3 U18 Championship Qualifiers; 1 U16 Championship Qualifier; 15 Club Competition matches (5 UC, 8 UCL (5 G), 2 UIC)
3 Old Firm matches

Jim McBride
Date of Birth: 22nd April 1958
No. of seasons on SFA List: 11 (1992-93 to 2002-03)

No. of seasons as Specialist Assistant Referee: 5 (1998-99 to 2002-03)
No. of years as a FIFA Assistant Referee: 5 (1998 to 2002)
2 A Internationals; 1 U21 International
FIFA: 4 World Cup Qualifiers
UEFA: 1 European Championship Qualifier; 2 U21 Championship Qualifiers; 24 Club Competition matches (14 UC (1 S-F), 8 UCL (3 G, 1 S-F), 2 UIC)
1 Scottish Cup Final; 1 League Cup Final; 4 Old Firm matches

John McElhinney
Date of Birth: 24th July 1956
No. of seasons on SFA List: 15 (1986-87 to 2000-01)
No. of seasons as Specialist Assistant Referee: 3 (1998-99 to 2000-01)
No. of years as a FIFA Linesman/Assistant Referee: 5 (1996 to 2000)
4 A Internationals; 1 U21 International
FIFA: 4 World Cup Qualifiers
UEFA: 2 European Championship Qualifiers; U21 Championships (2000); 3 U16 Championship Qualifiers; 22 Club Competition matches (2 ECWC (1 Q-F), 4 UC, 16 UCL (14 G))
1 Scottish Cup Final; 5 Old Firm matches

Daniel McFarlane
Date of Birth: 3rd April 1992
No. of seasons on SFA List: 13 (2012-13 to 2024-25)
No. of seasons as Specialist Assistant Referee: 8 (2017-18 to 2024-25)
No. of years as a FIFA Assistant Referee: 7 (2019 to 2025)
FIFA: 1 World Cup Qualifier
UEFA: 4 European Championship Qualifiers; 3 Nations League matches; U21 Championships (2025); 3 U21 Championship Qualifiers; 35 Club Competition matches (3 UCL, 15 UEL (7 G and 4 LP), 13 UECL (4 G, 1 LP, 1 R16))
1 Scottish Cup Final; 2 League Cup Finals; 1 Challenge Cup Final; 6 Old Firm matches

David McGeachie
Date of Birth: 10th January 1986
No. of seasons on SFA List: 20 (2005-06 to 2024-25)
No. of seasons as Specialist Assistant Referee: 13 (2012-13 to 2024-25)
No. of years as a FIFA Assistant Referee: 13 (2013 to 2025)
4 A Internationals; 1 Women's A International
FIFA: 8 World Cup Qualifiers; U17 World Cup (2017)
UEFA: 8 European Championship Qualifiers; 9 Nations League matches; U21 Championships (2017); 5 U21 Championship Qualifiers; 3 U17 Championship Qualifiers; 97 Club Competition matches (27 UCL (17 G, 2 R16, 1 Q-F), 49 UEL (18 G, 4 LP, 5 R32, 6 R16, 2 Q-F , 1 S-F), 14 UECL (2 G, 2 LP, 2 R16) 1 UYL (R16)
1 Scottish Cup Final; 4 League Cup Finals; 1 Youth Cup Final; 13 Old Firm matches

George McGuire
Date of Birth: 4th December 1954
No. of seasons on SFA List: 8 (1989-90 to 1996-97)
No. of seasons as Class 2: 3 (1993 to 1995)
No. of years as a FIFA Linesman: 1 (1995)
UEFA: 1 European Championship Qualifier; 1 U21 Championship Qualifier; 3 Club Competition matches (2 UC, 1 UCL)

Ross MacLeod
Date of Birth: 18th February 1991
No. of seasons on SFA List: 13 (2012-13 to 2024-25)
No. of seasons as Specialist Assistant Referee: 4 (2021-22 to 2024-25)
No. of years as a FIFA Assistant Referee: 4 (2022 to 2025)
1 A International; 1 C International
UEFA: 1 European Championship Qualifier; 1 Nations League match; 5 U21 Championship Qualifiers; 2 U19 Championship Qualifiers; 6 U17 Championship Qualifiers; 12 Club Competition matches (3 UCL, 1 UEL, 7 UECL (2 G, 1 LP, 1 UYL)

1 Scottish Cup Final; 1 League Cup Final; 1 Challenge Cup Final; 3 Old Firm matches

Stuart MacMillan
Date of Birth: 7th March 1979
No. of seasons on SFA List: 11 (2005-06 to 2015-16)
No. of seasons as Specialist Assistant Referee: 4 (2012-13 to 2015-16)
No. of years as a FIFA Assistant Referee: 1 (2015)
UEFA: 3 U19 Championship Qualifiers; 3 Club Competition matches (1 UEL, 2 UYL (1 R16))
1 Challenge Cup Final

Kylie McMullan
Date of Birth: 1st December 1988
No. of seasons on SFA List: 9 (2012-13 to 2020-21)
No. of seasons as Specialist Assistant Referee: 7 (2014-15 to 2020-21)
No. of years as a FIFA Assistant Referee: 9 (2013 to 2021)
9 Women's A Internationals
FIFA: Women's World Cup (2019); 9 Women's World Cup Qualifiers; 2 U17 Women's World Cups (2016 and 2018)
UEFA: 9 Women's European Championship Qualifiers; U19 Women's Championships (2016); 6 U19 Women's Championship Qualifiers; 6 U17 Women's Championship Qualifiers; 9 Women's Champions League matches (4 R32, 7 R16, 3 Q-F); 1 Club Competition match (1 UYL)

Douglas Main
Date of Birth: 23rd December 1955
No. of seasons on SFA List: 17 (1982-83 to 1998-99)
No. of seasons at Class 3B/3: 11 (1987-88 to 1997-98)
No. of seasons as Specialist Assistant Referee: 1 (1998-99)
No. of years as a FIFA Linesman/Assistant Referee: 4 (1996 to 1999)
1 A International
FIFA: 1 World Cup Qualifier

UEFA: 2 U21 Championship Qualifiers; 1 U18 Championship Qualifier; 7 Club Competition matches (1 ECWC, 4 UC, 2 UCL)
1 League Cup Final; 1 Old Firm match

Alastair Mather
Date of Birth: 5th August 1977
No. of seasons on SFA List: 26 seasons (2000-01 to 2025-26)
No. of seasons as Specialist Assistant Referee: 14 (2010-11 to 2024-25)
No. of years as a FIFA Assistant Referee: 6 (2013 to 2018)
2 A Internationals
FIFA: 1 World Cup Qualifier; U17 World Cup (2017)
UEFA: 4 European Championship Qualifiers; 2 Nations League matches; U21 Championships (2017); 1 U21 Championship Qualifier; 6 U19 Championship Qualifiers; 16 Club Competition matches (4 UCL, 12 UEL (8 G and 2 R32))
1 Scottish Cup Final; 1 Old Firm match

Gordon Middleton
Date of Birth: 23rd June 1967
No. of seasons on SFA List: 19 (1994-95 to 2012-13)
No. of seasons as Specialist Assistant Referee: 13 (2000-01 to 2012-13)
No. of years as a FIFA Assistant Referee: 9 (2004 to 2012)
3 A Internationals
FIFA: 2 World Cup Qualifiers
UEFA: 1 European Championship Qualifier; 6 U21 Championship Qualifiers; 3 U19 Championship Qualifiers; 13 Club Competition matches (6 UC, 4 UCL, 2 UEL, 1 UIC); 1 Women's Champions League match
1 League Cup Final; 7 Old Firm matches

Alan Mulvanny
Date of Birth: 13th March 1983
No. of seasons on SFA List: 20 (2005-06 to 2024-25)
No. of seasons as Specialist Assistant Referee: 14 (2010-11 to 2023-24)
No. of seasons as Specialist Assistant VAR: 1 (2024-25)

No. of years as a FIFA Assistant Referee: 11 (2012 to 2014 and 2016 to 2023)
8 A Internationals; 1 U21 International
FIFA: 6 World Cup Qualifiers; U17 World Cup (2013)
UEFA: 4 European Championship Qualifiers; 1 Nations League match; U21 Championships (2013); 6 U21 Championship Qualifiers; 6 U19 Championship Qualifiers; 54 Club Competition appointments (13 UCL (10 G), 26 UEL (8 G, 4 R32, 4 R16, 2 Q-F), 11 UECL (6 G))
1 Scottish Cup Final; 2 League Cup Finals; 8 Old Firm matches

Tom Murphy
Date of Birth: 8th September 1965
No. of seasons on SFA List: 21 (1993-94 to 2013-14)
No. of seasons as Specialist Assistant Referee: 16 (1998-99 to 2013-14)
No. of years as a FIFA Assistant Referee: 8 (2003 to 2010)
9 A Internationals; 3 U21 Internationals
FIFA: 7 World Cup Qualifiers; U17 World Cup (2007)
UEFA: 3 European Championship Qualifiers; 2 U21 Championship Qualifiers; 3 U19 Championship Qualifiers; 38 Club Competition matches (1 ECWC, 18 UC (2 R32, 2 R16), 17 UCL (10 G)
1 Scottish Cup Final; 2 League Cup Finals; 8 Old Firm matches

Bobby Orr
Date of Birth: 6th February 1953
Died: February 2006
No. of seasons on SFA List: 24 (1979-80 to 2002-03)
No of seasons at Class 1/Category 1: 16 (1987-88 to 2002-03)
No. of years as a FIFA Linesman/Assistant Referee: 4 (1994 to 1997)
FIFA: 1 World Cup Qualifier
UEFA: European Championships (1996); 2 European Championship Qualifiers; 24 Club Competition matches (1 ECCC, 3 ECWC, 13 UC (2 Q-F, 1 F), 6 UCL (4 G, 1 Q-F, 1 S-F) 1 SC (F)
1 Scottish Cup Final; 1 League Cup Final; 1 Youth Cup Final; 1 Old Firm match

Mike Pocock
Date of Birth: 19th March 1958
No. of seasons on SFA List: 13 (1985-86 to 1997-98)
No of seasons at Class 1: 7 (1991-92 to 1997-98)
No. of years as a FIFA Assistant Referee: 2 (1992 to 1993)
1 A International
FIFA: 3 World Cup Qualifiers
UEFA: 1 U21 Championship Qualifier; 1 U16 Championship Qualifier; 9 Club Competition matches (1 ECCC, 4 UC, 3 UCL, 1 UIC)
1 Old Firm match

Dougie Potter
Date of Birth: 1st June 1985
No. of seasons on SFA List: 20 (2005-06 to 2024-25)
No. of years as Specialist Assistant Referee: 13 (2012-13 to 2024-25)
No. of years as a FIFA Linesman: 10 (2016 to 2025)
2 A Internationals
FIFA: 2 World Cup Qualifiers
UEFA: 2 European Championship Qualifiers; 3 Nations League matches; 5 U21 Championship Qualifiers; 6 U19 Championship Qualifiers; U17 Championships (2018); 36 Club Competition matches (4 UCL, 21 UEL (11 G, 1 S-F)), 6 UECL, 2 UYL (2 R16)
1 Scottish Cup Final; 1 League Cup Final; 9 Old Firm matches

Vikki Robertson
Date of Birth: 3rd November 1984
No. of seasons on SFA List: 2 (2005-06 to 2006-07 and 2024-25)
No. of years as a FIFA Assistant Referee: 11 (2015 to 2025)
8 Women's A Internationals
FIFA: 4 Women's World Cup Qualifiers
UEFA: 6 Women's European Championship Qualifiers; 1 Women's Nations League match; Women's U19 Championships (2017 (1 S-F)); 6 Women's U19 Championship Qualifiers; 3 Women's U17 Championship Qualifiers; 16

Women's Champions League appointments (2 G, 4 R32, 3 R16); 3 Women's Cup appointments

David Roome
Date of Birth: 29th April 1980
No. of seasons on SFA List: 14 (2011-12 to 2024-25)
No. of seasons as Specialist Assistant Referee: 9 (2016-17 to 2024-25)
No. of years as a FIFA Assistant Referee: 7 (2019 to 2025)
1 A International
FIFA: 2 World Cup Qualifiers
UEFA: 5 European Championship Qualifiers; 4 Nations League matches; U21 Championships (2019); 2 U21 Championship Qualifiers; 3 U17 Championship Qualifiers; 29 Club Competition matches (8 UCL (4 G), 10 UEL (5 G, 2 R32), 10 UECL (3 G, 1 LP), 1 UYL)
2 Scottish Cup Finals; 2 League Cup Finals; 1 Challenge Cup Final; 9 Old Firm matches

Derek Rose
Date of Birth: 21st July 1974
No. of seasons on SFA List: 13 (2002-03 to 2014-15)
No. of seasons as Specialist Assistant Referee: 6 (2008-09 to 2014-15)
No. of years as a FIFA Assistant Referee: 2 (2009 and 2012 to 2014)
1 A International
FIFA: 2 World Cup Qualifiers; U17 World Cup (2013)
UEFA: European Championships (2012); U21 Championships (2009); 2 U21 Championship Qualifiers; 3 U19 Championship Qualifiers; 14 Club Competition matches (9 UCL (4 G, 2 R16, 1 Q-F), 5 UEL (1 R32, 1 R16, 1 Q-F)
1 Scottish Cup Final; 1 League Cup Final; 1 Old Firm match

Alasdair Ross
Date of Birth: 4th July 1975
No. of seasons on SFA List: 15 (2005-06 to 2018-19)
No. of seasons as Specialist Assistant Referee: 10 (2009-10 to 2018-19)

No. of years as a FIFA Assistant Referee: 4 (2011 to 2014)
1 Women's A International
FIFA: 3 World Cup Qualifiers
UEFA: European Championships (2012); 3 European Championship Qualifiers; 3 U19 Championship Qualifiers; 15 Club Competition matches (11 UCL (4G, 2 R16, 1 Q-F), 4 UEL (1 G, 1 R16, 1 S-F)
1 Scottish Cup Final; 1 League Cup Final; 1 Challenge Cup Final; 2 Old Firm matches

Douglas Ross
Date of Birth: 27th January 1983
No. of seasons on SFA List: 20 (2005-06 to 2024-25)
No. of seasons as Specialist Assistant Referee: 13 (2012-13 to 2024-25)
No. of years as a FIFA Assistant Referee: 7 (2015 to 2021)
1 A International
FIFA: 5 World Cup Qualifiers
UEFA: 3 European Championship Qualifiers; 2 Nations League matches; 1 U21 Championship Qualifier; U19 Championships (2016 (1 S-F)); 33 Club Competition matches (10 UCL (6 G), 21 UEL (9 G, 3 R32, 1 R16), 2 UYL)
2 Scottish Cup Finals; 1 League Cup Final

Stewart Shearer
Date of Birth: 19th September 1960
No. of seasons on SFA List: 14 (1991-92 to 2004-05)
No. of seasons as a Specialist Assistant Referee: 7 (1998-99 to 2004-05)
No. of years as a FIFA Assistant Referee: 6 (1999-2004)
4 A Internationals; 1 Women's A International
FIFA: 2 World Cup Qualifiers
UEFA: 4 U21 Championship Qualifiers; 16 Club Competition matches (12 UC, 3 UCL, 1 UIC)
1 Scottish Cup Final; 1 League Cup Final; 1 Youth Cup Final

George Simpson
Date of Birth: 2nd May 1960
No. of seasons on SFA List: 17 (1983-84 to 1999-00)

No. of seasons as Class 1/Category 1 Referee: 8 (1992-93 to 1999-00)
No. of years as a FIFA Linesman/Assistant Referee: 6 (1993 to 1998)
1 A International
FIFA: 4 World Cup Qualifiers
UEFA: 2 U21 Championship Qualifiers; 3 U18 Championship Qualifiers; 13 Club Competition matches (1 ECCC, 1 ECWC, 6 UC, 4 UCL, 1 UIC)
1 Scottish Cup Final

Keith Sorbie
Date of Birth: 25th May 1965
No. of seasons on SFA List: 14 (1998-99 to 2011-12)
No. of years as Specialist Assistant Referee: 9 (2003-04 to 2011-12)
No. of years as a FIFA Assistant Referee: 6 (2005 to 2010)
3 A Internationals; 1 B International; 1 U21 International
FIFA: 2 World Cup Qualifiers
UEFA: 3 European Championship Qualifiers; 2 U21 Championship Qualifiers; 3 U17 Championship Qualifiers; 29 Club Competition matches (10 UC (2 R32), 8 UCL (3G), 7 UEL (3 G, 1 R32), 4 UIC)
1 Scottish Cup Final; 1 League Cup Final

Calum Spence
Date of Birth: 29th May 1989
No. of seasons on SFA List: 16 (2009-10 to 2024-25)
No. of seasons as Specialist Assistant Referee: 8 (2017-18 to 2024-25)
No. of years as a FIFA Assistant Referee: 6 (2020 to 2025)
1 A International
FIFA: 1 World Cup Qualifier
UEFA: 2 European Championship Qualifiers; 2 Nations League matches; U21 Championships (2025); 5 U21 Championship Qualifiers; 3 U19 Championship Qualifiers; 6 U17 Championship Qualifiers; 24 Club Competition matches (1 UCL (LP), 3 UEL, 16 UECL (5 G, 2 LP), 4 UYL (2 R16)
1 Scottish Cup Final; 1 League Cup Final

Stuart Stevenson
Date of Birth: 28th November 1981
No. of seasons on SFA List: 20 (2005-06 to 2024-25)
No. of years as Specialist Assistant Referee: 14 (2010-11 to 2024-25)
No. of years as a FIFA Assistant Referee: 7 (2012 to 2018)
5 A Internationals
FIFA: 3 World Cup Qualifiers
UEFA: 3 European Championship Qualifiers; 2 Nations League matches; 3 U21 Championship Qualifiers; 3 U17 Championship Qualifiers; 27 Club Competition matches (6 UCL, 21 UEL (13 G)
1 League Cup Final

Graeme Stewart
Date of Birth: 20th February 1985
No. of seasons on SFA List: 19 (2006-06 to 2024-25)
No. of seasons as Specialist Assistant Referee: 11 (2014-15 to 2024-25)
No. of years as a FIFA Assistant Referee: 11 (2015 to 2025)
4 A Internationals; 2 U21 Internationals
FIFA: 3 World Cup Qualifiers
UEFA: 6 European Championship Qualifiers; 7 Nations League matches, U19 Championships (2017); 3 U19 Championship Qualifiers; 6 U17 Championship Qualifiers; 69 Club Competition matches (19 UCL (10 G, 1 LP), 39 UEL (17 G, 1 LP, 2 R32, 3 R16, 1 Q-F), 10 UECL (6 G, 1 LP), 1 UYL (R16)
2 Scottish Cup Finals; 2 League Cup Finals; 1 Challenge Cup Final

Jordan Stokoe
Date of Birth: 7th June 1984
No. of seasons on SFA List: 10 (2010-11 to 2019-20)
No. of seasons as Specialist Assistant Referee: 4 (2016-17 to 2019-20)
No. of years as a FIFA Assistant Referee: 3 (2017 to 2019)
1 A International

UEFA: 1 European Championship Qualifier; 2 U21 Championship Qualifiers; 3 U19 Championship Qualifiers; 15 Club Competition matches (9 UEL (6 G), 6 UYL (1 R16)

Lists of FIFA Referees and Assistant Referees

The following tables set out, by length of service, Scotland's FIFA officials. 92 Scots have attained FIFA referee status - 87 through the SFA and five through other National Associations. FIFA changed its List from a seasonal basis to a calendar year in 1987.

Referee	No. of Seasons/Years	Seasons/Years
Bobby Davidson^	22	1954-55 - 1975-76
William Collum	19	2006 - 2024
Hugh Phillips^	15	1952-53 - 1966-67
George Smith	15	1974-75, 1978-79 - 1986-87, 1987 - 1991
Craig Thomson	15	2003 - 2017
John Beaton	14	2012 - 2025
David Syme	14	1977-78 - 1979-80, 1981-82 - 1986-87, 1987 - 1991
Kenny Clark*	13	1993 - 2005
Bobby Madden	13	2010 - 2020
Lorraine Watson*	13	2013 - 2025
Tom Wharton	13	1958-59 - 1970-71
Kevin Clancy	12	2012 - 2023
Stuart Dougal*	12	1996 - 2007
Kenny Hope	12	1978-79, 1981-82 - 1986-87, 1987 - 1990
Brian McGinlay	12	1976-77 - 1985-86, 1991 - 1992
Jack Mowat	12	1948-49 - 1959-60
John Paterson	12	1966-67 - 1977-78
Dougie McDonald	11	2000 - 2010
Willie Brittle	10	1953-54 - 1959-60, 1961-62, 1963-64 - 1964-65
Hugh Dallas*	10	1993 - 2002
Bill Mullan	10	1962-63 - 1963-64, 1965-66 - 1972-73
Bob Valentine	10	1978-79 - 1986-87, 1987

Referee	No. of Seasons/Years	Seasons/Years
John Gordon	9	1967-68, 1971-72 - 1978-79
Jim McCluskey	9	1987 - 1995
Michael McCurry	9	1996 - 2004
Morag Pirie*	9	2009 - 2017
Don Robertson	9	2017 - 2025
Andrew Waddell	9	1998 - 1996
Ian Foote	8	1973-74 - 1980-81
Alistair MacKenzie	8	1962-63, 1969-70 - 1975-76
Nick Walsh	8	2018 - 2025
Bill Crombie	7	1986-87, 1987 - 1993
Steven McLean	7	2010 - 2016
George Mitchell^	7	1948-49 - 1954-55
Charlie Richmond	7	2003 - 2009
Willie Young*	7	1994 - 2000
Hugh Alexander	6	1976-77 - 1977-78, 1981-82 - 1983-84, 1985-86
Iain Brines	6	2003 - 2008
Alan Ferguson	6	1981-82 - 1986-87
Doug Gerrard	6	1951-52 - 1956-57
Les Mottram	6	1991 - 1996
John Rowbotham	6	1995 - 2000
Willie Syme	6	1963-64 - 1968-69
Jimmy Barclay^	5	1953-54, 1958-59 - 1959-60, 1961-62 - 1962-63
Jimmy Callaghan	5	1968-69 - 1972-73
Andrew Dallas	5	2015 - 2019
Charlie Faultless	5	1949-50 - 1954-55
Alan Freeland	5	1997 - 1999, 2001 - 2002
David Munro	5	2020 - 2024
Calum Murray	5	2005 - 2009

Referee	No. of Seasons/Years	Seasons/Years
Euan Norris	5	2009 - 2013
Bill Anderson	4	1968-69 - 1970-71, 1977-78
John Bissett^	3	1953-54 - 1954-55, 1958-59
Gibby Bowman	3	1957-58, 1960-61 - 1961-62
Willie Davidson	3	1948-49 -1950-51
David Dickinson	3	2023 - 2025
Jimmy Duncan	3	1986-87, 1987 - 1988
Douglas Hope	3	1989 - 1991
Rollo Kyle	3	1974-75 - 1976-77
Alan Muir	3	2009 - 2011
Joe Timmons	3	1992 - 1994
Willie Webb	3	1947-48 - 1949-50
Archie Webster	3	1964-65 - 1965-66, 1973-74
Willie Brown	2	1950-51 - 1951-52
Frank Crossley^	2	1955-56, 1960-61
Douglas Downie	2	1979-80 - 1980-81
Peter Fitzpatrick	2	1955-56, 1958-59
Willie Harvie^	2	1955-56 - 1956-57
Bob Henderson	2	1966-67 - 1967-68
Matthew MacDermid	2	2024 - 2025
Tommy Marshall	2	1971-72 - 1972-73
Tommy Muirhead	2	1979-80, 1984-85
Eddie Thomson	2	1973-74, 1975-76
John Underhill	2	2001 - 2002
Bert Benzie	1	1948-49
Bobby Calder	1	1947-48
Bob Carruthers	1	1947-48
John Cox	1	1950-51
Peter Craigmyle	1	1947-48

Referee	No. of Seasons/Years	Seasons/Years
Arthur Crossman	1	1961-62
Alex McClintock^	1	1956-57
Ross Hardie	1	2025
Abbie Hendry	1	2025
Jimmy Martin	1	1947-48
Eddie Pringle	1	1980-81
Paul Robertson	1	2014
Hugh Williamson	1	1992
Ernie Youngson^	1	1956-57

^ These referees were in the "Deputy" category, which operated in the 1950's. Their periods of service were:

Jimmy Barclay: 1953-54
John Bissett: 1953-54 and 1955-56
Frank Crossley: 1955-56
Bobby Davidson: 1954-55
Willie Harvie: 1955-56 and 1956-57
Alex McClintock: 1956-57
George Mitchell: 1953-54 and 1954-55
Hugh Phillips: 1955-56
ErnieYoungson: 1956-57

* these officials served as FIFA Linesmen/Assistant Referees prior to becoming FIFA referees. Their periods of service were:
Kenny Clark: 1992
Hugh Dallas: 1992
Stuart Dougal: 1993-1994
Morag Pirie: 2004-2007
Lorraine Watson: 2010-2011
Willie Young: 1992-1993

The five Scots who became FIFA Referees through other National Associations are:

Referee	National Association	No. of Season/Years	Seasons/Years
Alistair Coutts	Hong Kong	2	1986-87, 1987
David Galloway	Zambia	4	1969-70 - 1972-73
Willie Laidlaw*	Canada	7	1993 - 1999
Eddie Lennie	Australia	9	1996 - 2004
Stanley Tait	Canada	3	1966-67, 1969-70, 1974-75

* Willie Laidlaw was a FIFA Assistant Referee in 1992

Assistant Referees
58 Scots have gained FIFA Linesmen/Assistant Referees status:

Assistant Referee	No. of Seasons/Years	Years
David McGeachie	13	2013 - 2025
Martin Cryans	12	2003 - 2014
Frank Connor	11	2015 - 2025
Alan Mulvanny	11	2012 - 2014, 2016 - 2023
Vikki Robertson	11	2015 - 2025
Graeme Stewart	11	2015 - 2025
Dougie Potter	10	2016 - 2025
Vikki Allan	9	2017 - 2025
Kylie McMullan	9	2013 - 2021
Gordon Middleton	9	2004 - 2012
Francis Andrews	8	2004 - 2011
James Bee	8	2004 - 2008, 2010 - 2012
Graeme Chambers	8	2009 - 2016
Willie Conquer	8	2008 - 2015
Tom Murphy	8	2003 - 2010
Sean Carr	7	2016 - 2022
George Drummond	7	2006 - 2012

Assistant Referee	No. of Seasons/Years	Years
David Roome	7	2019 - 2025
Douglas Ross	7	2015 - 2021
Stuart Stevenson	7	2012 - 2018
Alan Cunningham	6	2001 - 2006
Andy Davis	6	2000 - 2005
Wilson Irvine	6	1998 - 2003
Alastair Mather	6	2013 - 2018
Gordon McBride	6	1997 - 2002
Daniel McFarlane	6	2019 - 2024
Calum Spence	6	2020 - 2024
Stewart Shearer	6	1999 - 2004
George Simpson	6	1993 - 1998
Keith Sorbie	6	2005 - 2010
Graeme Alison	5	1993 - 1997
David Doig	5	1999 - 2003
Jim Dunne	5	1998 - 2002
Bob Gunn	5	1995 - 1999
Joe Kelly	5	1994 - 1998
Stuart Logan	5	1999 - 2003
Jim Lyon	5	2003 - 2007
John McElhinney	5	1996 - 2000
Jim McBride	5	1998 - 2002
Molly Alexander	4	2017 - 2020
John Fleming	4	1995 - 1998
Jim Herald	4	1992 - 1995
Stuart Macaulay	4	2003 - 2006
Ross MacLeod	4	2022 - 2025
Douglas Main	4	1996 - 1999
Bobby Orr	4	1994 - 1997
Derek Rose	4	2009, 2012 - 2014

Assistant Referee	No. of Seasons/Years	Years
Alasdair Ross	4	2011 - 2014
Jonathan Bell	3	2023 - 2025
Kevin Bisset	3	1995 - 1996
Iain Cathcart	3	1992 - 1994
Martin Doran	3	2000 - 2002
Jordan Stokoe	3	2017 - 2019
Gavin Harris	2	2013 - 2014
Hayley Irvine	2	2015 - 2016
Mike Pocock	2	1992 - 1993
Chris Rae	2	2024 - 2025
Jim Carlin	1	1992
Stuart MacMillan	1	2015
George McGuire	1	1995

Video Match Official:

Referee	No. of Years	Years
John Beaton	1	2025
Kevin Clancy	1	2025
William Collum	1	2022
Andrew Dallas	1	2025
Bobby Madden	1	2022
Steven McLean	1	2025

Futsal

Referee	No. of Years	Years
Gordon McCabe	8	2017 - 2025

FIFA

When the four British Associations returned to membership of FIFA in 1946, the door was opened for British referees to be included in its List of International Referees, which had been operating for many years. Prior to rejoining FIFA, the SFA had only been in membership of FIFA for two brief spells from 1910 to 1920 and 1924 to 1928. As a consequence, the scope for the appointment of Scottish referees was essentially restricted to matches played in the British Isles.

The FIFA Referees' Committee formally came into being in 1946, essentially replacing a previous version, and was empowered to "compile a List of qualified referees from which officials will be selected to officiate in international matches" and "to try to establish a universal system of refereeing". This latter power heralded the start of a standardisation process which carries through to the present day. In the late 1940's and early 1950's Sir Stanley Rous, the Football Association Secretary and a member and then Chairman of the FIFA Referees' Committee, was an extremely influential figure and he did much to shape how refereeing would develop. In many ways, there was an imperialistic approach taken by him to refereeing, being of the belief that British referees (and English ones in particular) could teach the rest of the world how matches should be controlled. In fairness, this position was readily accepted in many parts of the world given that the game had emerged in Britain and its football and referees were held in high regard.

Badge

FIFA, rightly, recognised that referees were a key and important component of football. A FIFA Bulletin of 1951 stated that "Referees, we must reiterate, are the flag bearers and best supporters of the FIFA around the world." The wearing of the FIFA Referees' badge was therefore seen as having great significance. Gaining the badge was held to be very symbolic of the referee's connection to FIFA and the exercise of authority on its behalf. The badge had to be earned. In the post-War years it was only presented to referees who had refereed at least two international matches of representative A teams. For a brief period in the late 1950's, this requirement was tightened up – a referee had to have controlled at least six A matches before receiving the badge. This condition was soon relaxed outwith Europe where less international football was played and by the early 1960's the "two match" qualification had returned to universal use, but with the caveat that a referee's name had to have appeared twice on the FIFA List.

The significance of wearing the badge still held strong at this time, with FIFA conveying that it "will indicate membership of a referee fraternity" with the badge being "an insignia of that office".

Over the ensuing years, there were other adjustments made to the conditions of the award of the badge. By the mid-1970's, the conditions had been extended to include two matches officiated in the Olympics (Qualifiers or Finals) or other amateur tournaments organised by FIFA and subsequently further extended to include matches in the FIFA World Youth Championship and the Championships of the member Confederations. These conditions were in place until 1989 when FIFA decided to simplify the process by automatically issuing the FIFA badge to all referees included in its List, with the badge having to be worn at all the matches officiated at during the year of tenure as an international referee. The badge is always proudly worn by the recipients. Some issues arose in Scotland in 2010, due to a number of younger Category 1 referees becoming FIFA referees before fully establishing themselves in domestic football. For a brief period, these referees were given permission by the SFA Referee Committee not to wear their FIFA badge in domestic football to give them some protection from criticism that might go their way at games.

Up to the change in 1989, FIFA sent a badge automatically to the referee's National Association as soon as he had complied with the conditions. During the 1970's, the SFA invited the referees to Council meetings to be presented with their badge. This happened, for example, with John Gordon in 1974 and Ian

Foote in 1976. For a period, FIFA published its annual International List with an asterisk against the name of a badge holder.

In 2010, the SFA Referee Committee instituted a Dinner in the early part of each year to honour the FIFA Listed officials, to recognise their achievement and to present their badges to them. Football politics intervened in 2020 when UEFA required all FIFA referees officiating in its competitions to wear a "UEFA Match Official" badge instead of the FIFA badge.

Nominations

In the early 1950's, National Associations were able to nominate five referees for inclusion in the FIFA List, with FIFA stipulating that the "most important associations" (of which the SFA was one) could submit the names of three supplementary referees, hence the designation of Deputy in the Lists of the period. FIFA indicated that linesmen for international matches "may be chosen from national referees". In 1958, National Associations were enabled for the first time to nominate seven referees. Clarification was given on the appointments of linesmen for international matches: they need not be selected from the FIFA List but from "among other first class officials accustomed to acting as linesmen".

In 1989, FIFA increased the number of nominations National Associations could submit from seven to 10. This was effectively a means of enabling the larger associations to increase their number of FIFA referees and to better service the growing levels of international football at club and country level. The SFA decided to maintain its nominations at seven and it has done so consistently, with the exception of 2008 when only six nominations were submitted.

Conditions of Nomination

Whilst conditions for submitting nominations for the FIFA List no doubt existed in the years prior, the FIFA Referees' Committee confirmed the essential requirements in 1974, and these remained in place for a number of years. Proposed referees had to be at least 25 years of age and not older than 50 at 31st December in the year of nomination and had to have officiated regularly for at least two years in the First Division of their respective country. Medical and fitness tests had to be completed.

The standard of refereeing at the 1990 World Cup generated much discussion and led to significant changes to the construction of the FIFA List, chief of which was the inclusion of linesmen in the List for the first time in 1992 and, more importantly, the reduction of the age limit of 50 to 45 in 1993. Nominated referees and linesman being proposed for the first time could not be older than 40. This limit was reduced to 38 in 2006 and subsequently the minimum age for nomination of assistant referees was reduced from 25 to 23 years.

To be nominated as a linesman, the official had to have officiated more as a linesman rather than as a referee in the season before nomination. As the SFA had altered the operation of its own List in 1991, enabling Class 1 and 2 referees to act as linesman, this opportunity was taken full advantage of and a number of referees from these classes were nominated to be FIFA linesmen.

FIFA introduced a change of procedure for the 1997 List. A minimum one year period was now required to be served between being nominated as an assistant and as a referee. The SFA's creation of the Specialist Assistant Referee category in 1998 fed into the international sphere very quickly and a strong cadre of assistant referees soon emerged to represent the SFA on the FIFA List.

The last major change occurred in 2016 when FIFA dispensed with the retiral age limit of 45. In doing so, however, FIFA reserved the right to require referees over the age of 45 to undergo additional technical assessments as well as specific medical examinations and fitness testing on a case-by-case basis. Few referees have continued on the List after reaching 45 years of age.

Women officials were included in the FIFA List for the first time in 1995 with the Futsal category being introduced for 1996.

UEFA

The importance of UEFA to refereeing in Europe cannot be overstated. In the modern era, it has set the tone for referee development throughout the continent and it has always striven to produce top class referees so that the matches in its competitions can be officiated to the highest standards. As its wealth has grown in the last 30 years, it has devoted huge financial resources to develop football throughout Europe and refereeing, correctly, has been the recipient of a great deal of funding to achieve UEFA's aims.

Whilst UEFA was formed in 1954, it was not until 1968 that its Referee Committee was instituted. Its function was to oversee referees' appointments and to organise refereeing courses. In regard to appointments, it had been the case up to 1966 that UEFA invited the National Associations to designate a referee from their FIFA List for the match in question. On its creation, the Referees' Committee expressed concern at the general standard of referees nominated by the member associations for matches. This position was also shared by FIFA, with both bodies examining ways and means of bringing about improvement. Taking the view that some associations dealt with such nomination requests by sharing these appointments on a rotation basis amongst their referees, rather than by abilities, UEFA decided to introduce its own List of Referees for its competitions. The member associations were thus requested to submit the names of their three "most highly qualified" referees from their FIFA referees. The UEFA List operated through to the 1980's and its existence explains why it was difficult for new FIFA referees to break through and to receive sufficient appointments to provide a chance of establishing themselves at international level.

UEFA's first course for referees was held in Italy in 1969. Bill Anderson, Bill Mullan and John Paterson were selected by the SFA's Executive & General Purposes Committee to attend. Paterson spoke on the course at the 1970 Referees' Conference in an early example of cascading information out to the referee movement. The Executive & General Purposes Committee selected the referees to attend subsequent courses throughout the 1970's.

Over time, UEFA introduced categories for the European FIFA referees and these are hugely important in determining the progress and use of referees. Refined over the years, the categories are compiled annually and updated at the mid-point of each season. The initial style of courses organised by UEFA has also been developed over the years. Courses for the top categories are held at the start and mid-point of each season and in the early 1990's, a course was introduced for each year's intake of new FIFA referees. The course is effectively an induction course and is used to set the scene as to what is expected of the new referees at UEFA level. In the last decade, courses have been regularly held for assistant referees and to deal with the operation of Additional Assistant Referees and VAR.

A hugely important strand in the UEFA refereeing system is the assessment of referees, something which was recognised by the Referees' Committee when it was formed. Initially, it was not possible to cover each match with an Observer and the UEFA Delegate, generally a member of a UEFA committee, fulfilled the role though not competent to properly assess a referee. Slowly but surely, the inspection of referees was extended to the point that all UEFA matches have a Referee Observer in attendance. The growth in its wealth has enabled UEFA to increase the amount of Referee Observers, all of whom should be former international referees, with National Associations nominating potential Observers. Regular courses for Referee Observers are organised to ensure a standardised approach to assessment.

UEFA directly selected the referees from the Quarter-Finals onwards in the Club Competitions for the first time in season 1969-70. Thereafter, UEFA increasingly extended its control of appointments. In the 1970's and 1980's, for the first rounds of the club competitions, a National Association would be notified of the referees designated to some matches but would also be given free rein to nominate the referee for a particular match.

For the last decade or more, UEFA requests National Associations to submit a pool of referees, assistant referees and

Fourth Officials for appointment to the Group Stages, and now the League Phase, of its Club Competitions.

UEFA recognises that refereeing must develop constantly to meet the demands of the modern-day game. Due to the speed and movement of top-level football, allied to the intense media focus on the game, match officials have to be well-prepared, highly trained athletes (a huge focus has been placed on fitness training programmes) who also have tactical acumen, the mental strength to withstand pressure and the ability to make split-second decisions with confidence and consistency.

Attention is not just given by UEFA to referees on the FIFA List but also to those who stand a chance of reaching that standard. The introduction of its CORE (Centre of Refereeing Excellence) Course in 2010, aimed at developing young and promising match officials to prepare them for the intensity and ever-growing demands of elite-level football, has been of huge benefit to the many referees who have taken part in the course. It has given focus to each European association to identify future international officials at an early stage of their careers. The course offers a range of discussions, seminars and training sessions providing an excellent foundation to help them advance in their careers.

UEFA's refereeing activities have certainly kept pace with the game and for the good of football. This is something which might not always be understood and appreciated by clubs participating in its competitions when refereeing decisions are deemed to go against them (and National Associations too for that matter) together with, of course, the media which offers instant criticism of refereeing decisions.

SFA Nomination Process

In the post-war period, responsibility for deciding on the nominations for the FIFA List rested with the SFA Executive & General Purposes Committee, rather than the Referee Committee. The Referee Supervisors' Committee, all former referees and operating below the Referee Committee, had no role to play in the recommendation process, the SFA wishing to ensure a clean separation of responsibilities so that the decision making process was independent of any possible influence being exerted by a Supervisor in favour of a particular referee. That said, there can be little doubt that that Jack Mowat, once he became Chairman of the Referee Supervisors in 1962, had a significant role behind the scenes working in close co-operation with Secretary Willie Allan and his successor Ernie Walker.

Tom Wharton tried, unsuccessfully, to address the issue in 1977 when, speaking on his own behalf when Vice-Chairman of the Referee Supervisors, he requested that the Supervisors' Executive Committee be allowed to comment on the nominations before they were submitted to FIFA.

For many years, the nominations were entirely based on a referee's ranking in the domestic performance statistics over a rolling three season period. The top seven ranked referees determined by that process were the ones who were nominated. The underlying principle behind the use of this system was that the best performing referees would always rise to the top over that three season period. This generally proved to be the case and there was a degree of stability about the composition of the seven referees. New referees would obviously emerge over time and maintain their place on the FIFA List for a number of consecutive seasons but, every so often, a referee would briefly rise to the fore and serve only a season on the FIFA List due to falling outwith the top seven ranked referees. In such instances, it was difficult for the referee to establish himself in international football.

By the 1980's, the Disciplinary & Referee Committee had been given the responsibility of approving the FIFA nominations and the Referee Committee assumed the task when it was formed in its own right in 1993.

The process of selecting the nominees changed in the period after George Cumming became the SFA's Referee Training officer in 1988. There was a move away from rigidly using performance statistics to determine the seven nominees, to more of a talent identification process to better serve the purpose. This approach effectively ended the possibility of an official gaining a "surprise" entry into the top seven for a potentially brief period, and allowed the prospect of a referee with clear potential to have the opportunity of becoming a FIFA referee and the chance of developing a career in international football.

The Referee Supervisors were still not formally part of the decision-making process but were involved in general discussions about likely candidates and outcomes. There was close liaison between George Cumming and Tom Wharton, once he became the Chairman of the Referee Supervisors in 1990, on the likely nominations as issues were teased out between them. The changes to the FIFA List introduced by FIFA in the early 1990's confirmed the sense of the new approach being taken. The reduction of the age limit from 50 to 45 years of age combined with an upper age limit of 40 (and subsequently to 38) for nomination forced the hand of all National Associations to put forward younger referees for the List, a process which the SFA which has been successful in achieving.

The introduction of linesmen to the FIFA List generated a need to identify officials worthy of inclusion and brought with it a further level of necessary scrutiny of performance.

It also provided the opportunity of an official acting as an international linesman, gaining exposure to international football and all that that entails, and then progressing to be nominated as a FIFA referee. This change coincided with the SFA's restructuring of the List in 1991 which resulted in Class 1 and Class 2 referees acting as linesmen. The Class 1 referees Kenny Clark, Hugh Dallas and Willie Young were all selected as linesmen in 1992, with Stuart Dougal selected in 1993. All progressed from spells of one or two seasons as FIFA linesman to being a FIFA referee.

The Referee Committee was restructured in 2003, with the members of the Referee Supervisors' Executive Committee forming the majority of the membership. This provided the opportunity, for the first time, for former referees to decide on the nominations. An increased focus on the development and application of a strategy on the nominations resulted. To allow the referees to have the chance of developing a career at international level, a system of refreshing the nominees regularly by nominating younger referees to replace others whose international careers were not going to advance, was introduced. The same principle applies to the nomination of assistant referees.

From the perspective of a referee included in the FIFA List, the process is brutal when it results in not being re-nominated. A stagnation within UEFA's referee categories often signals that there is little prospect of advancement and a decision has to be taken if that referee should be kept on the List or not. If there is a definite candidate emerging to take his place and deserving of the opportunity to be nominated as a FIFA referee, then the likelihood is that a change will be effected. There is a certain cachet to be enjoyed by a referee when FIFA status is held and it is a huge blow to the person at times when that is lost, which is quite understandable. The Referee Committee understands full well the impact of removal from the FIFA List has on an official but it has to carry through the implementation of its strategy.

When a referee is not re-nominated for inclusion in the FIFA List, there is a parallel of sorts to a football club deciding to transfer one of its star players just as his career has peaked. The drive to produce younger referees for inclusion in the FIFA List is not confined to Scotland. All European associations are striving to do the same. It is extremely beneficial for a referee to establish him or herself quickly at UEFA level. When a referee is admitted to the FIFA List, it means he/she starts off at the lowest of UEFA's referees' categories. This equates to a referee being admitted to the SFA's List at Category 3 Development and having to be promoted a few times to reach Category 1. Progress through the categories is very much performance based and the competition is severe. To reach the top in UEFA is a huge achievement on the part of every referee who manages it.

The selection of the nominees is addressed extremely seriously, with a protocol being adopted in 2017 in respect of the nomination and decision-making process. There is an almost continual process of monitoring and evaluation of future prospective FIFA officials. The identification of future candidates starts early. It has to, to keep pace with developments at a higher level.

UEFA's CORE Course has played a pivotal and successful role in the development of future international match officials. The National Associations are required to identify potential candidates for future inclusion in the FIFA List. The officials on the course receive specialist advice on refereeing over two week-long courses and officiate at games in the lower Divisions of the French and Swiss Championships. The course has proved to be an invaluable stepping stone for referees in their careers. The possibility of being selected for each CORE Course is a great motivation for them. All the Scottish officials selected have progressed to the FIFA List. The early success of the CORE Course led to the SFA replicating a similar format which effectively starts the process of identification and development of young talented referees and assistant referees into future elite referees. Such programmes are now common throughout Europe as all the National Associations strive to do what is required produce referees for international football.

The World Cup

The World Cup is football's greatest competition. Just as every player dreams of representing his country at it, it is the same for a referee. Being selected for the World Cup is the pinnacle of every referee's career. Scotland has a proud record of being represented at the tournament by its referees.

There have been 22 editions of the World Cup and 10 Scottish referees have achieved selection. Two of them, Bobby Davidson and Hugh Dallas, have officiated at more than one. Davidson is in a select band of 22 referees who have been at three World Cups. Dallas is one of 95 referees who have taken part in two.

The list of referees, and their year of involvement, is:

George Mitchell (1950)
Charlie Faultless (1954)
Jack Mowat (1958)
Bobby Davidson (1962, 1970 and 1974)
John Gordon (1978)

Bob Valentine (1982)
George Smith (1990)
Les Mottram (1994)
Hugh Dallas (1998 and 2002)

One other referee, Brian McGinlay, should be included in this List given that he was selected for the 1986 World Cup. Regrettably, however, he had to resign from the SFA's List of Referees due to personal circumstances in April 1986.
Additionally, another Scot, Eddie Lennie, living in Australia, was selected for the 1998 World Cup.
Had McGinlay officiated at the 1986 tournament, Scotland would have had a referee chosen for 14 consecutive World Cups. Scotland is placed 13th equal in a world ranking of countries which have had referees selected for the tournament. In terms of European countries, Scotland is ranked 9th equal.
This section expands upon each referee's involvement in the World Cup. A picture emerges as to how refereeing at the World Cup evolved from 1950 to the modern era given reference to the selection of the referees and the developing manner of the instructions given to them. Refereeing had to keep pace with developments in the playing of the game. The World Cup expanded from 16 teams in 1978, to 24 in 1982, and to 32 in 1998. This expansion brought changes to the way referees were deployed, with, for example, the introduction of Fourth Officials and assistant referees in 1994. One thing which did not alter was the competition to achieve selection for the tournament. Such competition has always existed and always been intense. It undoubtedly helped Scotland's referees to have a voice at the table when Jack Mowat and Tom Wharton were members of the FIFA Referees' Committee during the period 1974 to 1990. Once the tournament gets underway, the competition between the referees becomes even more acute, especially to be retained for the knock-out stages. Whilst a Scottish referee has never taken charge of a World Cup Final, it is still nonetheless a terrific achievement that three Scots have officiated at a Final as either a linesman or a Fourth Official. It is a remarkable record for a relatively small country.

Within Scotland, there is understandably great pride taken by the Referees' Associations in respect of their members who have achieved selection for the World Cup. In this context, Lanarkshire RA has had five members chosen - Jack Mowat, Bobby Davidson, Hugh Phillips, Les Mottam and Hugh Dallas. Angus & Perthshire RA claim John Gordon and Bob Valentine, Glasgow RA has Charlie Faultless, Edinburgh & District RA George Smith and Stirlingshire RA, George Mitchell.

Brazil, 1950 – George Mitchell

FIFA invited the National Associations to nominate two referees for selection for the Finals and the SFA put forward the names of Willie Webb and George Mitchell. Webb resigned from the SFA List in November 1949 to become a Referee Inspector for the Scottish League, and Charlie Faultless was nominated in his stead. FIFA selected Mitchell to be one of 14 referees for the tournament.

The 1950 World Cup was played at a time when refereeing was starting to be given great focus by FIFA and when British referees were held in high esteem around the world. With Stanley Rous being the Chairman of FIFA's Referees' Committee, he was in a position to exercise great influence in how refereeing matters were handled. Out of the 14 selected referees, six were British –in addition to Mitchell four were English and one was Welsh. It was no surprise that three British officials were appointed to the opening match, Brazil v Mexico, in the Maracana Stadium, Rio de Janeiro. England's George Reader was the referee, with the linesmen being George Mitchell and Mervyn Griffiths of Wales. As a means of demonstrating the standards of British referees and to encourage the attainment of such standards, all the other referees had to attend the match to watch how the officials controlled the game. For the Finals, it had been decided that players could charge goalkeepers in possession of the ball. Common in Britain, such a practice had not been accepted by the South American associations up to the Finals.

Mitchell had one outing as referee at the Finals - a 2-2 draw in a Group match between Sweden and Paraguay in Curitaba, for

which he received praise for his handling of the match. A line appointment on Brazil v Spain in the Final Round of matches was Mitchell's next assignment. Refereed by England's Reg Leafe, the match was won easily by Brazil by 6-1 though it required firm handling due to some robust tackling.
The win set things up for the last set of the Final Round fixtures. With Brazil needing only to draw against Uruguay to win the competition, they were red-hot favourites with the whole country going wild in anticipation of victory. British referees were chosen to officiate the match – George Reader as the referee, Arthur Ellis (England) and George Mitchell as the linesmen. A world record attendance of 204,000 was in the Maracana. After a goalless first half, Brazil took the lead but were stunned by two late goals by Uruguay. The Brazil players were bewildered by their loss. In a newspaper article in the 1980's, Mitchell recalled that "when Uruguay won against all the odds, you could have heard a pin drop. The shocked silence was amazing."
To round the tournament off, a farewell dinner was held for all the referees at which they were presented with a World Cup medal and, of all things, a fountain pen. It was reported that the British referees had left a lasting impression of impartiality and efficiency which, the Brazilians said, had never been previously equalled in that part of the world. 10 of the 22 matches in the competition had been controlled by British referees.

Switzerland, 1954 – Charlie Faultless

Charlie Faultless was the SFA's successful nominee for the Finals, the first where matches were broadcast live on television. He was one of 16 referees chosen by FIFA. British referees formed a quarter of the officials - Arthur Ellis and Bill Ling from England and Mervyn Griffiths from Wales were the others.
In the pre-tournament build up, FIFA was aiming for consistent and uniform interpretation of the Laws of the Game by the referees, which might seem an obvious approach but at the time it was essential given the cultural differences in the playing of football around the world and the approach taken by referees in

each country. The issue of "charging" goalkeepers was still some way off being settled. Prevalent in British football, such actions were not tolerated in other countries, with the goalkeeper being left in possession of the ball. The approach taken by FIFA in these briefings was forward thinking. Visual aids were used to try and overcome the language difficulties in the referees' meetings. Films were shown of match incidents, first at ordinary speed, and then repeated in slow motion to generate discussion and to highlight the need for correct interpretation. Analysis of match incidents in this style became a staple cornerstone of modern referee education.

Faultless was appointed to referee Brazil's Group match against Yugoslavia, and had Arthur Ellis as his senior linesman. The match was drawn 1-1, with, unusually, extra-time being played. He then ran the line in a Group Play-Off match between West Germany and Turkey. Faultless was selected to referee Switzerland and Hungary in the Quarter-Finals. The match was won by Austria by seven goals to five, the highest ever scoring match in the World Cup. He was then chosen to run the line to Mervyn Griffiths in the Semi-Final between Hungary and Uruguay. Tensions were high before the match was played, due to player indiscipline in the Brazil v Hungary Quarter-Final, with FIFA impressing strongly on the teams that a repeat of such behaviour would not be tolerated. As it turned out, both teams put on a great spectacle of football, with Hungary winning after extra-time.

The Final is remembered for the surprise West German victory over the great Hungarian team of the time. Faultless later expressed the opinion that West Germany would never have won had the studs they were using had been properly checked. He held the view that their studs were as long as spikes which had given them a great advantage in the wet, slippery conditions in which the game was played.

Sweden, 1958 – Jack Mowat

Early in 1958, speculation emerged that the three referees being recommended by the SFA to FIFA were Jack Mowat, Bobby Davidson and Hugh Phillips. In the event, Mowat was selected by FIFA and, after missing out on the two previous Finals, he was able to get time away from his work to take part. 150 referees had been nominated the world's National Associations. There was still a strong British influence amongst the final selection of 22 referees. Four were British – in addition to Mowat, there was England's Arthur Ellis and Reg Leafe and Wales' Mervyn Griffiths (appearing at his third successive Finals). The referees were required to arrive in Sweden two days before the first matches were to be played for their "instructional session". The referees received a daily allowance of 50 Swiss Francs.

Jack Mowat refereed one match in the Group Stages – Sweden's 2-1 win against Hungary. He delayed the start of the match by 12 minutes as he insisted that the Hungarians change their studs. Perhaps he was mindful of Charlie Faultless' comments on the Final four years previously. He had two line appointments in the Group stages – Mexico v Sweden and Mexico v Hungary. The appointments certainly brought a degree of familiarity with the teams.

A report by the FIFA Referees' Committee on the Finals gives an insight to how the refereeing was viewed. Opinion was divided as to whether the standard of refereeing was higher than at the previous Finals. There were also divided opinions on the standard of refereeing of the British referees in 1954 and 1958 compared with the standard of the other referees. Some critics felt that the British referees had played a more prominent part in 1954 (10 of 26 matches had been handled by British referees) than in 1958 (only 7 of the 35 matches were refereed by British officials) and others affirmed that the standard of the European and American referees had much improved and that the differences between the two groups, if any, was very small. The main difference in outlook was that British referees had a more tolerant approach and interpretation of the charge in general and of charging the goalkeeper in particular, evidence that the conception of the game continued to vary in different countries. In this context, it is interesting to note that Jack Mowat had stated at the SFA's Referees' Summer School in 1956 that "foreign countries had a different outlook on pushing, charging and tackling" and that "it was really a farce for us to play on the continent or in the World Cup until FIFA applied the same rules as we did."

The report noted that the advantage rule was applied differently by referees and that there was a variance in the penalising of fouls – some referees penalised minor fouls whilst more severe fouls went unpunished. Overall, FIFA held that the referees had done a good job in the tournament. With the referees also acting as linesmen, it was felt that not all of them were accustomed to handling a flag and the report recorded that some even thought that being a linesman was below their prestige. It appeared that some linesmen would have liked to have assumed the responsibility of the referee and that some others did not assist the referee in the proper manner. It would not be for another 32 years before this important issue was properly addressed by the introduction of FIFA linesmen. The FIFA report recognised the importance of proper teamwork between the referee and his linesmen, with it being stressed that "under no circumstances should the spectators be given the impression that there is discord between them".

The number of referees was reduced after the Quarter-Finals, which was not liked by some referees, despite being informed in advance. The report hinted that a small number of referees did not wholly appreciate the quality of their accommodation. Some referees felt that better quality breakfasts and more baths being available would have been appreciated. In later life, Mowat would confide that the World Cup had not been the happiest of experiences for him and that he regarded Stanley Rous to have been his nemesis.

Chile, 1962 – Bobby Davidson

This was the first of a remarkable three World Cups for Bobby Davidson, with FIFA selecting him ahead of the SFA's two other nominees, Hugh Phillips and Tom Wharton. He was one of 18 referees chosen for the tournament. He and Ken Aston of England were the only British referees.

Aged 33 at the time, Davidson was chosen to referee the 0-0 draw between West Germany and Italy Group match, which was played in Santiago with an attendance of 65,000. It was a physical encounter with few goal-scoring chances. Davidson refereed West Germany again in the last of the Group matches, this time against the host nation, Chile. Either side of this match, Davidson ran the line in two other Group matches – Hungary v Bulgaria and Italy v Switzerland.

Whilst he did not referee any further matches in the tournament, FIFA retained his services after the Quarter-Finals and he was selected as a lineman for the Final, Brazil v Czechoslovakia. One memento Davidson kept from the match was his linesman's flag. So determined was he to retain the flag that he put it down his trouser leg when leaving the stadium.

On his return to Scotland, Davidson gave an interview to a newspaper on his experience at the Finals, He was critical of FIFA's Disciplinary Committee for not carrying out its intention to "get tough" with offenders after the Italy v Chile Group match, a game which became known as the "Battle of Santiago" due to the level of violence in it - two Italians were sent off, numerous punches were thrown by players and police intervention was required on four occasions. He was of the view that referees should receive better backing in future and that players should be properly punished if sent off. It seemed also that FIFA had still to properly get to grips with organisational arrangements for the referees. Davidson commented that they were housed three to a room and that there was nothing specifically organised to help fill in free time.

England, 1966 – Hugh Phillips

148 nominations were submitted by 62 member associations of FIFA for this World Cup. 25 referees were announced in February. British referees were again to the fore – in addition to Phillips, Jack Adair (Northern Ireland) and Leo Callaghan (Wales) were selected together with England's Ken Dagnall and George McCabe. England's five other FIFA Referees were chosen as linesmen. Each of the 16 competing associations had a referee at the Finals. There were nine referees selected from countries not at the World Cup.

Before the Finals got underway, in a somewhat grandiose arrangement to mark the holding of the tournament in England,

Harold Wilson, the Prime Minister, hosted a Dinner for 750 guests, including the match officials, at the London Guild Hall. The referees and the team managers were brought together the day after the Dinner for a briefing conducted by Sir Stanley Rous, now the FIFA President and still the Referees' Committee Chairman. Referees were requested "to keep on top of their job" and teams urged "to play the game".

Phillips was chosen to referee West Germany v Switzerland in the opening match in Group 2 and then was a linesman in the Spain v Switzerland match three days later. Switzerland protested about Phillips' appointment given that he had refereed its match against West Germany. The Swiss indicated that they had nothing against Phillips but, in principle, they felt his appointment was wrong. FIFA dismissed the protest saying the appointment was normal procedure.

FIFA continued that style of appointment procedure by appointing Phillips to West Germany's Quarter-Final against Uruguay at Hillsborough. At the conclusion of the tournament, all the referees received a replica of the World Cup, the Jules Rimet Trophy.

Phillips, from Motherwell, kept a local newspaper up to date with regular bulletins to convey his experiences during the Finals.

Mexico, 1970 – Bobby Davidson

Confirmation of the referees selected for the World Cup was issued by FIFA in February. Chosen for his second Finals, Davidson was one of 30 referees selected from a short leet of 53, evidence of a shift in approach by FIFA in the selection process. The days of requesting nominations from National Associations had come to an end.

The referees were required to arrive in Mexico City a week before the opening match. Davidson took with him a phrase book, containing football and refereeing phrases in six languages, which he had used throughout his career. At the tournament, all the referees were aided in regard to dealing with any language difficulties by the introduction of yellow and red cards for cautions and sendings-off. When they arrived in

Mexico, the referees went through a medical examination, lecture sessions and training to become acclimatised to the high altitude. They were told that they must conform to a definite pattern of match control in accordance with instructions laid down by the International FA Board, another sign of a more focussed approach being taken by FIFA.

Davidson refereed only one match in the competition, Israel v Uruguay in the Group Stages, but it was a game in which he won considerable praise, so much so that he was tipped for the Final by some. He had refused to be taken in by the "acting" of the Uruguayans each time they were felled in a tackle. Davidson reportedly shouted "get up" to players pretending they were injured and refused trainers on to attend them. The message quickly got through to the players and they returned to their feet to play on. Uruguay won the match 2-0.

Davidson received two line appointments after refereeing his match. Firstly, he ran the line in the USSR v Belgium Group Stage match and then encountered USSR and Uruguay again in a Quarter-Final. Both matches were played in the Azteca Stadium in Mexico City.

West Germany, 1974 – Bobby Davidson

Bobby Davidson completed his hat-trick of officiating at the World Cup when he was selected as one of 30 referees for the tournament in West Germany.

As with previous Finals, the referees did not receive any fees for officiating, with it being it was reported that they would receive a daily allowance of £16. In the days before commercial deals and free provision of kit, the referees had to bring their own. An article in a newspaper featured Davidson and his kit expenditure – altogether it was costing him a minimum of £55.

Frankfurt was used as the referees' base for the Finals. They had a week-long preparation course, with FIFA wanting to ensure a common and consistent interpretation of the Laws by the referees. High standards were expected from them. FIFA was seeking to build upon the similar course held prior to the 1970 World Cup. Clarification was given on how certain match situations should be handled. Films were used to illustrate the correct decisions referees should take. Many clips were used from previous Finals to highlight past mistakes. Referees travelled from Frankfurt to the match venues, with match appointments being announced 36 hours before each match.

Davidson, surprisingly perhaps, did not referee a match in the First Group Stage, but had line appointments to the Poland v Argentina and East Germany v Chile matches. He was chosen to handle the opening Second Group Stage match between the Netherlands and Argentina, one of the games of the Finals as Netherlands dismantled Argentina 4-0. Davidson was then a linesman in the Netherlands v Brazil match.

Davidson had gone to the World Cup with high hopes of being appointed to the Final. Alas for him, the tournament ended in major disappointment. On the day before the appointments for the Final and $3^{rd}/4^{th}$ Place match were to be announced, Ken Aston, the Vice-Chairman of the Referees' Committee, had told Davidson during a train journey between Frankfurt and Munich that he more than likely would be the referee for the Final. Davidson phoned his wife in Airdrie to let her know. Then, the following morning, things fell apart. Davidson and Jack Taylor, the English referee, were room-mates in the Munich hotel. The appointment of the referee to the Final somehow had been leaked to the British press and Davidson was dumfounded when a journalist came to his and Taylor's room to tell Taylor that he had been appointed. Davidson reacted badly. The appointment was soon formally announced. It was said that none of the South American referees had been completely satisfactory in the tournament, although it would have been ideal to have appointed one for a match between two European countries. Reference was made to Taylor's great experience. Six officials had been named – three for the Final and three for the $3^{rd}/4^{th}$ Place match. Davidson was not among them and he packed his bags and flew home to Scotland in anger. In comments made to a newspaper, Davidson said he was "sick and disgusted, having been told I was to be given the game". He hinted that he would give up refereeing due to how he had been treated but, after a period of reflection, he did not carry this through and refereed for a further two seasons.

In the aftermath, sources from the Netherlands team denied that they had exerted any influence on the appointment for the Final, although it was conveyed that they were not happy with Davidson's handling of their match against Argentina. It also emerged that FIFA's Disciplinary Committee was not entirely satisfied with Davidson's performance in the Netherlands v Brazil match, being of the view that, as he was close to the incident, he should have seen a Brazilian player knocking out Johan Neeskens with a punch. Linesmen had been warned to look out for foul play off the ball, and Davidson missed that punch. Another important factor in the selection for the Final which probably counted against Davidson was that with the Netherlands reaching the Final against West Germany, he had officiated in three of their matches – one as a referee and twice as a linesman. Taylor had not been involved in any of the Finalists' matches. Davidson's disappointment at not getting the Final can be understood, with there being a serious issue over the Referees' Committee handling of the situation by Aston letting him know that he was in line for the Final, but the general context requires to be taken into account. Such are the vagaries at the top of refereeing as a tournament progresses to its conclusion.

Argentina, 1978 – John Gordon

John Gordon's selection as one of the 28 referees for the Finals was confirmed in February. In a newspaper interview he said he was "absolutely thrilled at the prospect of going to the World Cup". In a prescient comment he added: "The success of the World Cup as a spectacle could depend on the refereeing so everything will be done to keep a tight control." He outlined his thoughts on the approach he would take "Although it will be a whole new experience, I'll basically be doing what I do in every match. I'll be trying to read each game. I'll have to weigh up the teams, the tensions and the possibilities of trouble. Yet I'm hoping to keep the games flowing as smoothly as possible, because that's what football is all about. But all the time, I'll be trying to snuff out any trouble before it starts."

The referees arrived in Argentina a week before the Finals got underway. Gordon was not the only Scot to be involved. Jack Mowat had been tasked by the FIFA Referees' Committee with drawing up the instructions for the referees. Mowat considered them to be the strictest instructions ever given to referees saying "I have brought every instruction on football up-to-date: tackling from the side, from behind, obstruction on the goalkeeper and all the points which are likely to occur. FIFA is determined to make the Finals a football spectacular." The daily allowances for these Finals had reached £36 per day but referees were reportedly unhappy about the low rate and a modest increase was achieved after negotiations with FIFA.

In the first Group Stage, Gordon was in charge of Tunisia's 3-1 win over Mexico in Rosario and was a linesman in the Italy v Hungary match. He refereed Netherland's opening match in the Second Group Stage, a resounding 5-1 win over Austria in Cordoba. No sanctions were issued by him in his two matches.

Spain, 1982 – Bob Valentine

Bob Valentine was one of 41 referees chosen for the Finals. In a remarkable twist of fate, Valentine followed in the footsteps of John Gordon at the previous World Cup, which he was particularly pleased about as Gordon had been his instructor when he attended the training classes in Dundee.

The referees once again arrived one week before the tournament started and were based in a hotel close to Real Madrid's training complex. Armed police guarded the hotel. The now-standard fitness tests, medicals, training and discussions were undertaken as preparation. Valentine's first appointment was as a linesman for the 1-1 draw between Czechoslovakia and Kuwait. He was then chosen to referee West Germany and Austria, the last in the opening group games and regarded at the outset as one of the plum ties in the competition. It was felt that it would be a hard fought match but, as things turned out, it was anything but.

By the time the match came round, Austria had beaten Chile and Algeria. West Germany had beaten Chile and Algeria's 3-2 win over Chile meant that if Austria drew or defeated West Germany, Algeria would qualify. If West Germany won by more than one goal Algeria would qualify due to a better goal difference than Austria. The only score which would knock Algeria out would be a 1-0 win for West Germany, meaning West Germany and Austria would qualify.

The match was played in Gijon, with searing temperatures. Many Algerians were in attendance in anticipation of their team qualifying for the next stage.

West Germany scored after 10 minutes, eased back a little and allowed Austria to come into the match although little threat was offered. There was a chorus of boos at half-time. The second half started at a sedentary pace. The booing became incessant and people tried to scale the fence surrounding the pitch due to the way the game was being played. Riot police became involved. Bedlam erupted from the Algerians as the game finished with the fateful 1-0 result. Valentine was glad that he had come through the game without any difficulty or controversy about any of his decisions. How wrong he was. Algeria and other associations called for West Germany and Austria – and Valentine – to be thrown out of the tournament due to the approach they had taken to playing the game. The Algerians called the affair "a sinister plot". Michel Hidalgo, the French manager, suggested wryly that both teams should be nominated for the Nobel Peace Prize. Valentine was accused of complacency by the Algerians, who thought he should have intervened with the two teams on their lack of effort. Valentine later commented "It may seem astonishing, but while I was aware that it was not the most physical or hard fought match in which I had ever officiated, I was never aware of how it was coming over in such a bad way to spectators, other than the Algerians with their vested interest. I was at least praised for my concentration in spite of such terrible distractions going on all around the stadium."

Although the circumstances of the match were discussed by FIFA, no action was taken against the two teams. One significant outcome did follow for future tournaments, however. It was the last time that the final group matches were played at different times so as to avoid any possible repetition of what had happened. The match continued to cause interest for many years afterwards. As the referee, Valentine was very much a

central figure and he was contacted regularly by journalists from all over the world wishing to gain his views on the match.
Valentine was one of 12 referees retained to officiate in the second round of Group Matches and the later stages onwards. He was appointed to referee the USSR v Poland match in the Camp Nou, Barcelona. The match was very fraught given the political background at the time in view of the emergence of the "Solidarity" movement in Poland. Polish supporters displaying "Solidarity" banners around the stadium generated complaints from Russian TV. Scuffles broke out as Spanish police tried to remove the banners. A 0-0 draw enabled Poland to progress to the Semi-Finals. Valentine, a trim figure, lost over half a stone in weight during the game due to the heat, even though the match had kicked-off at 9.00pm.
Valentine's involvement in the Finals concluded with his selection as a linesman for the Semi-Final match, West Germany v France in Seville. This was one of the greatest ever World Cup matches – a 3-3 draw after extra-time and won 5-4 on penalties by West Germany.

Italy, 1990 – George Smith

George Smith was one 29 referees selected for these Finals. In March, FIFA gathered all the officials for a preparatory meeting in Italy where medical and fitness tests were undertaken. Smith had the misfortune of sustaining a calf injury during the fitness test on a flooded running track due to the awful weather conditions. As part of the advance preparations for the Finals, all the referees had to act as a linesman in five matches in their home country.
The referees were split between two centres, Milan and Rome, for the Finals. Smith was based in Rome and, during his time there, he was part of a group taken to the Vatican to have an audience with the Pope.
Smith refereed one match in the competition – Czechoslovakia's 1-0 win over Austria in Florence, a match in which he cautioned seven Austrian players. He was a linesman in Italy's match against Czechoslovakia in Rome's Olympic Stadium. He was among a large group of referees who did not

progress to the knock-out stages. On his return home to Edinburgh, Smith revealed his thoughts on his involvement at the World Cup in a newspaper interview, expressing natural disappointment at not having officiated at more games. The Finals had set new records for the number of cautions and sendings-off (two Argentinians were sent off in the Final) and although FIFA had issued a "get tough" edict, Smith reckoned that it was a difficult tournament. He suggested that the problems being experienced in Scottish football were mirrored worldwide. "There is so much money in the game, and the prizes are so great that it's win at all costs. Players have a lack of respect for their fellow professionals and sadly this results in many of them doing some rather nasty things to each other." It was certainly a watershed tournament for refereeing, given the changes FIFA instigated in the following couple of years. The referees were afforded ultra-tight security with their hotels placed under round-the-clock armed guard and they travelled to matches in a five car motorcade with police outriders. At times Smith had found it a bit oppressive. "You couldn't even go out for a stroll without alerting a FIFA official and even then you were accompanied by a guard. But football rivals Catholicism as the No. 1 religion in Italy and the game is subject to the most intense external pressures."

USA, 1994 – Les Mottram

By this World Cup, FIFA had implemented major changes to the FIFA List – lowering the retiral age from 50 to 45 and introducing linesmen – and had further refined the selection process for the Finals.
In November 1993 Les Mottram was included in an initial selection of 30 referees and 25 linesmen for the Finals, for which 24 and 22, respectively, were to be chosen. The final selection was determined following a gathering in Dallas in March where the customary fitness and medical examinations were undertaken. In the Fitness test, Mottram, always an extremely fit referee, was ranked 6th overall. At the discussion sessions, FIFA used an SFA referee training video.

Mottram had fly to Dallas, the referees' base for the tournament, just a few days ahead of the opening match. For the Finals, FIFA issued two new and influential directives to the referees which were designed to make the game safer for the players and more entertaining for spectators: i) the violent tackle from behind – when the legs are taken with no attempt to play the ball – was to receive an immediate red card for serious foul play and ii) if an offside is unclear, it should not be awarded.

Mottram refereed two Group matches – a 0-0 draw between South Korea and Bolivia in which he sent off a Bolivian player for two cautions and cautioned five other players, and Nigeria's 2-0 win over Greece. Both matches were played in Foxborough, Massachussetts in front of capacity crowds of 53,000. In-between these matches, Mottram was the Fourth Official for the Republic of Ireland's famous match against Italy match at the Giants Stadium in New York where the 0-0 draw put the Republic through to the knockout stages.

France, 1998 – Hugh Dallas and Eddie Lennie

34 referees were selected for the Finals, two of them being Scots. Hugh Dallas was one of 15 referees from UEFA with the Australia-based Eddie Lennie the sole representative of the Oceania Confederation. A week long course at Gressy, near Paris, was held for the referees in March to go through the fitness and medical tests and undertake discussions. FIFA wanted to ban the tackle from behind (again!), with the referees being instructed to send off any player who committed such a tackle. The interpretation of this requirement and how to apply it caused concern and to help matters, FIFA produced a video to show players exactly what constituted a sending-off for the offence. The video was distributed to referees, the participating National Associations and team coaches. In connection with this, Hugh Dallas was invited by the Scotland team manager, Craig Brown, to speak to the Scotland squad on the referees' instructions before they travelled to France. In a sign of the wealth now generated by football, FIFA was now paying a sum of over £15,000 to each referee to more properly recognise their

important function at the tournament. Assistant referees received approximately £12,000. Daily allowances continued to be paid. As well as the kit now being provided by FIFA, the referees were also issued with a leisure suit supplied by the French designer Yves St. Laurent.

Hugh Dallas' first appointment was as the Fourth Official for the Saudi Arabia v Denmark match and was followed by refereeing Belgium and Mexico in Bordeaux, in which he sent off a player from each team and cautioned three other players.

Eddie Lennie's first appointment was also as a Fourth Official in the opening Group matches – Morocco v Norway in Montpellier. He returned to the same venue to referee Italy's 3-0 defeat of Cameroon and then officiated at Romania and Tunisia in the Stade de France in Paris before 77,000 spectators. After being Fourth Official for the Round of 16 tie between the Netherlands and Yugoslavia in Tolouse, the Stade de France was Hugh Dallas' next destination. One of eight referees retained for the knock-out stages, he was selected to control the Quarter-Final between the hosts France and Italy. The match, played in front of 77,000 spectators, was won by France on penalties after a 0-0 draw. Dallas was highly praised for his handling of the game and, although that seemed to put him into contention for the Semi-Finals or Final, it was not to be.

Dallas and Lennie each came away from the Finals with great appreciation of what they had experienced. Dallas said "I've been a professional referee for the last five weeks and tasted the benefits. Training every morning, attended to by physios and advance looks at teams on videos. There's time to concentrate fully and prepare. We also see other games and study refereeing styles. The day after our matches we met the Observer and analysed what went on. Good and bad points were discussed to help us improve our performance."

Eddie Lennie considered that the camaraderie which developed amongst the match officials had the greatest impact on him, living and working together as they did for the duration of the tournament.

South Korea/Japan, 2002 – Hugh Dallas

FIFA selected 36 referees and 36 assistant referees for this tournament with Hugh Dallas being chosen for his second consecutive Finals. He was one of 14 UEFA referees picked.

Dallas was not the only Scot to play a part in the refereeing at the World Cup. George Cumming had left his position as the SFA's Development Director in 2000 to become FIFA's first-ever Head of Refereeing. At the Finals, working under the FIFA Referees' Committee, he was responsible for the education and training of the match officials. Cumming had also had a role at the 1998 World Cup, having been appointed by FIFA as a Technical Adviser tasked with making an instructional film for referees.

Dallas was based in South Korea for the opening period of the tournament and his first appointment was as a Fourth Official – for the Paraguay v South Africa match in Busan. His selection as the referee for Portugal's match against Poland generated some controversy. Portugal protested due to Dallas' role as Fourth Official in their European Championship Semi-Final against France in 2000 and his becoming embroiled with the Portuguese bench following the award of a penalty kick on an assistant's signal. FIFA dismissed the spurious protest and Portugal ran out comfortable 4-0 winners.

In the Round of 16, Dallas was the Fourth Official in the Germany v Paraguay match and was then put in charge of the Quarter-Final between Germany and the USA, won 1-0 by the Germans. There were a couple of incidents in the game which generated interest. The USA claimed that a clear penalty had been denied them for a handling offence but FIFA supported Dallas' decision not to award a penalty as the handling was deemed unintentional. Dallas had also cautioned the German player Oliver Neuville after consulting an assistant referee but, post-match, FIFA transferred the caution to Neuville's team mate Jens Jeremies.

This latter incident certainly did not impact on Dallas at all, for he was selected to be the Fourth Official for the Final, Germany v Brazil, in Yokohama, Japan. The appointment was viewed as a clear statement of support for Dallas given the incidents in the

Germany v USA match. Dallas thus became the third Scot to be part of the refereeing team for a World Cup Final.

The European Championships

The European Championships, first held in 1960, have developed greatly over its 17 editions, and is a good barometer as to how football has grown over that time – progressing from just four countries competing in the Semi-Finals, the $3^{rd}/4^{th}$ Place match and the Final in 1960 to 24 countries participating at the 2016 Championships.

Bill Mullan was Scotland's first referee to be involved in the Finals, when he was selected as one of four referees for the four-team tournament held in Belgium in 1972. He refereed West Germany's 2-1 win against Belgium in the Semi-Finals, and had as his linesmen John Paterson and John Workman who had been appointed by the SFA.

The Finals expanded to eight teams for 1980 in Italy, where they were split into two Groups with the winners and runners-up of each group qualifying for the Semi-Finals. Brian McGinlay was one of 12 referees chosen by UEFA for the tournament. UEFA again requested the referees' National Association to select the linesmen to accompany the referees. The SFA appointed David Syme and Tommy Muirhead as McGinlay's linesmen. McGinlay handled West Germany's last Group match, a 0-0 draw with Greece in Turin.

UEFA maintained the same format of the 1984 Finals in France, with Bob Valentine earning selection as one of 14 referees. The same approach continued in regard to the selection of linesmen, with the SFA choosing Brian McGinlay and Hugh Williamson. To prepare for the Finals, Valentine and his linesmen had to work as a team in six domestic matches. Valentine was put in charge of the host nation's Group match against Belgium, played in Nantes, and a resounding 5-0 home victory.

Valentine confirmed his standing as one of the elite European referees of his era when he was selected for his second successive Finals in 1988, played in West Germany. UEFA again picked 14 referees, with the Finals maintaining the same format as the previous two tournaments. Kenny Hope and Andrew Waddell were selected by the SFA to be Valentine's linesmen. The team once again had to control a number of domestic matches as preparation in advance of the Finals. As in 1984, Valentine found himself appointed to a match involving the host nation in the Group Stage – Germany's match against Denmark in Gelsenkirchen, a game won 2-0 by the hosts.

Les Mottram was the next Scot to officiate at the Championships, in 1996 in England. The Finals had now expanded to 16 teams in four groups, with Quarter-Finals being introduced. The number of referees was increased also – 24 referees were selected by UEFA. The National Associations were again invited to appoint the linesmen, with Bobby Orr and John Fleming chosen by the SFA. Additionally, Hugh Dallas was picked as the Fourth Official. The team built up good experience of operating together before the competition, officiating at the UEFA Super Cup Final 2nd Leg between AFC Ajax and Real Zaragoza and at a UEFA Cup Quarter-Final, SK Slavia Praha v AS Roma. Handling the Lanarkshire Cup Final was small beer by comparison, but it was still a match together! Mottram was appointed to Italy's 2-1 win over the USSR in a Group match played at Anfield Stadium. As the tournament developed, it was thought that Mottram was in with a chance of being appointed to the Final. That possibility was hampered by England's progress to the Semi-Finals and Mottram and his team were appointed to the other Semi-Final, France and the Czech Republic, played at Old Trafford and won by the Czechs on penalties after a 0-0 draw.

UEFA moved firmly into the modern era for the 2000 Championships, played in Belgium and the Netherlands. Whilst the format of the Finals was not changed, the approach to refereeing was. 13 referees were selected, together with 17 assistant referees and four Fourth Officials. Additionally, the pool included a referee and an assistant from the Confederation of African Football. A significant change was the introduction of a tournament camp, in Brussels, for the match officials. Up to this point, the match officials for previous Finals were flown in and out of the host nation for each game.

Hugh Dallas was selected as one of the referees. As one of the top European referees of the time, he was invited by UEFA, along with Italy's Pierluigi Collina, to be part of a panel, including coaches and former players, to assist in the drawing up of the refereeing guidelines for the Finals. Focus was given to various forms of tackling. At this time, concerns about endangering the safety of an opponent as a result of tackles were coming into vogue. During the course of a five-day pre-tournament gathering in April, the referees were shown a variety of such incidents and given guidance on how they should be dealt with.

Dallas was appointed to two Group matches – Italy's 2-1 win over Turkey in Arnhem and Yugoslavia's 1-0 victory against Norway in Liege. In each match, he had Eddie Foley (Republic of Ireland) as one of his assistants. Foley had been appointed by UEFA to work with Dallas in two Club Competition matches that spring to develop teamwork. Dallas was one of eight referees retained by UEFA after the Group Stages and, whilst it was thought at one stage that he was in the running for the Final, he was only deployed as a Fourth Official for the Quarter-Final between Spain and France and France's Semi-Final against Portugal.

The 2004 Championships in Portugal saw Stuart Dougal selected as one of four Fourth Officials. UEFA selected 12 referees and 24 assistant referees, with two assistants coming from the same association as each referee. Dougal was appointed to four Group Matches and to the Quarter-Final between France and Greece, the eventual surprise winners of the tournament.

Craig Thomson was chosen as a Fourth Official for the Championships held in Austria and Switzerland in 2008, with UEFA this time increasing the number of such officials to eight. UEFA maintained the principles established at the previous Finals – 12 referee teams from different associations. Thomson was appointed to three Group matches. His selection stood him in good stead as he was chosen as a referee for the 2012 Finals in Poland and Ukraine. UEFA announced the 12 referees and four Fourth Officials in December 2011 and confirmed the assistant referees and Additional Assistant Referees in late

March. Thomson's assistants were Alasdair Ross and Derek Rose, with William Collum and Euan Norris selected as his Additional Assistant Referees.

Thomson was appointed to two Group matches – Denmark v Portugal and Czech Republic v Poland. Collum was also deployed as a Fourth Official – to the Czech Republic v Poland match where the French referee Fredy Fautrel deputised for him as an Additional Assistant Referee – and the Spain v Italy Group match.

The Championships of 2016 were the first to be contested by 24 teams and as a consequence UEFA increased the referees from 12 to 18. William Collum was chosen and his team was completed by assistants Damien McGraith (from the Republic of Ireland and who had been part of Collum's team for two seasons) and Frank Connor and Additional Assistants Bobby Madden and John Beaton. Collum refereed two Group Matches – France v Albania (continuing the sequence of Scottish referees handling a home nation's match at the Finals) and Czech Republic v Turkey. He was also deployed as the Fourth Official on the Turkey v Croatia game. Bobby Madden also acted in that role in the Germany v Ukraine Group match.

A Internationals

A Internationals, matches played between the senior representative teams of a National Association and more colloquially known as friendly internationals, have played a hugely important part in football and for the referees who handled these games. For many years, there was a great deal of prestige associated with the playing of such matches, particularly as football developed and the ability to travel increased to open up the opportunity of National Teams testing themselves against others. It was considered a tremendous honour for a referee to be appointed to such matches.

Tom Robertson has the distinction of being the first Scot to referee an A International between two continental European teams when he came out of retirement to control Sweden v Denmark in 1923. Prior to the Second World War, there were only two other occasions when a Scot handled internationals involving a team from outwith the British Isles. Willie Webb refereed the Republic of Ireland's match against Germany in 1936 and two years later, Jimmy Martin refereed England v Norway, a match played in Newcastle.

After the Second World War, there was a gradual increase in the opportunities for Scottish referees, no doubt assisted by the SFA's return to FIFA membership. Jimmy Martin became the second referee to officiate in Europe when he was appointed to referee Belgium v England in 1947. He was followed by George Mitchell when he officiated at Netherlands v Finland in 1951.

Slowly but surely the playing of A internationals increased. Generally it was customary for a National Association to invite a neighbouring association to appoint the referee and it is no surprise that Scots have refereed many internationals in England, Wales, Northern Ireland and the Republic of Ireland. Jack Mowat refereed four internationals in England between 1949 and 1951, three against major countries such as Italy, France and Austria. Bobby Davidson handled three matches in the early 1960's – Sweden, Yugoslavia and Mexico. In the 1990's, Jim McCluskey refereed England against Denmark, Brazil and Greece.

Scots have been in demand also from the western European and Scandinavian associations for internationals. Since the Second World War, 10 matches have been handled in the Netherlands, nine in Belgium and Norway, eight in France and six each in Denmark and Sweden. Iceland leads the way, however, with a remarkable tally of 28. The relative proximity between the two countries was no doubt a major factor in invitations being extended to the SFA. The 1960's and 1970's were the peak decades for many of these matches and they provided an excellent opportunity of giving referees the chance to referee an international match. Iceland played a diverse range of opponents, including Bermuda, refereed by Bill Anderson in 1969, Japan, controlled by Tommy Marshall in 1971 and Israel, handled by Joe Timmons in 1992. Often, an Iceland international proved to be the only one a Scot would handle in his time as a FIFA referee.

From the 1990's onwards, there was an increasing use of reciprocal arrangements between National Associations for international matches which was beneficial to both parties and their referees. The selection of the referee, in the context of the match, could be tailored to suit – either by appointing one of the top FIFA referees or judiciously introducing a lesser experienced referee into the international arena to aid their development. Recent examples of the latter approach are the appointments of Nick Walsh to Gibraltar v Estonia in 2019 and Matthew MacDermid and David Dickinson to Sweden v Northern Ireland and Poland v Moldova, respectively, in 2025.

34 National Associations have invited a Scot to referee one or more of its international matches. The quality of many of these matches reflects the standing of Scottish referees in European and world football. By way of illustration, the following list provides a flavour of such matches:

Year	Match	Referee
1958	Belgium v Netherlands	Jack Mowat
1961	Belgium v Netherlands	Bobby Davidson
1968	Netherlands v Yugoslavia	Bill Mullan
1971	Sweden v West Germany	Tom Wharton
1973	West Germany v Spain	Alistair MacKenzie
1978	West Germany v USSR	John Gordon
1984	Italy v Poland	Bob Valentine
1994	Germany v Italy	Jim McCluskey
2002	Germany v Netherlands	Hugh Dallas
2013	Belgium v France	Craig Thomson
2018	Germany v Spain	William Collum

Scots have also refereed many internationals in Europe involving non-European countries as the opposition. Five have refereed Brazil, the world's greatest football nation – George Smith (Norway 1988), Jim McCluskey (England 1992), Hugh Dallas (Netherlands 2002), Stuart Dougal (Norway 2006) and William Collum (Austria 2014). Three referees have taken charge of Argentina internationals – Bob Valentine (Republic of Ireland 1979), Brian McGinlay (England 1980) and Stuart Dougal (Republic of Ireland 1998).

Other South American countries to feature are Chile, Paraguay and Uruguay. George Smith and John Beaton refereed Chile in matches against Northern Ireland (1989) and Denmark (2018); Kenny Clark and Dougie McDonald refereed Paraguay when they played Belgium (1998) and Wales (2006) whilst Uruguay's matches against Poland (2012) and the Republic of Ireland (2017) were controlled by William Collum and Craig Thomson. Four referees have handled USA matches in Europe – Craig Thomson (Denmark 2009), William Collum (Belgium 2011 and France 2018), Andrew Dallas (Republic of Ireland 2018) and Nick Walsh (Republic of Ireland 2020). Hugh Dallas travelled to the USA in 1994 to referee its international against Bolivia.

This century, some international matches have been played in Britain which have not involved the home nations. This provided the chance for Iain Brines to referee Ghana v Nigeria (2007) and William Collum to handle Nigeria v Republic of Ireland (2009), both these matches being played in London. Dougie McDonald did not have to travel far to take charge of Ghana against South Korea in 2006 as the match was played in his home city of Edinburgh. The first referee to take charge of a friendly involving an African country was Hugh Dallas when he refereed Belgium v Zambia in 1994. Craig Thomson and William Collum have each refereed South Africa – in matches played in 2009 against Norway and the Republic of Ireland.

There have been instances of the SFA having to assist the Football Association by providing officials to service matches. Bobby Madden was Fourth Official when Australia played Ecuador in London in 2014 and Kevin Clancy and David Munro also acted in that capacity when Saudi Arabia played matches against Costa Rica and South Korea in Newcastle in 2023. Alan Mulvanny and Graham Chambers were assistant referees in Portugal v Cameroon (a match played in France) and Germany v Chile, respectively, both matches being played on 5th March 2014.

Scottish referees developed a fine reputation for the quality of their refereeing and the amount of invitations received by the SFA for their services in international friendlies speaks volumes for their abilities and how well they have been regarded throughout football. There is always a choice to be made by a

National Association when it comes to determining which country should be asked to provide the referee for a match and it reflects well on Scottish referees that so many have handled so many matches. Specifically, 57 referees have been in charge of 177 A Internationals since 1923.

William Collum leads the way with 15 matches over 16 seasons. Bobby Davidson's total of 13 matches over a 14 season period is a fantastic achievement and a real reflection of his place in the game given the comparatively low number of international friendlies played during his career. Being appointed to an international friendly is a significant pinnacle for a referee to reach in his career. Not every referee was appointed to an international and many only managed to gain one or two appointments. Hugh Phillips, for example, one of the leading referees of the 1950's and 1960's, only received one appointment to an international friendly. There was a period in the 1990's and 2000's when the top referees of the time received around five or six appointments as the volume of international friendlies grew. With the number of friendlies being played now largely reduced by the introduction of the UEFA Nations League, it is likely that the opportunity of building a substantial total of A International appointments during a career will also be much reduced. Scottish referees will surely remain in demand, however, when friendly internationals are arranged.

British International Championship

The British International Championship, instituted in 1884-85, was the only international competition for British players and indeed referees until the home nations rejoined FIFA after the Second World War and participation in the World Cup slowly gained greater significance. The Championship assumed huge importance in the British football calendar. Receiving an appointment was greatly prized by a referee.

The four associations agreed the basis of the appointments on an annual basis once the fixture schedule was agreed. For many years, an association generally nominated three referees to the "home" association for it to select the referee it wished. Of the 528 matches played in the Championship over its 88 editions until it ended in 1984, 50 Scottish referees handled 163 matches. Of the "early pioneers", Tom Park (1889-95) and James McKillop (1885-90) each refereed six matches, and John Campbell (1889-94) was in charge of five.

Once true referees emerged, the scene was utterly dominated by Tom Robertson who refereed 24 matches between 1896 and 1908, which fully reflects his popularity and standing as a referee within Britain. Over this period, the only other Scots to referee games were Robert Murray (two matches) and John Marshall (one match).

Robertson was followed by Alex Jackson, who refereed 12 matches between 1910 and 1923, and Tom Dougray who handled seven matches over 15 years from 1912 to 1927. Willie Webb's popularity as a referee was reflected in his being chosen to referee nine matches between 1935 and 1948. His tally would surely have been greater but for the Second World War.

In the post-war period, Bobby Davidson and Hugh Phillips were the pre-eminent Scottish referees, each handling eight matches. Jack Mowat, John Gordon and Brian McGinlay each took charge of three matches with George Mitchell, Willie Brittle, Bill Mullan, John Paterson and Ian Foote all having two matches each. Many of the top referees only handled one match in the Championship, an indicator of the tough competition for selection given the low number of matches available to each association.

The biggest match in the Championship was the England v Scotland fixture. Six Scots refereed the match – Tom Robertson, John B. Stark, Alex Jackson, Tom Dougray, Willie Bell and George Mitchell. Dougray refereed four consecutive matches from 1920. Bell refereed the Wembley Wizards match of 1928. George Mitchell was the last Scot to referee the game in 1951.

Brian McGinlay was the last Scot to take charge of a match in the Championship when he refereed Wales v Northern Ireland in 1984.

Ireland

Scotland's international referees have enjoyed a long association with football in Ireland, and particularly Northern Ireland.

The Scotland international Bob Parlane was the first Scot to referee a major match there – the 1888 Irish Cup Final between Cliftonville and Distillery. He was a linesman in the following year's Cup Final.

Deployment of Scottish and English referees in Irish football took off in the 1900's, with English referees being the more dominant of the two groups. The use of "Cross-Channel referees", as they were referred to in Ireland, was borne out of a combination of factors – largely a distrust of the local referees, with the thought that they were not good enough, and the feeling that the English and Scots were better. The issues concerning their use reverberated within Irish football for many years, with the clubs given the ability to decide if they wanted to engage a Cross-Channel referee. All this came at a cost to them, as they had to meet the referee's fee and travel expenses. The local referees were largely content to accept the position though as the years went past they often started to rebel against their use and the lower fees they received.

Referees were required to apply for inclusion in the Irish League's List of Referees. In 1904, nine Cross-Channel referees were accepted into membership of the Irish Referees' Association – six English referees and three Scots – Tom Robertson, Robert Murray and John Deans.

Tom Robertson refereed extremely regularly in Irish football from 1900 to 1913. His popularity was such that he refereed eight Irish Cup Finals, six played in Belfast and three played in Dublin. But for the postponement of the Final in March 1908 due to snow and not being available for the rescheduled match, he would have refereed nine Finals. He also refereed five Finals of other Cup Competitions in Northern Ireland.

During the 1900's, other referees who officiated in Ireland were John B. Stark and David Philp. Tom Dougray and Alex Jackson refereed occasionally there in the early 1910's. Up to the formation of the League of Ireland in 1921, the referees would handle matches in Dublin as well in the North but thereafter they only officiated in Northern Ireland. There was a resurgence in Scots going there in the late 1920's through to the early 1930's. Peter Craigmyle was a regular visitor, along with Hugh Watson and Mungo Hutton. Jimmy Thomson was appointed to the 1931 Irish Cup Final and, in 1934, Craigmyle won a vote over one of the top Northern Irish referees, William McClean, to referee the Final. Other Scots were regularly used during this period. The situation got so bad that the Scottish League put an embargo on referees going over to Northern Ireland as its own appointment system was becoming so hampered by the regular absences of referees. On one occasion, in 1933, the SFA removed two referees from Irish League matches to referee ties in the Qualifying Cup.

During the Second World War, Jack Mowat made a name for himself refereeing in Northern Irish football while stationed there.

Scots returned to Northern Ireland in the post-war period. Craigmyle was appointed to the 1948 Irish Cup Final and rounded off his career by refereeing the 1949 Final. Charlie Faultless officiated on a fairly regular basis for a few seasons, handling several Cup Semi-Finals and the 1953 Irish Cup Final. John Cox was the referee who officiated most regularly during this period, establishing a fine reputation amongst the clubs. He refereed the 1950 Irish Cup Final and the Irish Gold Cup Final the following season. Cox handled many matches involving Derry City, a reflection of the system where the clubs could agree on a referee.

Cox and Faultless, along with Peter Fitzpatrick and two other Scots referees, flew over to Belfast from Glasgow on Boxing Day in 1949 to take charge of the Irish League's Christmas holiday programme of matches. They had all been on Scottish matches on Christmas Eve and all had wished to spend Christmas Day with their families. They resolved any travel problems by chartering the plane.

Travelling to Northern Ireland for matches was generally quite an undertaking for the referees, particularly for Craigmyle who lived in Aberdeen. Sailing from Glasgow was a common means of travel. Many of the games were midweek matches and one cannot help but wonder at the commitment shown by them to undertake the appointments. Arranging time away from work adds to the situation. It speaks volumes for the referees. Doing so could not have been easy. An English referee, Harry Nattrass, was sacked from his job at a colliery a few weeks before refereeing the 1936 FA Cup Final referee because he had been away from work too much due to refereeing. He had just returned from a match in Northern Ireland.

The use of Scots referees petered out after the early 1950's though English referees continued to referee in Northern Ireland until the early 1970's when the Troubles put an end to things. There is one tale from 1955. The day before an Irish Cup Quarter-Final between Glenavon and Ards, the Irish FA contacted the Scottish League requesting a referee. Willie Brittle was free so was appointed to the match, flying over on the Saturday morning.

South America

South America provides an extremely interesting and largely unknown tale of Scotland's international referees. In the late 1940's, at a time when the prestige of British referees was at its peak, the Argentine FA, due to the inhospitable environment faced by native referees in their football (facing intimidation and violence was an unfortunate and constant way of life for them), was drawn to the United Kingdom to offer contracts to referees. Consequently, a good number of English referees went out to Argentina and, in the first two years, were supplemented by five Scottish referees, Willie Brown, John Cox, Jimmy Provan, Bobby Calder and Willie Crawford.

The Argentine FA established contact with the Football Association and assistance was readily given to publicise the opportunity on offer, news of which also reached Scotland. A representative of the Argentine FA, Manuel Gonzalez, came to Britain in January 1948 to conduct interviews with interested referees and visited Scotland to meet three referees, Brown, Cox and Provan, who had expressed a willingness to go to Argentina. A newspaper report set the scene for the interest in obtaining British referees and quoted Gonzalez: "Our referees know the rules perfectly but we feel that British referees can teach them a great deal, particularly with regard to keeping a tight grip on the behaviour of players. We are offering good terms to the right men. They will have their fares paid, of course, and that of their wives, too, if necessary. They will be based in Buenos Aires, where we already have an academy for referees. In addition to officiating at a match each week, they would be required to take classes of referees. They will have to learn a bit of Spanish but that should not take them long. The pay will about £57 per month and when they travel to matches all expenses will be made. We have only had one British referee out there, Isaac Caswell of Blackburn, who was there just before the war. He created a very fine impression. So far, I have had about a dozen applications from all over Britain, three of them from Scotland. A year's contract will be offered with the option of staying another year if they so desire."

In the context of life in post-war Britain, the opportunity and money on offer to go to Argentina would have been an attractive proposition.

Eight referees were chosen from the applicants – the three Scots and five English referees. They all sailed from Southampton on 10th March 1948 and started their refereeing stint when the Argentine League got underway in early April. They quickly established an excellent standing within football in Argentina and, in comparison to the local referees, commanded respect. Accomplishing that was not easy at all given the behaviour of players and the feverish atmosphere created by spectators at the games. The use of tear gas and water hoses to control crowds was a regular feature of football in Argentina. Also, it was not uncommon for match officials to be set upon and assaulted. Around the time of the referees' arrival in Argentina, a linesman in a match in Buenos Aires had been beaten and kicked to death. In an early game, one of the English referees managed a remarkable achievement not being assaulted after disallowing a goal. John Cox had quite an experience in a match between Boca Juniors and San Lorenzo. The game was a 1-1 draw, with Cox having awarded a penalty to San Lorenzo. At the end of the match, the police offered to drive him away from the ground as the crowd was so menacing towards him. He declined the offer and left by taxi, though still under protection.

Between them, Brown, Cox and Provan refereed 92 First Division matches during the season, which ended in December. They were regularly in charge of major matches, with Willie Brown refereeing the famous derby match, River Plate and Boca Juniors.

In November, they were joined by Bobby Calder, who refereed four matches before the end of the season, one of which was also Boca Juniors v River Plate. Calder was invited to return to Argentina for the following season but had to refuse because of his anxiety for his wife's health back in Scotland.

The referees sailed back to Britain after the season finished. They had all made an impression, Cox in particular. In the mid-1950's a South American magazine mentioned Cox in an article reviewing the quality of British referees since 1948: "The British referees that performed with such success in our lands for various seasons were some very good ones. In the first group came two who were exceptional. They were two short fellows called Cox and Gibbs. How good they were on the eye, how correct they were spotting fouls, and what conscience they had to respect the advantage laws and at the same time make themselves respected on the field."

English referees continued to go to Argentina after the initial group in 1948. Peter Craigmyle was approached to go in 1949 but declined the offer. Only one Scot, Willie Crawford, took the chance thereafter to referee in Argentina. Having briefly been a Class 1 referee for three seasons in the mid-1940's, it would seem that being re-classified to Class 3 for season 1947-48 may have been the reason for him to take up the opportunity. He sailed for Argentina in April 1949 from Southampton with five English referees. During his season officiating in the Argentine Primera Division, he refereed 36 matches, with the Boca Juniors v River Plate featuring in his list of games.

Crawford evidently had a taste for adventure as, after Argentina, he accepted refereeing contracts in Chile, Mexico and Costa Rica throughout much of the 1950's, riding the wave of the popularity of British referees at that time in South and Central America. He established an excellent reputation, particularly in the initial period of his time in each country. He was held to be an exemplar of how refereeing should be carried out and controlling the behaviour of players, and indeed the crowds. In Chile he and an English referee, Walter Manning, were placed under constant scrutiny by the press and attracted great attention, regularly featuring in articles and cartoon caricatures from matches. Despite being lauded for their refereeing, the referees did not escape the ever-present dangers of Chilean football. In 1951 Manning was attacked after a match by a club director and in another was assailed by bottles thrown at him. There is a tale of Crawford in Chile, to demonstrate his impartiality before a match, getting one leg rubbed down by one team's physiotherapist and then getting his other leg rubbed down by the other team's physiotherapist.

Of all the British referees who went to Latin America, Crawford was perhaps the most well-travelled. He also became one of the most active British referees in international games in South and Central America during his time there. This was some feat as he was never a FIFA referee at any point. He refereed a World Cup Qualifier, Mexico v Haiti, in 1953 and 16 other international matches, in the 1952 Panamerican Championships (where he refereed Uruguay's matches against Mexico and Chile), the 1953 Central American and Caribbean Championships and the 1954 Central American Games (where he handled Mexico's matches against Cuba and Colombia). In these tournaments, he was a linesman in at least five matches. He also was in charge of a number of club friendlies involving touring teams. In 1951, he refereed three matches played by the Argentinian side Ferril Carril Oeste as they toured Chile and in 1953 he handled the Chilean club Everton's match against HNK Hadjuk Split of Yugoslavia. His last known match was a friendly played in Costa Rica on 1st January 1958 between Huracan of Argentina and Botafogo of Brazil.

During his time in Latin America, Crawford had regular contact with Scottish newspapers, keeping them informed of his tales, of which he had plenty to tell. In one match he awarded a penalty to the visiting club with two minutes to go, returned to his dressing room with his linesmen at the end to find that all their clothes had been torn to shreds. The culprit was the groundsman and damages were settled in a nearby pub afterwards. Oranges and a shoe were thrown at him at another match which ended with him being carried off the pitch by the home spectators. Their team had recovered from being three goals down to win the game and Crawford was deemed to be a hero for playing his part in the comeback.

In Mexico, when refereeing a friendly between a Mexican team and a Brazilian team, a Mexican player he had penalised for a foul became so enraged that he began hitting the Brazilian he had challenged. A fight ensued and the two teams joined in. That prompted hundreds of spectators to come pouring down from the stands on to the field to riot. It took the police 15 minutes to regain control. Ambulances took the injured to hospital and the game resumed with all the players wearing bandages of some sort.

Crawford typified the British approach to refereeing, being held as scrupulously fair, standing no nonsense and exercising fearless control. Most importantly, he could not be bought, something which was particularly prevalent in Costa Rica. It was expected when Costa Rican teams were playing teams from other countries that the referee would assist the home club to win. In advance of one game, Crawford feared for his landlady who had been threatened with her house being damaged if he gave any decisions against the home team. As the referee for the match was not to be announced until just before the kick-off (an indication as to how delicate the making of appointments were), it was deemed in the circumstances that Crawford should not be the referee. Crawford became a fluent Spanish speaker but retained a gallus Glaswegian approach in matches to address players and defuse situations in his games.

English referees were employed also in Brazil and other South American countries during the 1950's. Contracts were initially offered to the British referees, including George Mitchell, who had made such a great impression while officiating at the 1950 World Cup. These offers were declined but others took the opportunity to go to Brazil.

Three Scottish referees, Tom Wharton, Willie Syme and Archie Webster, spent over a month in Brazil in May-June 1966 to assist in Brazil's intensive preparations for the World Cup in

England. Brazil was totally focussed on winning the competition for the third successive time and put a huge amount of resource into their preparations. The Brazilians wanted to get their players accustomed to British refereeing. The planning had started the year before, as evidenced by a visit to England in November 1965 when Brazil played a friendly against Arsenal, a match refereed by Hugh Phillips. During a two month period from mid-April, Brazil played 14 preparatory matches against South American and European teams. The Scots took charge of 10 matches between mid-May and mid-June. Wharton refereed two matches against Wales and one against Chile; Syme refereed matches against Chile, Peru (twice), Poland and Czechoslovakia and Webster handled matches against Poland and Czechoslovakia. Six matches were played at the Maracana Stadium in Rio de Janeiro with two each being played in Sao Paolo and Belo Horizonte. Brazil's squad size was such that they played two matches in the Maracana on the same day against Peru and Poland.

The Old Firm

"He's entering the lion's den. A good referee enters the lion's den every Saturday. Good referees don't pick and choose matches. They just do them. If you're appointed by the authorities to be the referee they want to do this match, you do it. And that's it. You do it." Those are the words of Tom Wharton in a newspaper article in December 1999 in response to a journalist asking him about the appointment of Hugh Dallas to an Old Firm match. Dallas had come through a tumultuous time earlier in the year when he was struck by coins in a League match between the clubs at Celtic Park in May and then refereed the clubs again in the Scottish Cup Final three weeks later.

Wharton's comments reflect the great status held by the Old Firm match in Scottish football and the importance it has for referees as a consequence. If being appointed to a Scottish Cup Final is the pinnacle of a referee's domestic career, it is overshadowed somewhat perhaps by an appointment to an Old

Firm match. With obvious good reason, the match has been the preserve of Scotland's international referees, with some exceptions. Taking charge of the match is a huge honour for every referee and it always sets an examination of refereeing skills to the highest order. The referees undoubtedly benefit from the experience and it stands them in good stead for handling future matches. If an Old Firm match can be handled, then a referee will be well prepared for any other match. There is a valid argument to suggest that the absence of League fixtures between the clubs when Rangers spent four seasons from 2012 out of the top division in Scotland had an impact on the development of the referees during that period.

The rivalry between the clubs, and their supporters, soon took hold following the early matches from 1888 onwards. The build up to the matches is such that it generates great excitement and anticipation. There is a raucous and febrile atmosphere at the games. The matches are a powderkeg and from time to time they explode. There have been riots at Cup Finals (1908 and 1980) and countless occasions when player indiscipline boils over. League reconstruction in 1975 doubled the matches between the clubs each season and that increased the hype surrounding the fixture. In the modern age, the advent of social media has raised the levels of supporter interaction and involvement to absurd levels which has added another layer of activity surrounding the fixture as it ramps up the expectations and reactions to an insane degree.

And into this cauldron of emotion is placed the referee. He is put into an unenviable position once the appointment is announced. The appointment is scrutinised with the media always likely to cast up past events concerning the referee. In the fevered world of Scottish football, conspiracy theories and paranoia abound and all sorts can be crazily read into appointments and match decisions. The posturing attitudes of the two clubs towards referees add greatly to the mix with comments made to pander to their support. With managers now having access to the live match coverage in their technical areas, they are provided with an instant ability to offer comment in their post match media interviews, coloured as appropriate to denigrate any refereeing decisions that they take exception to.

The analysis of referees' performances goes stratospheric and perceived failings are long remembered by the clubs and supporters.

The history of the fixture is littered with a myriad of events of all sorts, and far too many to mention. Tom Robertson found himself having to give evidence in a court case in 1905 when a Celtic player, James Quinn, took a newspaper to court for slander in regard to the reporter's description of the offence for which Robertson had sent him off in a Scottish Cup Semi-Final. The match was abandoned due to crowd trouble and Celtic chose to forfeit the tie. The Sheriff dealing with the case found in favour of Quinn but only awarded him damages of one shilling. 80 years later, Jimmy Duncan gave evidence in the court case of three players he had sent off in a match at Ibrox Stadium. During a Victory Cup Semi-Final in 1946, Matthew Dale had to take evasive action when a Celtic supporter came on to the field of play and attempted to strike him with a bottle after a penalty had been awarded to Rangers. Referees have found themselves suspended after refereeing Old Firm matches – John B. Stark in 1908 and Jimmy Callaghan in 1969. There was an issue created by Celtic in 1975 when the club felt that a FIFA referee should have been appointed to the fixture instead of Bill Anderson, who was not at that time on the FIFA List.

Off-field issues have emerged in recent times which have placed undue focus on referees. The Celtic Supporters' Association hired a private detective to look into the background of Jim McCluskey before the 1990 League Cup Final, Celtic used a used a behavioural psychologist to analyse Hugh Dallas' performance in the League match of May 1999, John Beaton endured a torrid time in the aftermath of an match when social media was awash with stories that he had been seen drinking in a "Rangers" pub in 2019. All these things have a great impact on the private lives of the referees.

The demands of the game have over the years brought focus on the style of refereeing employed in matches. Whilst referees will judge the mood of the match in its early stages and act accordingly, a strict application of the Laws is generally called for to keep control. John Gordon received favourable comment in the press for his handling of the 1973 Scottish Cup Final, his first Old Firm match, by applying strict control throughout the game, awarding a much higher number of free-kicks than he would do in any other match. His approach was considered to have made the match an enjoyable spectacle. Yet, it can also be said that the threshold for intervention can be higher in an Old Firm match than in others, and in that respect, it may be argued that the Laws of the Games are applied differently in Old Firm matches. How that is done is down to the skill of the referees and the exercise of that skill is largely under-appreciated or goes unrecognised. All the referees who have handled Old Firm matches deserve great credit. Operating in the cauldron that the fixture generates and having to deal with whatever arises makes them battle-hardened and, as a consequence, elevates their ability to shine on the international stage, which many have done.

Around the World

"Join the Army and see the world" was a long used recruitment slogan in Britain. A similar one could equally apply to refereeing. Scottish referees have certainly been well travelled. They have officiated in all of UEFA's current membership of 55 National Associations. It is mind-boggling to think that when Scots go to Almaty in Kazakhstan, they are due north of India, such is the geographical extent of UEFA's membership. A minimum estimate of other countries where they have officiated is 30, making a total of 85.

Peter Craigmyle was an early voyager when he visited the Faroe Islands in 1936 and Malta twice in the late 1940's. The countries of South and Central America were prominent in the late 1940's and 1950's due to the referees who went to Argentina and Willie Crawford who operated in Chile and Costa Rica. George Mitchell was at the 1950 World Cup in Brazil, Hugh Dallas refereed a World Cup Qualifier in Uruguay in 2001 and William Collum was involved in the FIFA U20 World Cup in Colombia in 2011. Kylie McMullan was in Uruguay for the FIFA Women's U17 World Cup in 2018.

Mexico has been well covered with Willie Crawford, Bobby Davidson and Brian McGinlay all refereeing there. In addition to Les Mottram and Hugh Dallas officiating in the USA at the 1994 World Cup and 1996 Olympics, respectively, Brian McGinlay had a stint in the Major Soccer League in 1979, with Stuart Dougal refereeing three League matches there in 1999. Bobby Davidson and Tom Wharton each refereed club matches in Canada.

The Far East has also seen Scots in action. FIFA sent Ian Foote to referee a World Cup Qualifier in South Korea in 1977. Brian McGinlay ventured to Japan in 1979 for a cup tournament, Les Mottram operated there after finishing his career in Scotland and Hugh Dallas was in Japan and South Korea for the 2002 World Cup. Alistair Coutts, based in Hong Kong, refereed an Olympic Qualifier in China. Bobby Madden and Morag Pirie have also officiated in China, at the World University Games and the Youth Olympics, respectively. Hugh Dallas and Willie Young refereed in Hong Kong at the Carlsberg Cup, an invitational club tournament. India was the destination for Bobby Madden in 2017 for the FIFA U17 World Cup.

Australasia has featured too. Bob Valentine went to Australia for the 1981 FIFA U19 World Cup and FIFA despatched David Syme to New Zealand in 1985 to referee in an Olympic Qualifying tournament. Eddie Lennie, based in Australia, adds some exoticness to the list of countries by having refereed in Fiji and Tahiti.

The Middle East has been visited by many Scottish referees since the 1980's. Bob Valentine refereed World Cup Qualifiers in Kuwait in 1981 and Abu Dhabi in 1985. Brian McGinlay officiated at the Arabian Gulf Cup in Abu Dhabi in 1982. The following year Kenny Hope and Hugh Alexander, along with Class 1 referee Alex McGunnigle, went to the United Arab Emirates for a few League matches. Bob Valentine refereed in the Gulf Cup played in Bahrain in 1986. Qatar became a regular destination for a number of years from 2006, with Craig Thomson having numerous appointments. Stuart Dougal and Charlie Richmond have also refereed in Qatar. In recent years, John Beaton, Andrew Dallas and Bobby Madden have all refereed in Saudi Arabia, with Madden refereeing eight matches in 2019 and 2020. The Middle East has also hosted international tournaments, with Kylie McMullan officiating in Jordan at the FIFA U17 Women's World Cup in 2016.

Africa is not overlooked. David Galloway, based in Zambia, handled a World Cup Qualifier in Mauritius. John Gordon and Les Mottram refereed World Cup Qualifiers in Zambia and Morocco in 1977 and 1993, respectively. Charlie Richmond handled a League match in Tunisia in 2009. Kenny Clark, William Collum, Hugh Dallas and Stuart Dougal have all refereed in Egypt, taking charge of the match between Al Ahly and Zamalek, the country's equivalent of the "Old Firm".

Newspapers

Newspapers have had an odd relationship with referees over the years. In football's early years, newspapers veered between the laudatory and the critical when commenting on referees and their performances. Whilst being critical of referees became the stock approach of newspapers, they were also portrayed in good light when the need arose. The importance of the role of the referee was recognised and understood, with "Knight of the Whistle" being a very common phrase to describe the best of the referees. Relationships were cultivated with referees to gain stories and information, with Peter Craigmyle being a prime example. The top referees often found their services to be in demand once they retired to provide a series of articles on their career. Tom Dougray, Peter Craigmyle and Willie Webb were to the fore in this regard in the 1930's and 1940's. Bob Valentine and Alan Ferguson followed suit in the 1980's. Many referees have been the subject of feature articles in newspapers to mark special appointments at home or abroad.

An early example of a referee's involvement with the press was Tom Robertson offering an opinion on the Scotland team to play England in 1909. It is remarkable to think that in 1977 the Daily Record asked Tom Wharton to give his views on the first Old Firm match of the season and to provide pen pictures of the players of each club. The paper was no doubt wishing to gain a neutral point of view given Wharton's experiences of the fixture, allowing that this was six years after he had retired. Brian McGinlay was used regularly by newspapers after his career finished to comment on the referee's performance in Cup Finals and Old Firm matches. For a couple of years following his retiral, Alan Ferguson was often used to give his views on refereeing matters.

Peter Craigmyle and Jack Mowat both had long associations with newspapers, dealing with readers' queries on the Laws of the Game. Charlie Faultless reported on football matches for a Sunday newspaper for many years. In 1981, Bill Anderson acted as a guest match reporter for the Sunday Post. David Syme, Willie Young and Kenny Clark had stints as newspaper columnists once their careers ended.

Family Connections

There is something about the pull of refereeing which has generated many family connections down the years, and there are a number of examples amongst Scotland's FIFA officials.

Father and Son
Willie and David Syme; Hugh and Andrew Dallas
Brothers
Kenny and Douglas Hope; Gordon and Jim McBride
Father and Daughter
Wilson and Hayley Irvine

There are further family connections as offspring followed in the footsteps of their fathers. The fathers of Stanley Tait, Rollo Kyle, Euan Norris, Vikki Allan and Ross Hardie all served on the SFA List. Willie Young's brother John was a Class 1 referee. Kenny Clark's and Jim Dunne's sons Ross and David, respectively, are currently on the SFA List, as is Matthew MacDermid's brother Michael. John Beaton and assistant referee Alan Mulvanny are brothers-in-law.

Referees' Associations' Awards

A number of the Referees' Associations in Scotland have instituted annual Awards in honour of past FIFA referees who were members of the association. These are:

Aberdeen and District RA – The Peter Craigmyle Award: given to the person who achieves the highest mark in the Introductory Examination

Ayrshire RA – The Jim McCluskey Trophy: awarded to the member who officiates at the highest level in youth football

Edinburgh & District RA – i) The Bill Mullan Trainer's Award: presented to the member who has fully applied themselves to training and improved their fitness levels; ii) The George Smith Development Award: given to the referee who has demonstrated significant future potential

Fife RA – The Archie Webster Shield: awarded to a member who has shown potential in the early stages of their career and who shows a commitment to the association

Glasgow RA - i) The Charles Faultless Award: given to the referee who is appointed to the highest level Cup Final in Scotland; ii) The Willie Davidson Award: given to the referee in minor football who has shown the most potential for progression; iii) The Tom Wharton Bursary: a financial award to assist in sending a referee to an international youth tournament

Lanarkshire RA – i) The Hugh Phillips Award: given to the member who has given outstanding service to the association, either during the season or during the term of their membership; ii) The Willie Brown Award: given to a member not on the SFA's List of Referees who has given outstanding service to the association either in their capacity as a member or as a referee.

Roll Of Honour

This section records all the appointments received by Scottish match officials to FIFA and UEFA tournaments for National Teams, the appointments to Finals in these competitions, and appointments from the Quarter-Finals onwards in the UEFA

Club Competitions. Information on Group Stage match appointments in the Club Competitions is also provided.

FIFA World Cup

1950	Brazil	George Mitchell
1954	Switzerland	Charlie Faultless
1958	Sweden	Jack Mowat
1962	Chile	Bobby Davidson
1966	England	Hugh Phillips
1970	Mexico	Bobby Davidson
1974	West Germany	Bobby Davidson
1978	Argentina	John Gordon
1982	Spain	Bob Valentine
1990	Italy	George Smith
1994	USA	Les Mottram
1998	France	Hugh Dallas and Eddie Lennie
2002	South Korea/Japan	Hugh Dallas

FIFA Confederations Cup

2001	South Korea/Japan	Hugh Dallas

Olympics

1912	Stockholm	Jimmy Phillip
1972	Munich	Bill Mullan
1976	Montreal	John Paterson
1980	Moscow	Bob Valentine
1984	Los Angeles	Brian McGinlay
1988	Seoul	Kenny Hope
1992	Barcelona	Kenny Clark (*Assistant Referee*)
1996	Atlanta	Hugh Dallas and Eddie Lennie
2004	Athens	Martin Cryans (*Assistant Referee*)

FIFA U16 World Cup

1987	Canada	Kenny Hope
1989	Scotland	Jim McCluskey

FIFA U17 World Cup

2003	Finland	Martin Cryans *(Assistant Referee)*
2007	South Korea	Craig Thomson
		Assistant Referees:
		Martin Cryans
		Tom Murphy
2013	UAE	Craig Thomson
		Assistant Referees:
		Derek Rose

2017	India	Alan Mulvanny
		Bobby Madden
		Assistant Referees:
		David McGeachie
		Alastair Mather

FIFA U19 World Cup

1981	Australia	Bob Valentine
1983	Mexico	Brian McGinlay
1985	USSR	David Syme
2001	Argentina	Michael McCurry

FIFA U20 World Cup

2011	Colombia	William Collum
		Assistant Referees:
		Graham Chambers
		Martin Cryans
2017	South Korea	William Collum (*AVAR*)

FIFA Futsal World Cup

1989	Netherlands	Bill Crombie

FIFA Women's World Cup

1991	China	Jim McCluskey
2019	France	Kylie McMullan (*Assistant Referee*)

FIFA Women's U17 World Cup

2012	Azerbaijan	Morag Pirie
2016	Jordan	Kylie McMullan (*Assistant Referee*)
2018	Uruguay	Kylie McMullan (*Assistant Referee*)

European Championships

1972	Belgium	Bill Mullan
		Linesmen:
		John Paterson
		John Workman
1980	Italy	Brian McGinlay
		Linesmen:
		David Syme
		Tommy Muirhead
1984	France	Bob Valentine
		Linesmen:
		Brian McGinlay
		Hugh Williamson

Year	Host	Officials
1988	West Germany	Bob Valentine Linesmen: Kenny Hope Andrew Waddell
1996	England	Les Mottram *Assistant Referees*: Bobby Orr John Fleming *Fourth Official:* Hugh Dallas
2000	Netherlands/Belgium	Hugh Dallas
2004	Portugal	Stuart Dougal (*Fourth Official*)
2008	Switzerland/Austria	Craig Thomson (*Fourth Official*)
2012	Poland/Ukraine	Craig Thomson *Assistant Referees*: Alasdair Ross Derek Rose *Additional Assistant Referees*: William Collum Euan Norris
2016	France	William Collum *Assistant Referee*: Frank Connor *Additional Assistant Referees:* Bobby Madden John Beaton

UEFA International Youth Tournament

Year	Host	Official
1978	Poland	David Syme
1979	Austria	George Smith

UEFA U18 Championship

Year	Host	Official
1981	West Germany	Eddie Pringle
1982	Finland	Kenny Hope
1983	England	Alan Ferguson
1984	USSR	Hugh Alexander
1994	Spain	Hugh Dallas

UEFA U19 Championship

Year	Host	Official
2003	Republic of Ireland	Jim Lyon (*Assistant Referee*)
2004	Switzerland	Dougie McDonald
2008	Czech Republic	William Collum
2014	Hungary	Kevin Clancy
2016	Germany	Douglas Ross (*Assistant Referee*)
2017	Georgia	Graeme Stewart (*Assistant Referee*)
2018	Finland	Andrew Dallas

UEFA U16 Competition

1984	Hungary	Tommy Muirhead
1986	Greece	George Smith
1987	France	Bill Crombie
1990	East Germany	Andrew Waddell
1992	Cyprus	Les Mottram
1995	Belgium	Kenny Clark
1996	Austria	Stuart Dougal
1998	Scotland	Michael McCurry
1999	Czech Republic	Stuart Logan (*Assistant Referee*)
2000	Israel	Dougie McDonald

UEFA U17 Championship

2006	Luxembourg	William Collum
2010	Liechtenstein	Euan Norris
2011	Serbia	Steven McLean
2018	England	Dougie Potter (*Assistant Referee*)
2019	Republic of Ireland	Don Robertson
2025	Albania	Chris Rae (*Assistant Referee*)

UEFA U21 Championship

2000	Slovakia	John McElhinney (*Assistant Referee*)
2007	Netherlands	Craig Thomson
2009	Sweden	Derek Rose (*Assistant Referee*)
2013	Israel	Alan Mulvanny (*Assistant Referee*)
2017	Hungary	Bobby Madden
		Assistant Referees:
		David McGeachie
		Alastair Mather
		Additional Assistant Referees:
		Andrew Dallas
		Don Robertson
2019	Italy	Bobby Madden
		Assistant Referees:
		Frank Connor
		David Roome
2025	Slovakia	Nick Walsh
		Assistant Referees:
		Daniel McFarlane
		Calum Spence
		VAR:
		Andrew Dallas

UEFA Regions' Cup

1999	Italy	Dougie McDonald

UEFA Women's Championship

2017	Netherlands	Lorraine Watson (*Fourth Official*)
2022	England	Lorraine Watson (*Fourth Official*

UEFA Women's U17 Championship

2010	Switzerland	Morag Pirie
2013	Wales	Lorraine Watson (*Fourth Official*)

UEFA Women's U19 Championship

2006	Switzerland	Morag Pirie (*Assistant Referee*)
2011	Italy	Morag Pirie
2015	Israel	Lorraine Watson
2016	Slovakia	Kylie McMullan (*Assistant Referee*)
2017	Northern Ireland	Vikki Robertson (*Assistant Referee*)

World University Games

1987	Belgrade	George Smith
2011	Shenzhen	Bobby Madden

Youth Olympics

2014	Nanjing	Morag Pirie

Finals

FIFA World Cup

1950	Uruguay v Brazil	George Mitchell (*Linesman*)
1962	Brazil v Czechoslovakia	Bobby Davidson (*Linesman*)
2002	Brazil v Germany	Hugh Dallas (*Fourth Official*)

FIFA U19 World Cup

1981	West Germany v Qatar	Bob Valentine (*Linesman*)
1985	Brazil v Spain	David Syme

FIFA U17 World Cup

2003	Brazil v Spain	Martin Cryans (*Assistant Referee*)
2013	Nigeria v Mexico	Craig Thomson

Assistant Referees:
Derek Rose
Alan Mulvanny

FIFA U16 World Cup

1987   Nigeria v USSR   Kenny Hope (*Linesman*)

FIFA Futsal World Cup

1989   Brazil v Netherlands   Bill Crombie

Olympics

2004   Argentina v Paraguay   Martin Cryans (*Assistant Referee*)

UEFA U23 Competition

1976   Hungary v USSR 1st Leg   John Gordon
                                                          Linesmen:
                                                          David Syme
                                                          Bill Cairns

UEFA U21 Championship

1992   Sweden v Italy 2nd Leg   Brian McGinlay
                                                          Linesmen:
                                                          Kenny Clark
                                                          Hugh Dallas
                                                          Fourth Official:
                                                          Hugh Williamson
2013   Italy v Spain   Alan Mulvanny (*Reserve Assistant Referee*)

UEFA U19 Championship

2008   Germany v Italy   William Collum

UEFA U17 Championship

2006   Czech Republic v Russia   William Collum (*Fourth Official*)
2025   France v Portugal   Chris Rae (*Assistant Referee*)

UEFA U16 Competition

1992   Germany v Spain   Les Mottram
1998   Italy v Republic of Ireland   Michael McCurry

UEFA Club Competitions

Scottish referees have an illustrious history in the UEFA Club Competitions, with 16 appointments to various Finals, whether played as a 1st or 2nd Leg or as a single match. 56 appointments have been received in Quarter-Finals and 23 in Semi-Finals. All these appointments are set out, with the full team of officials provided for each Final. Whilst the Inter-Continental Cup and the Inter-Cities Fairs Cup are included in these records, the competitions were not under UEFA's jurisdiction. Overall, it is a tremendous record of achievement.

Intercontinental Cup

1971	Nacional v Panathinaikos	Bill Mullan

European Champion Club' Cup

Quarter-Final 1st Leg

1962	Nuremberg v SL Benfica	Tom Wharton
1966	RSC Anderlecht v Real Madrid CF	Tom Wharton
1969	AFC Ajax v SL Benfica	Bobby Davidson
1976	SL Benfica v FC Bayern Munchen	John Gordon
1980	Hamburger SV v HNK Hadjuk Split	Ian Foote
1983	Sporting Clube de Portugal v Real Sociedad de Futbol	Bob Valentine
1985	IFK Goteborg v Panathinaikos	Brian McGinlay

Quarter Final 2nd Leg

1964	BV Borussia Dortmund v FK Dukla Praha	Willie Brittle
1965	Real Madrid v SL Benfica	Hugh Phillips
1989	AC Milan v SV Werder Bremen	George Smith
1991	Real Madrid CF v FC Spartak Moskva	Andrew Waddell

Semi-Final 1st Leg

1959	Real Madrid v Club Atletico de Madrid	Jack Mowat
1982	FC Bayern Munchen v PFC CSKA Sofia	David Syme

Final

1960	Real Madrid CF v Eintracht Frankfurt	Jack Mowat
		Linesmen:
		Donald Kyle
		Jimmy Fulton

European Cup Winners' Cup

Quarter-Final 1st Leg

1967	FC Bayern Munchen v SK Rapid Wien	Tom Wharton
1974	FC Magdeburg v PFC Beroe Stara Zagora	Alistair MacKenzie
1978	Rea Betis Balompie v FC Dynamo Moskva	Ian Foote
1991	FC Dynamo Kyiv v FC Barcelona	David Syme

Quarter Final 2nd Leg

1968	Olympique Lyonnais v Hamburger SV	Tom Wharton
1972	Dynamo Berlin v Atvidabergs FF	Bobby Davidson
1975	SL Benfica v PSV Eindhoven	John Paterson
1982	FC Porto v Royal Standard de Liege	Brian McGinlay
1985	FC Dynamo Moskva v Larissa	Bob Valentine
1986	Club Atletico de Madrid v FK Crvena Zvedza	Bob Valentine
1984	Malmo FF v AFC Ajax	George Smith
1993	FC Steaua Bucuresti v Royal Antwerp	Les Mottram
1993	Club Atletico de Madrid v Olympiacos	Jim McCluskey
1994	Bayer 04 Leverkusen v SL Benfica	Jim McCluskey
1998	Vicenza Calcio v Roda JC	Hugh Dallas
1999	Maccabi Haifa v FK Lokomotiv Moskva	Hugh Dallas

Semi-Final 2nd Leg

1973	AC Milan v AC Sparta Praha	John Paterson
1992	AS Monaco v Feyenoord	Brian McGinlay

Final

1962	Club Atletico de Madrid v AC Fiorentina	Tom Wharton
		Linesmen:
		Tommy Thomson
		Andrew Wright
1975	FC Dynamo Kyiv v Ferencvarosi TC	Bobby Davidson
		Linesmen:
		George Smith
		Bill Moulds

Inter-Cities Fairs Cup

Quarter-Final 1st Leg

1960	Birmingham City v Boldklub Kobenhaven	Frank Crossley
1964	Real Zaragoza v Juventus	Tom Wharton

Semi-Final 1st Leg

1963	Valencia CF v AS Roma	Tom Wharton
1970	RSC Anderlecht v Internazionale Milano	Tom Wharton

Semi-Final 2nd Leg

1964	Real Zaragoza v RFC Liege	Willie Syme
1971	Leeds United v Liverpool	Tom Wharton

Final 1st Leg

1961	Birmingham City v AS Roma	Bobby Davidson
		Linesmen:
		Alex Davidson
		John McNiven

UEFA Cup

Quarter-Final 1st Leg

1972	Ferencvarosi TC v FK Zeljeznicar	John Paterson
1973	OFK Beograd v FC Twente	Alistair MacKenzie
1979	FK Dukla Praha v Hertha BSC Berlin	Ian Foote
1983	Valencia CF v RSC Anderlecht	Brian McGinlay
1986	Internazionale Milano v FC Nantes Atlantique	Brian McGinlay
1988	Verona Hellas v SV Werder Bremen	Bob Valentine
1989	Victoria Bucuresti v Dynamo Dresden	David Syme
1996	SK Slavia Praha v AS Roma	Les Mottram

Quarter-Final 2nd Leg

1976	AC Milan v Club Brugge KV	Alistair MacKenzie
1984	HNK Hadjuk Split v AC Sparta Praha	Bob Valentine
1987	Vitoria Guimares v VfL Borussia Monchengladbach	Bob Valentine
1990	AJ Auxerre v AC Fiorentina	George Smith
1992	Torino v B1903 Kobenhavn	Andrew Waddell

Semi-Final 2nd Leg

1974	VfB Stuttgart v Feyenoord	John Paterson
1976	Club Brugge KV v Hamburger SV	Bobby Davidson
1980	Eintracht Frankfurt v FC Bayern Munchen	Brian McGinlay
1983	Universitatea Craiova v SL Benfica	Bob Valentine
1985	Real Madrid CF v Internazionale Milano	Bob Valentine
1989	FC Bayern Munchen v SSC Napoli	David Syme
1998	FC Spartak Moskva v Internazionale Milano	Hugh Dallas
2001	1.FC Kaiserslautern v CD Alaves	Hugh Dallas

Final 1st Leg

1979	FK Crvena Zvedza v VfL Borussia Monchengladbach	Ian Foote
		Linesmen:
		David Syme
		Tom Matthews

Final 2nd Leg

1986	1FC Koln v Real Madrid CF	Bob Valentine
		Linesmen:
		Alan Ferguson
		Jim McCluskey
1987	Dundee United f IFK Goteborg	Bob Valentine (*Standby Official)*
1994	Casino Salzburg v Internazionale Milano	Jim McCluskey
		Assistant Referees:
		Iain Cathcart
		Bobby Orr
		Fourth Official:
		Hugh Dallas

Final

1999	Parma AC v Olympique de Marseille	Hugh Dallas
		Assistant Referees:
		Bob Gunn
		John McElhinney
		Fourth Official:
		Willie Young

UEFA Intertoto Cup

Final 1st Leg

2001	Paris Saint-Germain v Brescia Calcio	Michael McCurry
		Assistant Referees:
		Stuart Logan
		Roddy Cobb
		Fourth Official:
		Kevin Toner
2005	Hamburger SV v Valencia CF	Stuart Dougal
		Assistant Referees:
		Wilson Irvine
		David Doig
		Fourth Official:
		Alan Freeland

Final 2nd Leg

2003	Villarreal CF v SC Heerenveen	Stuart Dougal
		Assistant Referees:
		Stuart Macaulay
		Martin Cryans
		Fourth Official:
		Calum Murray

UEFA Champions League

Quarter-Final 1st Leg

2002	FC Bayern Munchen v Real Madrid CF	Hugh Dallas
2011	FC Barcelona v FC Shakhtar Donetsk	Craig Thomson

Quarter-Final 2nd Leg

1995	IFK Goteborg v FC Bayern Munchen	Les Mottram
2000	FC Bayern Munchen v FC Porto	Hugh Dallas
2013	BV Borussia Dortmund v Malaga CF	Craig Thomson
2015	AS Monaco v Juventus	William Collum
2018	FC Bayern Munchen v Sevilla	William Collum

Semi-Final 2nd Leg

1995	AC Milan v Paris Saint-Germain	Les Mottram
2001	Real Madrid CF v FC Bayern Munchen	Hugh Dallas

UEFA Europa League

Quarter-Final 1st Leg

2010	Valencia CF v Club Atletico de Madrid	Craig Thomson
2011	FC Twente v Villarreal CF	William Collum
2013	Fenerbache SK v SS Lazio	William Collum
2014	Olympique Lyonnais v Juventus	William Collum

Quarter-Final 2nd Leg

2012	FC Metalist Kharkiv v Sporting Clube de Portugal	William Collum
2017	KRC Genk v RC Celta de Vigo	William Collum
2019	Valencia CF v Villarreal CF	William Collum

Semi-Final 1st Leg

2011	SL Benfica v SC Braga	Craig Thomson
2012	Club Atletico de Madrid v Valencia CF	William Collum
2019	Olympique de Marseille v FC Salzburg	William Collum

UEFA Super Cup

Final 1st Leg

1973	Rangers v AFC Ajax	Alistair MacKenzie
		Linesmen:
		Douglas Thomson
		John Dearie
1987	AFC Ajax v FC Porto	Bob Valentine
		Linesmen:
		George Cumming
		Graham Forrest

Final

2002	Real Madrid CF v Feyenoord	Hugh Dallas
		Assistant Referees:
		Wilson Irvine
		David Doig
		Fourth Official:
		Stuart Dougal
2015	FC Barcelona v Sevilla	William Collum
		Assistant Referees:
		Damien McGraith (IRL)
		Frank Connor
		Fourth Official:
		Graham Chambers
		Additional Assistant Referees:
		Bobby Madden
		Kevin Clancy

Since it replaced the European Champion Clubs' Cup in 1992, the UEFA Champions League has become the pre-eminent competition in club football. Scottish referees have a proud record of officiating in the competition, as evidenced by the following summary of Group Stage appointments: William Collum (30), Craig Thomson (26), Hugh Dallas (24), Stuart Dougal (11), Les Mottram (7), Bobby Madden (6), Michael McCurry (4) and Jim McCluskey (2). Nick Walsh refereed a match in the new League Phase format during season 2024-25.

Scots have fared well also in the Group Stages of the UEFA Europa League. The tally of appointments is: Bobby Madden (19), John Beaton (17), William Collum (14), Andrew Dallas (5), Dougie McDonald (5), Kevin Clancy (5), Craig Thomson (3), Steven McLean (3), Nick Walsh (3) and Don Robertson (1). In the new League Phase format in season 2024-25, John Beaton had four matches and Nick Walsh one.

Since its introduction in 2021, the summary of Group Match appointments in the UEFA Europa Conference League is: Nick Walsh (5), Don Robertson (3), John Beaton (3), Kevin Clancy (2), Bobby Madden (2) and William Collum (1). The League Phase format introduced for season 2024-25 resulted in the following appointments: David Dickinson (2), Nick Walsh (2), John Beaton (1) and Don Robertson (1).

Across these three competitions, Scottish referees have handled many important Play-Off matches and ties in the Rounds of 32 and 16.

Bibliography

Websites

Websites are a wonderful modern resource and they played an invaluable part in the research for the book. The following were all of great use:

britishnewspaperarchive.co.uk
scottishfa.co.uk
fifa.com
uefa.com
scottishfootballmuseum.org.uk
englandfootballonline.com
rsssf.org
worldfootball.net
eu-football.info
11v11.com
worldreferee.com
uk.soccerway.com/competitions
londonhearts.com
welshsoccerarchive.co.uk
nifootball.blogspot.com
websites.mygameday.app/assoc
dailyrecord.co.uk
wikipedia.org
playmakerstats.com
irishleaguegreats.blogspot.com
irishleaguearchive.org
scottishsporthistory.com
thethistlearchive.net
olympedia.org
playupliverpool.com
the1888letter.com
nonleaguematters.co.uk
Scottish Football Historical Results Archive (sfha.org.uk)
tournoimauricerevello.com
glasgowfa.co.uk
ratetheref.createaforum.com

thescotsfootballhistoriansgroup.org
killiefc.com
footballvictoria.com.au/rep-teams-1970-76
afcheritage.org
footballaustralia.com.au
footballhalloffamewa.com.au

Books

Beyond accessing a myriad of football documents held in the Scottish Football Museum, the following books provided invaluable information:

The Men Who Made Scotland – The definitive Who's Who of Scottish Football Internationalists 1872-1939 by Andy Mitchell
History of Queen's Park Football Club 1867 – 1917 by Richard Robinson
Schoolboys International Who's Who 1911-1997 Graeme Liveston/Scottish Schools' FA
A Lifetime of Soccer by Peter Craigmyle
The Remarkable Story of Peter Craigmyle - The Fearless Aberdonian by Gordon Mellis
Rangers: The Gers' Greatest Old Firm Victories by Jeff Holmes
Jack Taylor – World Soccer Referee by Jack Taylor with David Jones
Dear Scotland – On the Road with the Tartan Army by Ally McCoist

www.ingramcontent.com/pod-product-compliance
Lightning Source LLC
Chambersburg PA
CBHW052012070526
44584CB00016B/1716